RAINWATER HA[RVESTING]

The collection of rainfall an[d runoff]

Arnold Pacey with Adrian Cullis

WITH ILLUSTRATIONS BY PHIL CLARK

[I]NTERMEDIATE TECHNOLOGY PUBLIC[ATIONS]

Intermediate Technology Publications, 9 King Street,
London, WC2E 8HW, UK

© IT Publications, 1986

ISBN 0 946688 22 2

Typeset in Great Britain by Photobooks (Bristol) Ltd
and printed by WBC Print

CONTENTS

ACKNOWLEDGEMENTS   vi
PREFACE   vii

CHAPTER 1   Technical perspectives on
             rainwater collection   1

CHAPTER 2   Water, livelihood and organization   22

CHAPTER 3   Data collection and design criteria   43

CHAPTER 4   Rainwater tanks and
             technical assistance   72

CHAPTER 5   Design for drinking water systems   99

CHAPTER 6   Traditions in runoff farming   127

CHAPTER 7   Replication of runoff farming   158

CHAPTER 8   Rainwater economics and
             future prospects   181

REFERENCES AND BIBLIOGRAPHY   196
INDEX   209

ACKNOWLEDGEMENTS

The publishers would like to thank the organizations and individuals named below for giving permission to use or to draw upon published material; illustrations have been redrawn, based upon originals in works by the authors cited in captions (for full details of works in question see Bibliography, starting page 196).

A passage from '*Who puts the water into taps?*' by Sumi Krishna Chauhan: Earthscan, London (p. 67); quotations from '*Why the poor suffer most: Drought and the Sahel*' by Nigel Twose: Oxfam, Oxford (Chapter 8); Heinemann Educational Books, London (Figure 1.1); GRET, Paris (Figure 4.4); Water Resources Research Centre, Honolulu (Figure 1.2); IRC, The Hague (Figure 3.1); Institute for Rural Water, c/o USAID, Washington (Figures 3.4, 3.5, 5.3 and Boxes 5.1 and 5.2); VITA, Washington (part of Box 5.1); YDD, Yogyakarta, Indonesia (Figures 4.3, 5.2, 5.8); CIEPAC, Paris (Figure 7.5); D. M. Farrar, U.K. (Figure 1.6); Geographische Gesellschaft Trier, W. Germany (Figures 1.3, 1.4, 6.6 and 6.8); Chicago University Press, Illinois (Table 7.1); The City Engineer, Public Works Dept., Gibraltar (Figure 1.7); *African Environment*, c/o ENDA, Senegal (Figure 6.2a); IWACO, Rotterdam (Box 4.2); Friends' Rural Training Centre, Hlekweni, Zimbabwe (Box 4.1); UNICEF in Thailand (Figures 4.1 and 5.9 and illustrations in Fricke's work 1982); UNICEF, Nairobi (Box 3.1); Food and Agriculture Organization of the United Nations, Rome (Figure 7.3); W. R. S. Critchley, Baringo Pilot Project, Kenya (Box 6.2 and Figure 6.10); Experimental Farm for Desert Agriculture, Wadi Mashash, 6114 Groß-Umstadt, Bodenäcker 10, West Germany (Figure 2.2); *Geographical Journal*, Royal Geographical Society, London (Figure 6.9); *Journal of Arid Environments*, Academic Press, London (Figure 6.3); Professor Rama Prasad, Indian Inst. of Science, Bangalore (Box 6.1); Tycooly International, Dublin, Eire (Figures 3.5 and 5.10).

The publishers also wish to thank the following for the plates which appear between pages 120 and 121.

PREFACE

Rainwater collection and storage has been a long-standing interest of ITDG, stemming from the work in the 1960s of one of its earliest advisers, Michael Ionides, on low-cost water storage reservoirs in the Sudan. ITDG subsequently initiated a rainwater harvesting and micro-irrigation demonstration project with the Department of Community Development in Botswana in 1967. Further project work followed in Swaziland, Jamaica and Brazil (with the financial support of the Ministry of Overseas Development and Oxfam) and at the end of the 1970s Peter Stern, founder chairman of ITDG's Water Panel, proposed a research project for a rainwater harvesting publication to continue investigating the subject. Funding for the proposal was secured from the Shell Grants Committee in 1982 (as a contribution towards the U.N. International Drinking Water Supply and Sanitation Decade, 1981–90) and Adrian Cullis undertook a major literature search as well as carrying out practical work in Kenya. Arnold Pacey then used the results of this research in writing this book. The opinions, estimates and definitions expressed in the book are the responsibility of the authors and should not necessarily be taken to represent the views of ITDG.

Rainwater harvesting has attracted considerable attention in recent years in work covering a wide range of techniques — from the collection of rainwater from roofs to the retention of surface and sub-surface flow in rivers. The main interest of the authors has been methods of collecting and conserving rainwater at as early a stage as possible in the hydrological cycle to ensure the best use of rainfall, before it has run away into rivers and groundwater, or has disappeared as evaporation. Additional benefits from such measures of water control will often include a reduction in both soil erosion and in the damage caused by flooding. The authors believe that the systems they describe could hold out the greatest immediate hope for thousands of scattered, small communities that cannot be served by more centralized water supply schemes in the foreseeable future. For the purpose of this book, therefore, rainwater harvesting, or 'collection', has been defined as 'the gathering and storage of water running off surfaces on which rain has directly fallen' and not the 'harvesting' of valley floodwater or stream flow.

At the outset of our research ITDG was planning to produce a handbook which would describe in mainly technical terms the different methods of harvesting rainwater for domestic, livestock and crop production purposes. During the literature search it became clear that there were already plenty of documents in existence which adequately described the technical details, especially for domestic systems. What was missing, however, was material on designing and implementing schemes which were socially, technically, economically and environmentally appropriate for use in different patterns of livelihood and organization. This book aims to present the subject from these various perspectives in order to emphasize the importance of such interdependent dimensions of rural development.

Equally neglected, we concluded, was the subject of how systems, once established, could be sustained or copied by other groups so that larger numbers of people could benefit from the same ideas. These observations, together with the known limitations of a purely technical text, led us to shift our emphasis towards a more people-oriented treatment of the subject. This does not mean, however, that this book will not interest the technician — on the contrary, the mixture of technical and non-technical matters should help to stimulate the awareness of factors often overlooked by the single-subject specialist. The book is intended for rural development workers, especially those involved with water resources for domestic and agricultural purposes. The authors have tried to avoid a dull 'official' account of the subject and believe that the ideas presented will be stimulating to practical field-workers, project planners or managers, policy makers and academics — indeed to anyone with a commitment to rural development with the poor.

During the research and production of this work ITDG has been helped by numerous individuals and we are particularly grateful to the following: Jack Lawrence for his guidance during the initial stages; John Gould, Brian Latham, Steve Layton, Derek Ray, Angela Sinclair, Jeremy Swift (in connection with Chapter 2) and Peter Wright (Chapter 7) for contributing case study material; and Peter Stern for his invaluable advice throughout. My special thanks are due to Arnold Pacey, who not only edited the material which appears in the book but also provided invaluable assistance at all stages of the project. ITDG is, of course, greatly indebted to the Shell Grants Committee for their financial support.

Readers may be interested to know of other outcomes of this project, which are the assembly of a unique collection of documents on rainwater harvesting (kept at ITDG's Head Office in Rugby and accessible by arrangement) and the fact that ITDG has again become involved in a rainwater harvesting project overseas, in Turkana, north-west Kenya — with the possibility of involvement with other projects in Kenya and India. It is my hope that at least some of the lessons learned through the research and publishing of this book can be applied in practice in order to support the poor in their struggle for survival.

John Collett
Programme Officer, The Intermediate Technology
Development Group (ITDG)
Rugby, UK
August 1985

1. TECHNICAL PERSPECTIVES ON RAINWATER COLLECTION

RAINFALL AND WATER RESOURCES

Modern technologies for obtaining and using water are concerned chiefly with the exploitation of river systems and the development of ground water by means of wells and boreholes. On average, however, river flows together with the annual turnover of groundwater account for less than 40 per cent of the rain and snow which falls on the world's *land* surfaces. The remainder is lost to the land by evaporation from the soil, or from pools, marshes and lakes, and by evapotranspiration from the leaves of growing plants. In some of the world's driest areas, rivers account for as little as 4 per cent of precipitation.

Yet civil engineers have concentrated their efforts on the major rivers, seeing them, perhaps, as 'a sort of challenge', and considering how many dams they could build on them, how great a command area could be created, and so on. 'But for the vastly greater areas of the world's surface that are outside big river systems, they had virtually nothing to offer' (Ionides 1976).

Clearly, if rivers only represent a small proportion of annual precipitation, one method to try outside the big river systems is to collect rainwater immediately it falls, and before large evaporation losses occur. In earlier phases of human civilisation, major rivers were certainly exploited, but there was also a complementary and more extensive pattern of settlement in areas where rivers were few, and where the direct collection of rainfall was one of the few methods available for securing a water supply. Rainfall was collected from house roofs (Fig. 1.1) and was also sometimes directed into cisterns from paved courtyards, from hill and rock surfaces, and even from specially surfaced areas sloping towards cistern inlets (Fig. 1.2).

More surprisingly, among earlier civilizations, productive agriculture extended much further into the semi-desert areas of Arabia, Sinai, North Africa and Mexico than has seemed possible in more recent times. Moreover, this is explicable not by a markedly better climate in the past, but by the use of rainwater collection and conservation techniques. Figure 1.3 illustrates one approach, where a channel dug across a hillside intercepts water running downslope during storms, and directs that water

PLAN

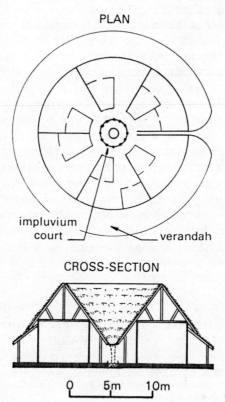

impluvium
court _____ _____ verandah

CROSS-SECTION

0   5m   10m

Fig. 1.1   A traditional, though rather rare, example of collecting rainwater from roofs – found in a house in Senegal about 1940. (Denyer, 1978) Water dripping from the eaves falls directly into the circular tank in the courtyard or sometimes into the impluvium court itself, from where it drains to an underground cistern. Square houses using the same principle have been common in the Yoruba and Benin regions of Nigeria. There are also houses with larger courtyards where the paving serves as a catchment surface. Runoff from the roof then enters the cistern only after flowing over the paved area. (UNEP 1983)

onto a field on flatter ground. Many variants of this technique, referred to as 'runoff farming' are known to have existed, and new methods have been developed in recent years.

Agriculture in the Old World originated in a climatically dry region in the Middle East, and may have depended to some degree on irrigation or runoff farming methods from the start (Evenari/Mashash 1975). The techniques involved seem to have been forgotten in subsequent agricultural development located in moister regions of Europe, Asia and America. The most notable evidence about such techniques has emerged from research into runoff farming and rainwater collection systems in the Negev Desert, in southern Israel. It is clear that in this region, rainwater provided a livelihood for a considerable population more than 2,000 years ago, continuing until about 700 A.D. The restoration of ancient farms where the techniques were used and the application of lessons learned has made new settlements possible in the desert, and has stimulated research elsewhere. However, conditions in the Negev Desert are atypical, and techniques developed there are not easily applicable in other regions, as will be explained in Chapter 6. Runoff farming should not, therefore, be thought of as *generally* applicable in deserts and 'arid' regions. Other areas where it has been successful have moister climates then these terms imply, though not moist enough for reliable crop production without use of runoff.

In North America, some notable research on runoff farming has been stimulated by realization that people living in what is now Mexico and the south-western United States prior to European settlement had methods of directing runoff water onto plots where crops were raised, thereby making a productive agriculture possible in an otherwise unpromising, semi-arid environment. In a few instances, similar systems are still used, and much research has been devoted to elucidating their operation (see Chapter 6) and in devising new but analogous methods of rainwater collection, for example, utilizing chemical soil treatments. There have also been important innovations in Australia, where something like a million people, mostly in remote areas, are today dependent on rainwater as their most important (but rarely their only) source of supply (Perrens 1982). Other work on rainwater collection techniques has been supported by the Intermediate Technology movement in Britain, and it is from this that the present book has stemmed. Again, ancient precedents were important. The initiator of this work, Michael Ionides, traced the origin of his ideas

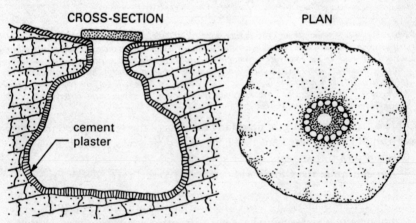

CROSS-SECTION   PLAN

cement
plaster

Fig. 1.2   An underground cistern filled by rainwater from an artificial catchment area laid on the ground surface. This is a traditional technique in the Yucatan peninsula of Mexico. The underlying rock is limestone, and in the absence of a prepared catchment, rainwater infiltrates into the ground without significant runoff. Cisterns are excavated in the rock and waterproofed with a thin layer of cement plaster. Many of them are very old, dating back to pre-conquest times. (Gordillo et al. 1982)

Note: *Drawing is not to scale.*

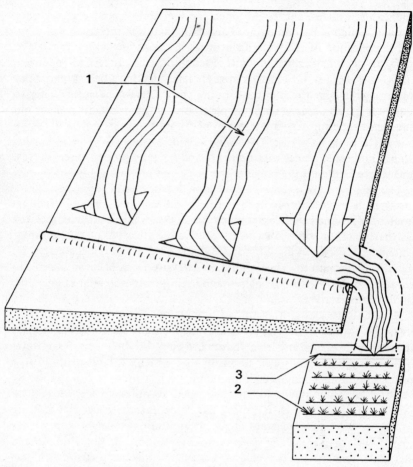

Fig. 1.3   The concept of runoff farming. Rain falling on the catchment area (1) is collected at the foot of the slope and conveyed to the cultivated plot (2) where its flow is checked and spread out by a bank (3). There may be additional banks to control flow over the plot.

Note: *Diagram is schematic and not to scale.*

back to 1926, when he was working in Iraq on 'the reconstruction of an ancient Babylonian irrigation canal' (Ionides 1976), and to his work on old water supply systems in Jordan (Ionides 1939).

He always stressed that the storage of rainwater in enclosed tanks was 'an ancient way' of enabling a water supply to last through a long dry season. He argued that a revival of the technique was inevitable for two reasons. 'The first reason is need. There are great tracts of semi-arid territory where population growth is pressing on the water supplies for drinking. . . . The second reason is opportunity'. Modern materials made possible a new approach to the construction of storage tanks and catchment surfaces, and could 'open the way for a massive attack on a problem which is becoming more and more acute as the years go by'.

The collection of rainwater from roofs has been a common practice in many moist climatic zones, not just in semi-arid areas. In Kenya, Indonesia and elsewhere, use of water from roofs has sometimes been a particular advantage at busy times in the farming year. There is most rainwater to collect at the very season when people are working hardest on the land, and have least time for carrying water from distant sources; thus even a small rainwater tank may ease a seasonal labour bottleneck. There are also islands and other places with no rivers and no good groundwater sources, and where rainfall is the only feasible means of providing a water supply.

The technique of rainwater collection for domestic supply or runoff farming, is essentially small in scale. It utilizes the roofs of individual houses, or ground catchments, which, because they are small, maximize the efficiency of runoff collection. Thus a scatter of small rainwater catchments, each serving an individual farm, homestead or hamlet, is the characteristic pattern. This implies an *extensive* form of development, in contrast to the *intensive* irrigation and hydropower potential of big dams built on major rivers.

Where large concentrations of population have to be supported, intensive forms of development are inescapable, and must sometimes include large dams and river basin projects. In such areas, rainwater collection will have only a small role to play, perhaps complementing other water sources or giving individual families a private source of supply. By contrast, on small islands and in a few other exceptional places where there are no significant rivers, ingenuity has sometimes been used in devising rainwater catchment schemes to supply substantial towns. Gibraltar has one of the largest rainwater systems in existence, and on both Gibraltar and Bermuda, regulations compel householders to collect water from their own roofs. In the limestone districts of Jamaica, there are many small rainwater supplies, some private and some communal.

Despite these exceptions, when studying the socio-economic conditions under which rainwater can be most effectively used, we are quickly brought back to the semi-arid areas where rivers may be few or only seasonally flowing, and where climatic conditions and environmental resources tend to restrict settlement to a scattered, extensive pattern. In such areas, rainwater collection offers its greatest technical advantage in terms of the conservation of the scarce water resource. The fact that it also fits the settlement pattern so well tends to confirm its appropriateness.

DEFINING RAINWATER COLLECTION

The principle of collecting and using precipitation from a small catchment area is often referred to as 'rainwater harvesting'. This term derives from a more general name, 'water harvesting', first used in Australia by H. J. Geddes to denote, 'the collection and storage of any farm waters, either runoff or creek flow, for irrigation use'. This nomenclature has since been used very loosely, as if the collection of rainfall and all other water harvesting amounted to the same thing. Yet in the above definition, water harvesting includes stream flow in creeks and gullies, not just rainwater at the point where it falls. Other definitions include water arising from all kinds of precipitation, not just rainfall. This book deals only with water running off surfaces on which rain has directly fallen, not with stream flow, and utilization of this runoff will be referred to as 'rainwater collection' (or concentration). Something needs to be said, however, about other forms of precipitation. For example, in Afghanistan, the winter snow is sometimes 'harvested' by manually collecting and packing it into a deep watertight pit. With the top sealed, the snow melts very slowly during the following summer, and water is withdrawn from the bottom of the pit. However, this book is concerned with countries where snow is a rare occurrence, so this technique is not further considered.

It is also sometimes said that dew and mist can usefully contribute to water supplies. Having himself shaken enough dew off long grass for a scanty morning wash, at least one of the present authors is not inclined to dismiss the idea. In the Negev Desert, where mean rainfall is less than 150mm, dew is equivalent to a further 20-30mm of precipitation. From this general region comes the Biblical story about harvesting dew by spreading a fleece on the ground in the evening. Next morning, enough dew could be wrung from it 'to fill a drinking cup' (Judges 6:38). In a place in Africa where the eaves of buildings are observed to drip in the early mornings after a dew, it was estimated that a roof area of $29m^2$ could yield 320 litres of dew water in a year. An Indian publication suggests lining a small depression with a plastic sheet and piling stones on this, so that dew forming on the stones drips onto the plastic (CCSK 1983).

However, the amounts of water which can be collected in these ways will always be very small. Dew may sometimes contribute a little extra water to a system designed for collecting rainfall, but the number of situations where it is worth devising structures specifically to collect dew and mist will be rare indeed. The so-called 'dew ponds' of southern England were filled mainly by rainwater, and ground surface catchments were constructed to drain into them. However, their linings, which were made by compacting clay over a layer of straw, favoured rapid cooling of the sides and bottom of an empty pond at night, and hence some increased condensation of dew may have contributed very slightly to their contents.

Because of the marginal relevance of snow and dew collection, this book deals only with precipitation in the form of rain, and particularly with rain close to the point where it is intercepted by the ground or by a roof. The concern is with collecting rainwater before it has flowed very far over the ground, in order to avoid as far as possible the losses to which runoff is subject. Stern (1978, 1979) points out that in the semi-arid regions within or close to the tropics, runoff water from a *small* catchment may amount to half the rainfall, even though only around 5 per cent of the rain may ultimately enter a river system. This is because the smaller the catchment area from which runoff water is collected, the less water is lost by evaporation or interception in depressions. Shanan and Tadmor (1979) observe that in the Negev Desert, watersheds of 300 to 500 hectares in extent produce less than 3mm of runoff on average each year. By contrast, a 'micro watershed' of 0.02ha may produce 10-30mm of runoff per year depending on slope, shape of catchment, soil conditions and the intensity of the storms.

Analysing this in more detail Shanan and Tadmor consider three main ways by which rain falling on a watershed is detained and 'lost'. Firstly, it may be intercepted by the leaves of plants growing on the watershed, evaporating without reaching the ground. In a dry area, vegetation is usually sparse, and interception losses are likely to be less than 2 per cent of rainfall. In a moist area with more vegetation, they may be more than 5 per cent.

Secondly, as already noted, runoff accumulates in any depression on the watershed to form puddles. On steep slopes, this may happen to only a small extent. On flatter land, there will usually be many large puddles after a storm, and where these are observed it may well mean that around 2-4mm of rainfall from that storm is accounted for by 'depression storage'.

The third way in which runoff is diminished is by infiltration into the soil. At the beginning of a storm, the dry soil may absorb all the rain that reaches it. However, some soils crust over under the impact of raindrops, in which case, infiltration diminishes almost to nothing, and runoff begins quite quickly. Even with soils which do not form a crust, the infiltration rate diminishes considerably once the surface has been thoroughly wetted.

Much therefore depends on local conditions. Moreover, infiltration occurs at a faster rate in hot weather than in cold; it is affected in complex ways by stones on the watershed, and usually reduced quite considerably if vegetation is removed.

Referring to the comparison made earlier between small (0.02ha) and large watersheds, one may comment that the proportion of rainfall lost due to interception by vegetation is likely to be independent of catchment size, whereas the proportion accounted for by depression storage and infiltration will tend to become greater the further the runoff flows across the ground surface. It may perhaps be added that while a small watershed is a more *efficient* collector of rainfall, in areas where showers are very localized and precipitation is patchy, a large catchment area may sometimes produce runoff on occasions when individual small watersheds do not receive rain at all.

It needs to be made clear that the rainwater collection methods discussed in this book are mainly (but not exclusively) concerned with *small* catchment areas or watersheds. To establish the distinction between techniques relevant with these applications and other forms of water harvesting, it is useful to consider the following example. In Yemen, when rains fall in the mountains, which rise to 2,500m, torrents of water rush down steep valleys, or *wadis*, towards the Red Sea. Much of the water soaks into the sandy soil of the coastal plain and evaporates, but a proportion is diverted onto fields, where enough infiltrates the soil in most years to support a crop. Some of the diversion structures used are again very ancient, and this type of irrigation may have been practised in the area for 3,000 years. However, the water is only utilized in this way after it has flowed some distance as a well-defined stream, and after some has already been lost. It is a method which fits the general definition of water harvesting, and may be appropriately described as 'floodwater harvesting', or 'spate irrigation'. But if the same water were to be collected as *rainwater*, this would be a matter for people living in the mountain areas where the rain falls. They could collect water from house roofs, or from small areas of ground whose slope and surface are suited to a high rate of runoff into an excavated tank, or onto cultivated terraces, and all these techniques are in fact used to an extent. But clearly, the latter are very different techniques from those involved in using floodwater far down the wadis.

Typically, floodwater flows are collected behind dams or by means of diversion weirs. In many semi-arid areas, sand accumulates in the beds of the larger ephemeral streams, and a flow of water persists in the sand long after the floodwaters have subsided. These 'sand rivers' are regularly exploited by the inhabitants of semi-arid areas, often simply by digging a hole in the dry river bed to reach the water. Such supplies may be improved by constructing subsurface dams in stream beds to hold back the flow in the sand, or by constructing silt-trapping dams across gullies. All these techniques, together with more conventional means of using dams and bunds to hold back floodwater, come into the general category of water harvesting. None of them, however, may be described as rainwater collection.

Shanan and Tadmor imply a very specific way of defining the distinction between rainwater collection and the harvesting of floodwater flows. They point out that when rain is falling on a small catchment, water will move downslope in a sheet of roughly even depth, often described as 'overland flow'. Some distance from the top of the slope, however, as the sheet flow becomes deeper and swifter, turbulence and erosion of the soil surface begins, and the water tends increasingly to flow in rills. In one case analysed, the transition from sheet flow to turbulent flow occurred 90m from the top of the slope and more generally we can expect it within 50–150m of the top of a gentle (1 per cent) slope.

In runoff farming, a careful balance has to be struck between the efficiency of a catchment in producing runoff and its susceptibility to erosion. While it is always possible to increase runoff by clearing slopes of vegetation and compacting the surface, the dangers of this leading to erosion are greater with longer slope lengths and steeper gradients. The precise distance downslope at which erosive flow begins not only depends on the gradient, though, but also on the soil, the intensity of the rain and many other environmental conditions. In designing catchment systems, a considerable margin of safety is needed to allow for unusually intense storms, and with 'microcatchments' in their local desert environment, Shanan and Tadmor specified a maximum slope length of 25m on a 1 per cent slope, and 14m with a 3 per cent incline. For the purpose of definition rather than design, however, the 50m-150m slope length can be taken to differentiate rainwater collection from other ways of manipulating runoff or harvesting floodwater.

In the work described by Shanan and Tadmor (though not in the programmes discussed in Chapters 6 and 7 below), the microcatchment is the most characteristic method of using rainwater directly to support growing crops. It must be explained, then, that this term refers to a bare catchment area on a gentle slope demarcated by a low bank or bund. The catchment has a small cultivated plot at its lowest point, watered by runoff from the whole area. The collection of sheet flow or overland flow, 'differentiates the design of microcatchments' from the design of runoff systems in which water is utilized, 'after it has collected in channels'.

To summarize these points, rainwater collection is defined here so that it comprises the harvesting of runoff only on the basis of what might be called 'microcatchment principles', that is runoff from:

- roofs;
- artificial surfaces at ground level:
- land surfaces with slopes less than 50-150m in length.

In practice, however, there is no easy distinction between runoff farming on short and long slopes. A more practical distinction is between runoff from *within-field catchments* and *external catchments*. The first category refers to systems where patches (or strips) of catchment area alternate with cultivated plots inside the field boundary. The most common version is where strips of bare ground are aligned with the contour, and runoff from these areas is used by growing crops on parallel, cultivated strips. On steeper slopes, the cultivated strips become terraces. Figure 1.4 compares this arrangement — in diagram i(a) — with other runoff farming methods. Microcatchments — in diagram i(b) — are also within-field catchments, in contrast to the *external* catchments shown in both parts of Figure 1.4ii. Within-field catchments invariably have short slope lengths and conform with the definition of rainwater collection given above. External catchments, by contrast, often (but not always) have slope lengths greater than

a.

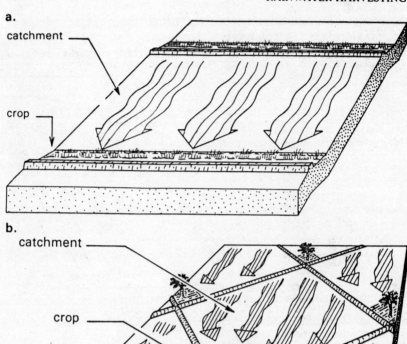

b.

Fig. 1.4   (i) Within-field catchments. Rainwater collection on contour strips (a) and micro-catchments (b). (Adapted from Kutsch 1982)

Note: *Diagrams are schematic and not to scale (slopes are much exaggerated).*

50-150m. On these longer slopes, runoff is a smaller proportion of the total rainfall because of losses from depression storage and infiltration, but as already noted, it may be capable of causing erosion. According to Critchley (1984), this has been a considerable problem in experiments carried out in Kenya, because when inflow to the cultivated plot 'becomes turbulent', there may be serious 'damage to earthen structures'.

In Figure 1.4ii, diagram (b) represents the diversion of flood flows from a natural gully onto cultivated land, and is an example of 'floodwater harvesting'. This distinction can be emphasized by saying that in diagram 1.4i, the aim of both systems is to *concentrate* rainwater on cultivated areas, whereas in 1.4ii, it is necessary to *distribute* an already concentrated flood flow onto a field.

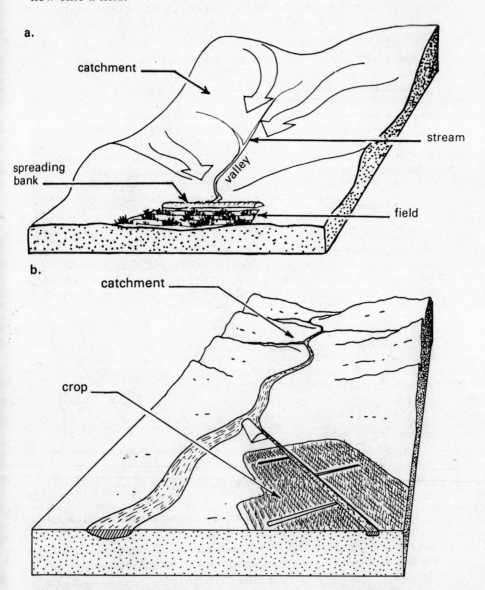

Fig. 1.4 (ii) External catchments. Floodwater harvesting by water spreading (a) and diversion of spate flow (b). (Adapted from Kutsch 1982)

Note: *Diagrams are schematic and not to scale.*

CLASSIFYING TECHNIQUES AND USES

With these definitions in mind, we can examine the uses of rainwater in more detail. It is tempting to think of just two contrasting applications. In one, water from a house roof is collected in a tank owned by the household and is used for drinking and cooking. The other is exemplified by the various runoff farming and microcatchment techniques. In these latter systems, the soil of the cultivated areas itself provides the storage medium, and water is abstracted directly by the plants' roots.

We can get a better perspective, however, by thinking briefly about the whole range of water sources which might conceivably be used for domestic or agricultural purposes. If the water sources available are rivers on the one hand or wells on the other, relevant techniques are clearly outside the scope of this book, as Figure 1.5 indicates. When it comes to surface runoff, the preceding paragraphs make a distinction between turbulent, erosive runoff from long catchments (which raise problems of soil conservation) and sheet runoff from short catchments. Figure 1.5 shows this further subdivision and indicates how the scope of this book is chiefly limited to application of sheet runoff, whilst recognizing that with most types of runoff farming (except microcatchments), there is some overlap between short and long catchments.

However, it would be wrong to make too sharp a division between domestic and agricultural applications, or between roof and ground surface catchments. Sometimes water from roofs is used to irrigate crops, if only on a garden scale. An example is a house in Botswana which has two rainwater tanks. One stands on the ground and collects water directly from the roof to provide water for drinking and cooking. The other is an excavated tank filled by overflows from the first tank as well as by runoff water from hard ground near the house. This tank is used to provide small amounts of water for the garden, as well as some water for washing and laundry. The principle is illustrated by Figure 1.6, which shows a slightly improved version of its application.

In other situations, especially where a larger supply is required than a single roof can provide, a ground surface catchment may be fenced to prevent contamination by livestock and may then produce water for domestic purposes. Thus one cannot say that roof catchments are associated solely with the domestic use of rainwater and ground surface catchments with its agricultural use. Nor can one totally separate systems which store water in the soil for use by growing crops from systems employing tanks or cisterns for storage. At one particular farm in the Negev Desert investigators found a conduit carrying water from a hillside catchment which had two branches, one supplying a cistern within the farmhouse, and the other discharging onto the fields.

Another example is reported from the southern United States where

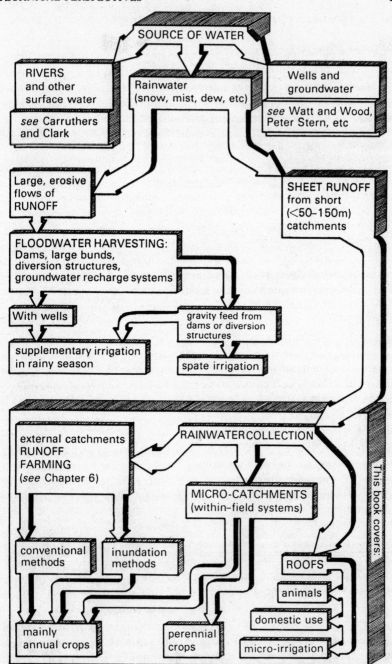

Fig. 1.5   *Rainwater collection in relation to other water resource development. (Note that some categories in this diagram overlap, especially the 'inundation method' of crop production which can be used with either runoff from an external catchment or spate irrigation.)*

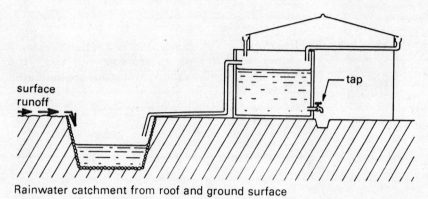

Rainwater catchment from roof and ground surface

Fig. 1.6   Two rainwater tanks used in conjunction. Water for drinking and cooking is drawn from the tank fed directly from the house roof, whilst water for other purposes is taken from the excavated tank. (Farrar 1974)

experience has shown that runoff onto cultivated strips is sometimes too great when the crop is at an early stage in its growth. To deal with this, arrangements have sometimes been made to divert part of the runoff into tanks and hold it in reserve for use in irrigating the crop later (Luebs and Laag 1975). This illustrates the distinction between irrigating crops from water stored in a tank and the runoff farming principle of storing water as soil moisture. When that distinction is collated with the differences noted earlier between the use of large and small catchments, we are confronted with a considerable variety of ways of using rainwater and runoff, as Table 1.1 seeks to indicate.

The possible range of techniques and their combination is increased when options for domestic supply and livestock watering are added to the table. Some of the most striking examples are to be seen where rainwater is collected from large rock surfaces. In parts of Kenya, this is done by building small dams directly on the rock (Nissen Petersen 1985). In one case, a whole village, including its livestock, is supplied throughout the year. In Zimbabwe, there are instances of the collection of rainwater from granite massifs (Richards 1972), and rock catchments are also used on several Caribbean islands. Their efficiency is commonly improved by the application of a coat of cement plaster to badly fissured areas of rock surface.

One especially good example of a large modern rainwater system is to be seen on Gibraltar, where two kinds of catchment surface are in simultaneous use. On the west side, water collected directly from rock surfaces is channelled into underground tanks. On its other main slope, Gibraltar has a sandy subsoil which produces very little runoff, so here an artificial catchment has been formed by laying some 14 ha of corrugated iron sheeting on timber battens, with 'gutters' at two levels to collect the water (Fig. 1.7). These catchments produce about 10 per cent of the local

Table 1.1   A classification of rainwater collection systems according to catchment, storage and use. The different uses to which rainwater is put are indicated as follows:

DD — drinking water and all domestic uses
S — water for livestock
G — garden irrigation from cistern, tank or dam
F — field irrigation from tank or dam
R — runoff farming with *external* catchments
M — use of runoff from *within-field* catchments
      (as on contour strips and microcatchments)
W — floodwater distribution to support crops
      (spate irrigation, water spreading, etc.)

	SMALL CATCHMENTS with sheet runoff (typified by micro-catchments)		LARGE CATCHMENTS with turbulent runoff and / or channel flow	
	ROOFS of all kinds	GROUND SURFACES less than 50-150m length; within-field catchments	SLOPES longer than 50-150m and minor rills and gullies	FLOW in WADIS, GULLIES, RIVERS and all natural drainage channels
WATER STORAGE TECHNIQUES				
TANKS ABOVE GROUND	DD	DD•	n.a.	n.a.
EXCAVATED TANKS, CISTERNS and HAFIRS	DDSG	DDSG	n.a.	n.a.
SMALL DAMS ('tanks' in INDIA)	n.a.	DD•SG	SFDD	(SFDD)
SOIL MOISTURE[1]	n.a.	M	R	(W)

•   especially on rock catchments
( ) floodwater harvesting techniques outside the scope of this book
n.a. not usually applicable
[1]   This area is elaborated in Table 6.2.

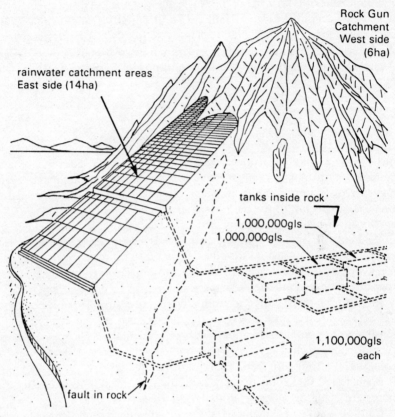

Fig. 1.7   Rainwater collection on Gibraltar. Apart from rainwater collected from house roofs and from rock surfaces on the west of the peninsula, there is a large artificial catchment on the east side consisting of corrugated iron sheeting supported on wooden piles driven into the sandy subsoil. (F.J. Gonzalez 1972)

community's potable water requirement, the rest being obtained from groundwater, desalination and importation (Doody 1980).

Elaborate rainwater catchments such as this are only justified when the need is for a domestic water supply and other sources are very limited. On a smaller scale, the cisterns or tanks which collect water from house roofs are also relatively costly and are justified chiefly when the water is used for high priority domestic purposes. Excavated cisterns, suitably lined with cement plaster or other impermeable material, can be cheaper and may collect large volumes of water from ground surfaces. As with the example in Figure 1.6, such tanks are well suited to purposes with lower priority than drinking water — such as laundry, watering gardens, or providing for livestock.

Small dams are often built for collecting water from the larger types of catchment, where the volume of water is too large for storage in a tank.

Examples include farm dams in Australia and the small dams in India which are generally known as 'tanks'. In both countries, most examples are sited in gullies or 'creeks', and are classed as 'floodwater harvesting' here. As Table 1.1 notes, such dams or tanks are used for watering livestock (in Australia) and for irrigation (in India), although domestic water may be obtained from them also.

CATCHMENT SURFACES

Detailed accounts of the various components of rainwater systems are distributed among subsequent chapters. For example, conveyance and storage for drinking water systems are described in Chapter 5. First, however, it is important to consider catchment surfaces in more detail because, according to the definitions given earlier, it is the nature of the catchment which most clearly distinguishes rainwater collection from other kinds of water harvesting. Specifically, catchments used to collect rainwater (as opposed to floodwater or surface water generally) are frequently artificial surfaces, or else are ground surfaces which have been specially prepared and demarcated.

Rainwater may be collected from any kind of roof. Tiled or metal roofs are easiest to use, and may give the cleanest water, but it is perfectly feasible to use roofs made of palm leaf or grass thatch. The only common type of roof which is definitely unsuitable, especially to collect water for drinking, is a roof with lead flashings, or painted with a lead-based paint. It is suggested that roofs made of asbestos sheeting should not be used if fibres are being detached from damaged areas (IRC 1981).

Caution is advised in many texts regarding thatched roofs, which are said to harbour sources of contamination, but there seems to be no evidence that water from a well thatched roof presents significantly greater hazards to consumers than water from other roofs. Greater precautions may be advisable to ensure that debris from the roof does not enter the tank, and the water should usually be boiled before drinking. The most important consideration, however, is that if a project is to help low-income groups, there may be no choice but to tackle the problems of collecting water from thatch or palm-leaf roofs, either by use of a low level collecting tank (Figure 1.1), or by devising means of attaching gutters (Figure 1.8).

In West Africa, rainwater has long been collected from thatched roofs and there appears to be no strong objection on grounds of taste to its use for drinking (Novieku 1980). In other places, with thatch of other types, water from roofs is often discoloured and although it may be fit to drink, people may dislike it. In a survey of 150 households in three Botswana villages, many families were found to collect rainwater from roofs in some informal way by placing buckets, basins or oil drums under the eaves. However, while this was done at 43 out of 51 households which had metal roofs, only

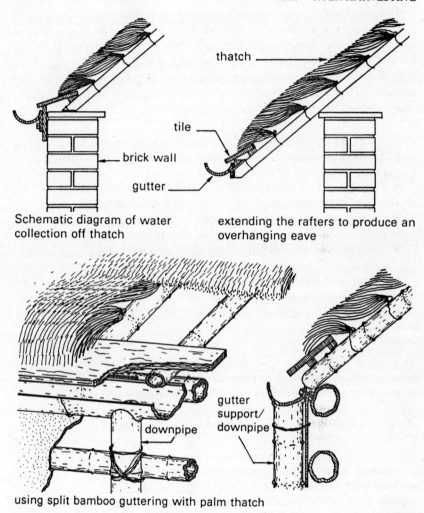

thatch

tile

brick wall

gutter

Schematic diagram of water
collection off thatch

extending the rafters to produce an
overhanging eave

downpipe

gutter
support/
downpipe

using split bamboo guttering with palm thatch

Fig. 1.8   Gutters for rainwater collection from thatch. (Hall 1982)

9 of the 99 households with thatched roofs collected water from them, and
only at one did the householder admit drinking the water (Gould 1983).

One advantage for the household in collecting rainwater from its roof is
that the roof has already been paid for, and so additional investments are
limited to gutters and tanks. Such investments may be more than people
can afford, however, and even when storage tanks have been obtained,
gutters may only be attached to one side of the building, or sometimes only
to short lengths of roof. Indeed, lack of guttering is sometimes said to be
one of the primary limiting factors restricting the wider adoption of
rainwater collection (Chapter 5).

The collecting of rainwater from ground-level catchments is sometimes possible using a hard surface created for some other purpose. School playgrounds and threshing floors have both been used in Botswana. More usually, though, a catchment area or watershed is developed for rainwater collection by applying some more specific form of treatment to the ground surface. UNEP has proposed a classification of surface treatments which, with one addition, is as follows:

- clearing sloping surfaces of vegetation and loose material;
- improving vegetation management by planting with different species or by cropping;
- mechanical treatment of the soil, including smoothing and compacting the surface, as on contour strips and microcatchments;
- making a hard surface using traditional soil stabilization techniques (as used on Botswana threshing floor catchments);
- reducing soil permeability by application of chemicals (e.g. sodium salts);
- applying chemical binders such as asphalt to seal the surface;
- covering the catchment with conventional paving materials;
- covering the catchment with other rigid materials;
- covering the catchment with flexible/plastic material.

Most of these techniques fall into one or other of two main groups — firstly, those which involve *treatment* of the soil itself, either mechanically or with chemicals, to reduce infiltration by rainwater and achieve greater runoff, and secondly, those which entail *covering* the soil with another material, as with the last three items in the list (compare Table 3.1 in Chapter 3).

As regards treatment of the soil, much research has been carried out in the United States on substances which can be mixed with, spread or sprayed over the soil (Frasier 1975). Experiments have been made with sodium salts (which encourage surface crusting on soils containing clay); with silicones (which are water repellent); and with oil, paraffin wax, bitumin or asphalt (which bind soil particles together). The sodium treatment is cheap but may not last for more than a year and can lead to increased soil erosion. The other methods tend to be expensive, though most are less costly than such alternatives as covering ground surface catchments with plastic sheeting, butyl rubber, or even aluminium foil, all of which have occasionally been tried (Maddocks 1975). Not only is the use of these last materials expensive, but unless supervision and maintenance is meticulous, their durability is not good — weed growth from below or stray animals can easily puncture surfaces.

More significant than research findings with the materials is to notice what is done in practice. Where public water supply is an urgent need and ample funds are available, ground catchments have been successfully surfaced with smooth concrete, butyl rubber or plastic sheet. These materials are now used in preference to corrugated iron catchments of the Gibraltar type for economic reasons. Butyl rubber, which also makes a good lining for excavated storage tanks, may be the most widely used of the modern materials. On Hawaii, over 300 butyl catchments and reservoirs have been constructed. Plastic sheeting — usually black polythene — has been less successful because of its vulnerability when exposed to wind and sun. One method of countering this has been to cover the plastic catchment surface with a 3cm layer of pea-sized gravel. Less runoff is obtained, but there is a marked gain in durability and encouraging results have been reported, for example, from trials in Jamaica.

Where a ground catchment must fill a farm pond from which livestock drinking water is supplied, or where it supports the cultivation of crops by runoff farming methods, plastic surfaces are rarely used except on a very small scale. In Australia, for example, rainwater harvesting is widely practised on farms, but one commentator emphasizes that the technique is used by 'commercial farmers' and must therefore be 'economically attractive' (Laing 1981). This excludes most exotic materials, and means that improvement of catchment surfaces to obtain greater runoff must depend very largely on earth forming, smoothing and compaction.

One particularly notable Australian technique was developed by analogy with road-building and is referred to as the 'roaded catchment'. The point is that a well-constructed highway must have a camber and surface capable of disposing of rainwater quickly into the roadside drains. If a small catchment is covered with a series of parallel, cambered roadways surfaced with smooth, compacted soil, ditches laid out between them can collect rainwater and discharge it into a suitable storage reservoir. Early results were highly satisfactory, especially on clay or clay-loam soils, and since the 1950s, roaded catchments have been widely adopted in Western Australia. Individual catchments of 2-4ha have been constructed for livestock water supply, and larger ones are also to be seen, some over 40ha.

With mechanical earth-moving equipment needed for construction, roaded catchments may not be immediately applicable for low-income developing communities, where it might make more sense to look at traditional technologies, at least for small catchments. For example, in Botswana, the ground within household compounds is surfaced with a clay/cow-dung mixture which can be smoothed to form a hard, polished, impermeable surface from which some provision for rainwater drainage has to be provided. As already noted, threshing floors made this way have recently been utilized as catchments. In other countries, various mixtures of soil with clay, lime, dung or even cassava flour are used as 'cements' for sealing flat roofs as well as making floors, and these traditional soil stabilization techniques deserve to be better appreciated. Where cow-dung is used, it is probably inert by the time floor surfaces have dried thoroughly, and is not a source of contamination.

In many places, ground catchments must be made at low cost and with very basic techniques. Sometimes all that can be attempted on a large catchment is the filling of obvious depressions, and construction of banks or bunds to divert runoff into storage, or to retain it on cultivated land. Even so, 20 to 30 per cent of rainfall may often be collected as runoff. In low-rainfall areas where the priority is to maximize runoff, vegetation may be completely removed. Where rainfall is higher, control of erosion is often more important and trees or grass are planted on catchments (as sometimes in India). Where it is possible to obtain sufficient runoff from grassed catchment areas, they may be used by grazing animals, though of course, this would not be considered where the water is for domestic use because animals are invariably a source of contamination, and so are fertilizers if they are used.

Here an important distinction can be made between multi-purpose and single-purpose catchment surfaces. The roof of a house is designed primarily to provide shelter and privacy. Sometimes it is also a status symbol. Flat roofs in some countries are used for sleeping, storage and drying clothes. Thus when a roof is used to collect water, it is very much a multi-purpose structure, and may serve some purposes which conflict with requirements for rainwater collection, especially regarding contamination. Other examples of multi-purpose catchments, apart from those used for grazing, include school playgrounds and public roads. Most catchments of these kinds are appropriate only for agricultural (or industrial) application, not for domestic supply.

These points about how catchments are used, and more generally, about how rainwater is applied, make it clear that rainwater collection is not something that can be analysed in a purely technical manner. Its relevance in any situation depends critically on whether it is compatible with other economic and domestic activities, on whether people have the organization necessary to build and maintain the system, whether they have adequate housing, and above all, whether they regard a water supply of this kind as a high priority. Many of these factors arise from the way in which the people obtain their livelihood, and that must be a central concept in any examination of where and how rainwater collection techniques have most to offer.

2. WATER, LIVELIHOOD AND ORGANIZATION

THE GEOGRAPHICAL RELEVANCE OF RAINWATER

All water resources are limited, but the nature of the limiting factors varies greatly from one part of the world to another. The relatively low proportion of rainfall reaching river systems in climatically dry regions is one factor already mentioned. Groundwater is much favoured for drinking water supplies because of its freedom from contamination, but in the more arid parts of the world, potable groundwater is not always available. Sometimes it can be found, but is too salty for human consumption. There are also 'extensive areas in Africa, the drier parts of South America, the Indian sub-continents and many islands in the sub-tropics where groundwater can be found but the recharge rate of wells is inadequate to meet demands' (Stern 1982). It may also be very deep, and hence costly to exploit, and to pump. Not surprisingly, places where rainwater collection has been most fully applied are frequently in regions where these other water resources are inadequate. However, sceptics are quick to point out that rainwater collection has limitations also, noting the questionable reliability of a system dependent on erratic rainfall, and the diseconomies of scale associated with rainfall storage when each household acquires its own small storage tank. As regards reliability, in almost no circumstances can stored rainwater be regarded as the sole source of supply. At some times, and for some purposes (such as laundry or garden irrigation), other water sources will have to be used. But for the individual household which wants the convenience of its own supply under its own control, and often for whole communities where the area lacks rivers or groundwater, the possibility of developing rainwater collection systems can be very attractive.

Islands may have water supply problems simply because there are no large catchments from which rivers can flow or aquifers can be recharged. Coral islands have highly permeable ground from which there is no runoff. Bermuda is notable as an island on which rainwater collection has been particularly well developed, and so is the quasi-island of Gibraltar. In both places, water is collected from the roofs of all households as well as from large corporately managed catchments (Figure 1.7) But even so, rainwater is not the sole source of supply. Seawater or brackish groundwater is used for secondary purposes, and desalination plant has been introduced. Furthermore, during periods of drought, water has been imported by ship. There are other islands, including several in the Pacific and Caribbean regions, where rainwater is an important source for drinking water supplies but where technologies for its collection are less advanced (Fujimura 1982, Layton 1984).

Places where geological conditions have so limited other sources of supply that rainwater collection is strongly emphasized include parts of Nova Scotia (Canada), Jamaica, Java (Indonesia) and the Yucatan Peninsula of Southern Mexico. In the three latter areas, the underlying rocks are permeable limestones, whilst in Nova Scotia, and also in West Java, the high mineral content of the groundwater makes it unfit to drink.

Climatically dry areas where rainwater is collected, not only for domestic supplies but for watering livestock, for runoff farming and even sometimes for irrigation, include much of Australia, parts of India, the Middle East, North Africa, parts of East Africa, Mexico and the south-western United States. These areas constitute a large proportion of the earth's surface with a fairly large (if thinly dispersed) population, often dependent on raising livestock, and they will be a considerable preoccupation in this book.

In all such areas, rainwater collection is frequently the 'least cost' form of water supply, largely because of the high cost of alternatives. Even where this cannot be claimed, it may be easier to mobilize household capital for a family rainwater tank than to secure large-scale investments in public supplies. Moreover, in some regions generally well-endowed with low-cost supplies, rainwater collection may fill a gap in existing provision. It may be that the quality of the water is advantageous for washing (where public supplies provide hard water), or for drinking (where borehole water is slightly brackish). Or in moist tropical climates, there is sometimes a particular season when work pressures and water needs are both critical, and the convenience of having a household tank of rainwater is very great. Rainwater collection may also have some insurance value against failure of other sources. Even in England there are some regions where water authorities encourage householders to store rainwater from roofs for use in times of drought, when watering gardens from the public supply may be prohibited (SWW 1984).

DISSEMINATION OF TECHNIQUES

With so many examples of the advantageous use of rainwater, it is puzzling to some commentators that there are still numerous villages in Asia, Africa and Latin America which experience desperate water shortages but where no effort appears to be made to exploit the rainwater resource. Equally, there are many areas where it might seem that agriculture could benefit greatly from runoff farming techniques. One reaction has been to carry out more research to improve the performance of available techniques or reduce their cost. Efforts have also been devoted to making more technical information available, and yet the spread of techniques still seems painfully slow. Three possible reasons for this situation need to be explored.

Firstly, although progress in *organized* projects for disseminating rainwater collection has been disappointing, it sometimes turns out that more people are collecting water from roofs or using runoff farming methods than is generally realized. Often they employ techniques which are informal or inconspicuous, or the spread of a new technique has been promoted by local craftsmen and traders whose activities have not been recorded. The latter is true in parts of Kenya, for example, where quite significant numbers of households have acquired tanks to collect roof runoff on their own initiative. Thus it may simply be the official version of rainwater collection which spreads slowly. Local people may have their own approaches — as later chapters will explain.

Secondly, it needs to be noticed that much of the research done on rainwater collection has been of a purely technical kind. There has been relatively little investigation of the processes by which a successful water tank construction project might be 'replicated' or 'extended', spreading from one village to another over wide areas. Such processes not only involve the spread of information, but also depend on village organization, on the organization of support services and technical assistance, and on manpower, skills, money and material resources. These various aspects of the extension or replication process are well illustrated by programmes in Thailand and Indonesia and in publications influenced by them (Fricke 1982, Keller 1982), and are discussed in Chapter 4 of this book.

Thirdly, however, it is necessary to consider a facet of the culture of western technology which is sometimes hard to recognize and face up to — that our enthusiasm for the ingenuity of a technical device, or its performance under test, can often mislead us into believing that it is more relevant than is really the case. There is a distinct danger that we begin to interpret people's needs or to study environmental circumstances very selectively, examining only those facets of a problem which the favoured technique might remedy, and neglecting other aspects which ought to rule it out.

With regard to runoff farming in the Negev Desert, for example, nobody can fail to be impressed by techniques which allow crops to be grown wihout conventional irrigation, solely by using the low desert rainfall of less than 150mm per year. The old vision of the desert blooming as the rose seems within reach, and in our enthusiasm, we naturally think of the many other desert areas of the world which could be reclaimed for agriculture. Yet the Negev version of runoff farming is unusual both in the environmental niche it exploits (rainfall in a cool, winter growing season) and in its social and cultural origins. Thus, most fieldworkers attempting to apply the Negev techniques in other areas have had to modify them considerably or even abandon the attempt altogether (see Chapter 6).

Often our commitments to research and to particular innovations leave us open to the criticism that we find solutions first and then search for problems they may fit. Thus the nature of 'world hunger' and malnutrition has sometimes been misrepresented to suit the particular forms of agricultural innovation or 'food aid' that the West had to offer. And there is a similar danger of misrepresenting the special problems of semi-arid regions in Africa and elsewhere, in order to suit the particular techniques and patterns of organization favoured by western agencies. Rainwater technologies have long been used by the inhabitants of these regions and so are undeniably relevant — but there is still need to be wary of imposing alien and inappropriate versions.

For example, in semi-arid areas of Africa where pastoralism is the chief means of livelihood, traditional ways of using rainwater are by means of excavated cisterns, 'hafirs' (from the Arabic *hufra*), small dams and natural water holes. For African pastoralists south of the Sahara, natural water holes are probably most important, although small artificial excavations are also common. But in western Sudan and parts of Ethiopia and Kenya, the much larger hafir is used for collecting rainwater for all purposes.

Typically, hafirs are located on land with very gentle slopes where there are no well-defined drainage channels or sites for small dams. Thus a hafir has to be created by excavation, the spoil being used to build a bund around its perimeter (Figure 2.1). Long bunds extending upslope are also usually necessary to direct sheet runoff into the hafir. In small hafirs, livestock may gain access to the water by wading in at the inflow side, but this leads to erosion and rapid silting, and it is preferable for animals to be watered via a well and suitable drinking troughs, as indicated in the diagram. A further refinement is for inflow of water to be via a silting basin from which a pipe leads into the hafir; in this case, the bund may extend round all four sides of the excavation. The capacity of a hafir may be as little as 1,500m^3, e.g. in the Ogaden region of Ethiopia, or as much as 200,000m^3 in Sudan. In Botswana, where hafirs were introduced around 1970, a typical capacity is 9,000m^3 (Classen 1980).

Sandford (1983) notes that in the areas where traditional hafirs and cisterns were most highly developed, drinking troughs and other arrangements for distributing water to livestock were carefully planned and rules for maintenance and use of these water sources were meticulously enforced. Guards might be posted at hafirs, for example, which would be carefully fenced. He notes that such provision is neglected in many modern installations. In north-east Kenya, one result has been that of 100 hafirs or 'hafir-dams' built after 1969, most had silted up ten years later. At some of them, maintenance was adequately managed by local herdsmen for so long

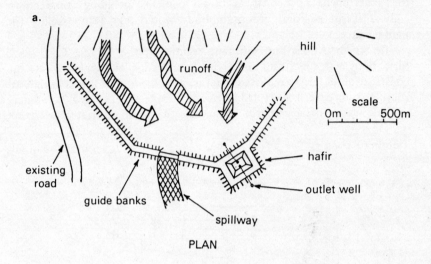

a.

PLAN

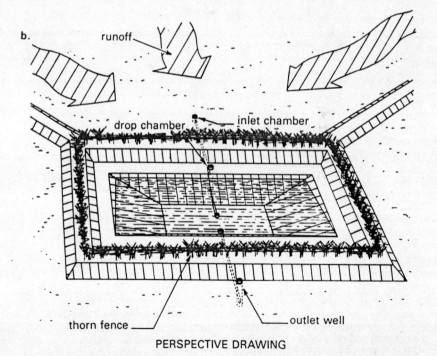

b.

PERSPECTIVE DRAWING

Fig. 2.1   Plan (a) and perspective view (b) of a Somali 'hafir' (or 'balli') with access to the stored water via a well. Hafirs of this sort are strongly fenced to prevent animals getting to the water and treading down the banks. (Based on a drawing provided by Gifford and Partners, Southampton)

as use of the hafirs was limited to their own social groups. However, once the government opened them to all comers, including some ethnically different pastoral groups, nobody would take responsibility for maintenance.

In North Africa and adjacent regions of the Middle East, rock formations with soft strata underlying harder rock lend themselves to the construction of large excavated cisterns, with the harder layers as natural roofing. Such cisterns are filled by runoff from hillsides (Fig. 2.2) and may provide water for large herds of animals. A major rainwater collection

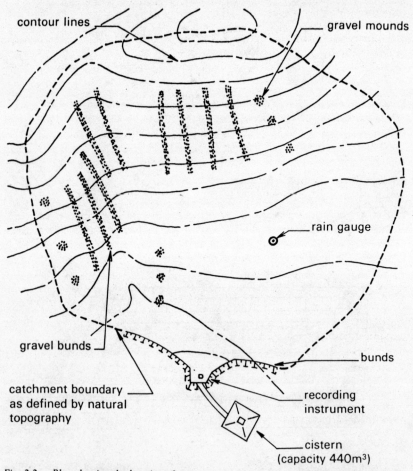

contour lines

gravel mounds

rain gauge

gravel bunds

bunds

catchment boundary
as defined by natural
topography

recording
instrument

cistern
(capacity 440m³)

Fig. 2.2   Plan showing the location of an excavated cistern in relation to its catchment area. This example in the Negev Desert was probably once used for watering camels on a caravan route. After restoration about 1960, it has provided water for 300–350 sheep during several months each year. Its capacity is 440m³ and the catchment is 1.2ha in extent. The plan shows how runoff from the catchment has been enhanced by raking gravel off the hillside, most of it being left in mounds or long heaps running down slope. There are two low bunds at the foot of the slope directing runoff into the cistern. (Evenari/Mashash 1981)

project completed before recent controversies about semi-arid areas came to a head was carried out in Libya between 1955 and 1962 (Stewart 1960; Ray 1983). One of its aims was to repair existing cisterns, and over 7,000 were either renovated or newly built. It was estimated that $0.75m^3$ of water in a cistern could support one sheep through about half the grazing season, and the cistern could be expected to fill three years in five. In other years, drought would limit the amount of water available and hence the number of animals which could be kept, and this was a very valuable and effective check on overgrazing at times when the growth of grass and forage was also limited by deficient rainfall. With a sharply changed political climate in Libya, no long-term assessment of the results of this scheme is available. Misrepresentation of the problems of pastoral peoples living in areas such as this is evident in many accounts of the 'environmental crisis' which confronts them, which is often labelled 'desertification'. In the countries immediately south of the Sahara Desert, for example, there has been a serious loss of tree cover, much soil erosion, and a general spread of desert-like conditions. Large numbers of people — many of them former pastoralists — became destitute in the long drought of the early 1970s, and with the underlying problems unresolved, widespread and tragic suffering has again resulted from the drought of 1983-5.

Yet simply to describe this as an *environmental* problem rather than a social or institutional one is part of the misrepresentation. Environmental problems are usually regarded as calling for technological solutions, which is principally what the developed countries feel they have to offer. But a more fundamental issue is the way in which the policies of government agencies in almost all these countries have for several decades weakened the traditional institutions through which pastoralists once regulated the grazing of their herds, and by which a balance was struck between the use of different areas by cultivators and pastoralists. In India as well as Africa, there has been a tendency for cultivated areas in semi-arid regions to expand at the expense of grazing lands.

In these circumstances purely technical responses to drought in the form of boreholes and rainwater conservation can achieve nothing. Proclaiming a 'crisis of desertification' as a problem requiring various forms of 'technical fix' is equally misleading. As Sandford (1983) says, there is no real agreement among experts as to how desertification should be defined, let alone how it should be measured, nor is there agreement as to its causes. Those who blame overgrazing by the herds of nomadic pastoralists cannot agree on how large those herds should be, and those who blame the extension of cultivated areas have few convincing remedies. Indeed, most statements about this widespread 'crisis' are one-sided interpretations angled towards favoured technical solutions.

But even with these warnings in mind, it is still possible to see a consensus among several commentators (Sandford 1983, Swift 1977, Ray 1984) about the relevance of rainwater collection, especially if it is complemented by appropriate institutional innovation. For example, Swift (1984) points to associations of herders formed in Niger during the early 1980s. Comprising about 20 pastoralist households each, these are managing grazing lands on a co-operative basis and appear to be the right units to manage small-scale rainwater collection systems on those lands.

In this part of Africa, natural rain-filled pools are the first source of water used by pastoralists after rain has fallen. There is scope for deepening some of these, for constructing artificial pools to complement them and for better management of their use by pastoral communities. Such rain-filled drinking points for livestock could help sustain pastoral lifestyles, and their advantage over borehole supplies is that the stored rainwater at any one point would be limited in quantity. Its exhaustion would force herds to move to another water point before vegetation in the vicinity is over-grazed — a matter of very considerable importance. Indeed one might say that rainwater collection is the most 'environmentally appropriate' technology for this application, and that boreholes are frequently quite inappropriate.

In India, as Ray points out, environmental problems are very different. There is drought and erosion on farms in central India, waterlogging and salinity in north India, and deforestation everywhere. Rainwater conservation could make a modest contribution to the solution of many of these problems, but faces major political and bureaucratic obstacles.

It is not, of course, the job of water engineers to initiate national programmes for institutional change, nor to campaign for political reform. But they do have a responsibility to ensure that the technological developments they favour are truly appropriate to the problems of local people, particularly disadvantaged groups, and are not being used by politicians and other interest-groups as a means of evading or disguising the need for more fundamental kinds of change.

At the local level, too, engineers or planners have a responsibility to consider whether their goals in promoting a specific technique are compatible with the needs and values of the people they seek to help. There is an increasing awareness of the way in which the objectives of planners, however well-meaning, may be in conflict with the aims of the people for whose welfare they plan. Such conflicts have been examined in the context of small water supplies (Thomas and Lockett 1978), rural sanitation (Pacey 1980) and the wider needs of pastoral communities (Sandford 1983).

Chauhan and Gopalakrishnan (1983) very effectively expose the illusions which arise when the lofty goals of the United Nations Water Decade are translated to village level: 'poor villagers . . . have their own clear perception of basic human needs . . . Earning enough from employment or land to buy more and better food for the family and to build a more durable house, is considered fundamental. Sanitation and even health are not.'

If people are simply asked whether they would like a better water supply and whether they would like a school for their children, they will, of course, say 'Yes'. Such things are certainly desirable. But, as Sandford notes, to ask whether the people want a school does not establish whether the school conflicts with other aims. New schools and water supplies almost invariably demand that people divert time and resources from some other activity, which may be of higher priority for them. Then the school may be badly attended and the water supply unmaintained. To avoid such situations, it is essential to discuss projects fully so that the people can see what obligations would be placed on them by the introduction of a new water supply, and so that planners and water engineers can appreciate the wider needs and goals of local people and identify potential points of conflict.

At this point, it is possible to identify two ways of safeguarding planning for rainwater collection (or any other specialized technique) against the danger of becoming merely a reflection of technological enthusiasms. The first involves the vexed question of participation by ordinary people in planning and implementing projects. Chapters 3 and 4 will argue that even if this does tend to slow down a project, the comments of local people should always be sought, both as a check on the social appropriateness of the project and as a means of obtaining practical information about the local environment, including water sources, building materials and so on.

The other safeguard is to check the economic appropriateness of projects in a more comprehensive way than has hitherto been usual, emphasizing especially their impact on people's livelihoods. This is the subject for the remainder of chapter 2.

PERCEIVING NEEDS AND UNDERSTANDING LIVELIHOODS

Economists make the point that when a new technology is introduced, its success depends on it being both technically effective and economically efficient. It must fit its environment and do what it sets out to do reliably and well. But it must also make sense in terms of the productivity with which resources are used. Over-enthusiasm for favoured techniques can lead to them being promoted solely for their environmental and technical effectiveness, with factors relating to efficient resource-use being forgotten.

However, Ray (1984) makes the further point that efficient resource-use in the context of rainwater collection will be seen differently according to whether the water is essential for survival or whether it is a means of profit. For some pastoralists and many islanders, rainwater collection is a pre-condition of life in their particular environments, and the same may be true of many scattered groups of farmers in dry regions. Such people may spend a much larger fraction of their limited resources on water supply than would be usual elsewhere, sometimes building cisterns and catchments that would seem extravagant by other standards. As Ray points out, survival is not conducive to economic analysis, 'particularly where the survivors are mainly subsistence-based poor farmers and labourers', or else pastoralists.

By contrast, in most of India, the relevance of rainwater technologies is mostly as a form of resource development for agriculture, with implications for erosion control and forestry. Survival is less often in question, and a hard-headed view of economic benefits is much more in order. But however hard-headed one's approach, there is still a choice to be made between economic analysis which considers mainly profit and cash income, and alternative economic views which focus more closely on the all-pervading problem of poverty. Cullis (1984) argues that existing rainwater projects have had least impact, 'where it really matters, amongst the lives of the rural poor'. There are few examples, he suggests, of modern rainwater technologies being 'actively maintained and widely used' by such people.

Economic analysis relevant to this priority arguably needs to be centred on the concept of *livelihood*, and some general points can be made by classifying different types of livelihood which rainwater collection may help to sustain. In the various environmental conditions already mentioned, these may fairly simply be identified as the following:

- In arid and semi-arid regions, livelihoods are commonly based on pastoralism, with small areas of irrigated crop production and some dryland farming based on drought-resistant crops. There may also be a rather small number of artisans and traders.
- In moister areas where rainwater collection is used mainly to provide a supplementary water source, its relevance seems often to be related to the seasonal pattern of crop production.
- On islands and in other places mentioned where rainwater collection is almost the only possible source of supply, livelihoods are often based on tourism and trade, and the main uses of water will thus be in domestic supply and cooking. There will often be some small-scale, but intensive, agriculture for which water is needed.

This approach gives us a list of economic activities which can be examined in order to check the relevance of rainwater collection to raising production, increasing incomes, or enlarging employment opportunities — and it is vital that all such prospective improvements in production or income should be thoroughly evaluated. As the economists quoted earlier have pointed out, many good ideas in technology are never taken up because the contribution they make to production, or to the more efficient use of resources is too small to justify their cost. Where rainwater collection is used to provide water for crops, it is possible to work out the value of the extra crop production and check this against the costs of the rainwater scheme.

Where water is used mainly in the household, however, it is not so easy to compare benefits and costs. People may benefit through better domestic hygiene, better health, and a reduction in the time they spend carrying water from distant sources. Some of these gains may be reflected in raised levels of production, especially if the time saved is diverted to work in the fields or to some form of small-scale manufacture. But it is a mistake to think that improved domestic supplies must always be justified by their contribution to increasing production.

Where concern is with the improvement of livelihoods, it has to be recognized that a family's livelihood is only *partly* dependent on production and income as these are conventionally understood. Hypothetically, one might imagine a group of herdsmen, farmers or even artisans living in the open, eating raw food, and having no children to care for. Such a group could, theoretically, provide the whole of its livelihood from its own production and trade without devoting any of its labour to domestic tasks. However, in normal communities, livelihoods depend heavily on domestic work which is not always regarded as 'productive'. Such work includes food preparation and cooking, maintenance of the home, domestic hygiene, and child care. Household water supplies contribute significantly to almost all these basic livelihood support activities. Thus if we are going to talk about the economic benefits of water supply, it is essential that we come to economic terms with the real significance of these various domestic tasks.

The activities which more conventionally count as 'production' all have a market value. Crops grown and goods manufactured can be sold (though in practice they may be partly retained for family consumption). Many kinds of service are paid for, and wages represent the market value of labour. By contrast, many activities which relate to the home, to cooking and to children are carried out by housewives working without wages, whose 'output' has no market value.

One way of thinking about this is to use concepts formulated in what is sometimes called the 'new home economics'. These are founded on the idea that two kinds of production are necessary to support people's livelihoods, 'market' production and 'home' production (Evenson 1981). The unpaid work which women do in the home may have no market value, but such 'home production processes' are economic activities in that they 'utilize resources which have real costs, i.e. they could be devoted to alternative income-generating pursuits'. One of the resources is water. Another is the women's own labour power, which is often subjected to conflicting demands from 'market' activities, (tending a crop or earning wages) and from home production duties. A third type of resource used in home production is the household's capital equipment — its cooking pots, stoves, brushes, water-carrying containers, and if it possesses them, pipes, taps, cisterns and so on. Finally, there are resources such as food which are regularly bought in and subjected to some form of processing in the course of the home production activity.

Arguments of this sort proceed by saying that although home production has no market value, a cash value can be ascribed to it by noting what kind of market opportunities are given up in order to undertake home production. If a woman has the chance to take paid work and might then earn up to six rupees per day, but instead she chooses to stay at home and care for her children, then she is said to be 'producing' a child-care 'service' which she values at more than six rupees.

Evenson (1981) argues that ideas about income and livelihood 'take on a quite different meaning in this approach. The conventional definition of income is oriented to market goods.' However, in the new home economics, the value of goods consumed in a household is not just what is paid for them. It also takes account of the resources applied to them within the household. The value of a meal is not just the market cost of the basic ingredients plus the cost of the fuel and water used in cooking. There is also some 'value added' as a result of the time and effort and capital used in preparing and cooking it. Thus the value of goods and services consumed in a household *exceeds* the value of the market goods involved in their production.

Theoretically, one might attempt to estimate the value of water used in the home by an extension of this approach. When water has to be carried some distance from its source to the household where it is used, water carrying must be regarded as an aspect of 'home production'. The low productivity of this activity will enforce *time* and *resource* constraints on other activities. There are many documented instances of malnutrition in young children occurring at busy times in the farming year because women have so much work to do in the fields that they spend less time preparing food. Mothers are torn between 'market' and 'home' production activities, and if water-carrying time can be reduced, this might allow production to rise in either or both sectors.

At the same time, when domestic water has to be carried some distance it is observed that families rarely use *enough* water for hygiene practice to be adequate. The high incidence of diarrhoeal and skin diseases in many countries may be directly attributed to this resource constraint. If the only water obtainable is contaminated, its poor quality may also be regarded as a resource constraint.

If a greater volume of water is made available to a family, domestic and personal hygiene can improve, there may be new possibilities with regard to cooking, home maintenance might be better, and garden vegetables might be watered. All these benefits could be valued either as home production, or, in the case of the vegetables, as market production and a benefit/cost ratio for the improved water supply could then be calculated.

More simply, we may look back at the different circumstances in which rainwater collection is commonly applied and ask: 'what is the significance of the techniques for people's livelihoods in relieving either time constraints or resource constraints?' For example, in semi-arid areas and on islands where rainwater harvesting is used, water shortages are likely to be a constraint on all forms of production, and the prime requirement is to make more of the resource available. By contrast, in moist climates, it may less often be necessary to think of rainwater collection as a means of relieving a resource constraint, e.g. supplying more water to crops, but it may be relevant to consider reducing time constraints, especially on 'home' production activities such as child care. Table 2.1 summarizes other livelihood support activities for which rainwater harvesting might have relevance, and for the sake of completeness, points out that many livelihoods depend not only on production but on receipts of welfare, interest or other 'transfers of resources'. Conversely, livelihoods are diminished to the extent that interest or taxes have to be paid out.

These arguments may again seem academic, but in Chapter 3, we will find that they are relevant to establishing *design criteria* for rainwater harvesting systems. For example, it may prove that a larger volume of water storage is required for each household when *resource* constraints are critical than when the problem is one of *time* constraints on production during a fairly short season.

There is not always a sharp distinction between the different categories in Table 2.1. In most respects, growing vegetables and other crops is certainly a 'market production' activity, because even when the food is grown for subsistence rather than for market, and the work is done without pay by women of the household, the crops have a market value and may be occasionally sold if a surplus is produced, or the family has an urgent need for cash. However, Ninez (1984) points out that many household gardens are used as what she calls 'budget gardens', meaning that they form part of a family's strategy for adapting to changing economic circumstances. When families are poor, or if a wage-earner loses his job, the household garden is likely to be intensively used for growing vegetables and even staples. If the family becomes more prosperous, vegetables and herbs may be increasingly oriented towards making meals taste better rather than as substitutes for food purchases, and flowers may also be grown. When such changes occur, there is a shift from use of the garden for 'market production' towards its use as a means of improving the quality of life within the home, which counts as a 'home production' activity.

Many of the other benefits of using rainwater come into the 'home production' category, especially where the water is cleaner or has a better taste than water from elsewhere. If better health results from using cleaner water, this too may have more significance as 'quality of life' than as higher production potential.

The point about household gardens is particularly relevant in that they

Table 2.1 Some basic livelihood support activities, with rough indications of the possible relevance of rainwater collection in relieving either 'time' (T) or 'resource' (R) constraints.

	arid and semi-arid regions	regions with moist climates	islands; isolated 'riverless' communities
SOURCES OF LIVELIHOOD			
Market production			
Animal husbandry	R	-	-
Crop production	R	T*	R
Services, trade, tourism	-	-	R
Manufactures, artisan trades	R**	-	R**
Water vending	(R)	(R)	(R)
Home production			
Carrying the family's water	T	T	-
Food preparation and cooking	R, T	T*R†	R
Child care	R, T	T*	R
Domestic hygiene, personal hygiene	R	R†	R
Home maintenance	R	-	R
Transfers of resources			
Total receipts less payments from:			
– inheritance			
– interest			
– rents			
– taxes			
– welfare handouts	-	-	-
Fixed water rates	R	R	R

* In moist climates, time constraints which can be relieved by rainwater collection are usually limited to short seasons when labour requirements for other work are at a peak.

** Manufacture of many types of rainwater tank requires water, e.g. for ferrocement or for puddling clay. Many tanks fail because cement or concrete is not 'cured' by being kept wet for a time after setting.

† resource constraints possibly due to contamination of available water

( ) Rainwater collection may have a negative effect on livelihoods unless water vendors control tanks.

will often be watered more frequently if the family acquires a tank for collecting rainwater from its own roof. Even if the water in the tank is reserved for drinking, water from other sources may more often be used to sustain a vegetable crop through a rainless period or for transplanting seedlings. Even with crop production on a *field* scale a rainwater tank which is too small for any sort of regular irrigation may allow a crop to be planted with water earlier than otherwise, leading to gains either in yield or in opportunities for a second crop. Ray (1984) considers that in the right circumstances, this use of rainwater for early planting may have a very high economic efficiency as measured in terms of benefits and costs.

Another instance where the sharp distinctions of Table 2.1 need to be qualified concerns payment for water. Where charges for a water supply or for irrigation water are levied at a fixed rate almost as a tax, they can be classed in the table as 'transfer' payments. However, when water is sold by vendors, it becomes a market commodity like food which some households depend on for a livelihood and others purchase. In these circumstances, water carrying should be classed as market production rather than home production.

This example serves as a reminder that in examining connections between rainwater collection and livelihoods, we need to be aware that an ill-designed project might lead to increased inequalities, or may actually worsen livelihoods for the poorest groups in society. There are several ways in which this may occur. Firstly, it is important to recognize that one person's time constraint is sometimes another's employment opportunity. Some people gain their livelihoods as water vendors or as well-diggers and may be thrown out of work when better-off people acquire rainwater tanks, unless the tanks lead to the creation of relevant, new kinds of employment.

Secondly, where tanks collecting rainwater from roofs are proposed, families with thatched roofs may not be catered for, and families without permanent homes, and hence lacking permanent roofs, cannot be served — yet they may be the poorest families who have most need of the water.

Thirdly, even when equipment is subsidized, it may still be too expensive for the very poor, and only better-off families will then benefit from the subsidy. There is thus a need to devise systems which have very low costs, or whose costs take the form of resources which the poor already possess, chiefly their own labour during seasons when employment opportunities are least.

THE SOCIAL RELEVANCE OF RAINWATER

While preceding paragraphs may classify the benefits of rainwater technologies, it is important to enquire whether local people see things in the same way. *Time* constraints, for example, may easily be misunderstood. Where women normally carry their household water, the time saved when supplies improve is not necessarily used for increased production. In one Indian village, better water supplies led to more water being consumed, so the women spent just as much time carrying it, even though the distance was shorter (Chauhan and Gopalakrishnan 1983). The question might then be whether the increased consumption led to an improvement in livelihoods.

On the other hand, there are undoubtedly situations, especially in sub-Saharan Africa, where labour shortages during peak times in the cultivation cycle are a constraint on agricultural yields and output. The problem is particularly great in those countries such as Botswana, Lesotho and Kenya, where migration of men to cities or industrial areas means that food production is largely left to women and children. There are also some places where it is usual for men to carry water — for example, Java (Latham 1984b); or where water is carted rather than being manually carried, in which case, water carrying will be more likely to compete for time with 'market' rather than 'home' production.

For such reasons, men and women will often see the benefits of rainwater collection differently, and neither may value the particular advantages which planners imagine to be important. There are other viewpoints to consider also. Rainwater projects must produce benefits that are valued by those whose support is needed if they are to be financed from public funds. Therefore, as well as benefits for individual householders or farmers, it may well be necessary to show that a rainwater project has something to offer the wider community. One limitation here is that although rainwater collection may lead to some increase in market production in the semi-arid hinterland area, the overall production increase for the nation is likely to be quite small. The question then is: 'how can policy-makers be persuaded to allocate scarce resources and improve water supplies with such little result?' On the premise that rainwater harvesting schemes in poor dry areas should also provide some tangible benefits to people in the better-off heartlands, Ray (1983) suggests that there can be wider gains in the following respects:

Resource conservation. Many semi-arid zones provide the upper catchments for rivers which flow through the towns and cities of the heartlands. Flood control, erosion control, groundwater recharge, and reduced silting at major dams are possible benefits from rainwater harvesting. Measures to reafforest watersheds and control grazing can be readily related to the direct interests of city-dwellers. Rainwater harvesting schemes which require public expenditure for conservation measures can be justified on these grounds.

Cost-effectiveness. For scattered settlements, rainwater
harvesting can often be presented as a cheaper alternative to a
much more costly piped water scheme which would be impossible
to justify on economic grounds.

Employment and skills. Populations in semi-arid areas may be
too dispersed to construct major schemes and works, but
perfectly adequate for small-scale rainwater harvesting
construction. The making of jars and cisterns helps build up local
skills as well.

Self-reliance. A further benefit which may be appreciated by the
planners responsible for committing public money to finance
rainwater collection in marginal areas is that with improved water
supplies, such areas become less likely to require famine relief and
health expenditures; they may become more politically stable and
more closely identified with the nation as a whole. At the same
time, if livelihoods in these areas improve, there may be less
migration to shanty towns on the fringes of cities. Even better,
past rural migrants to the towns may return home.

Ray (1983) concludes that these potential benefits, 'are not the
ones usually cited by donor agencies', but are present as implicit goals in
most rainwater collection schemes considered a 'success' by those involved.
The goals we mentioned earlier, concerned with alleviating poverty and
improving livelihoods, are often more explicitly recognized as the
objectives of rainwater and similar projects. However, in practice it is
important to demonstrate that rainwater harvesting 'is also a worthwhile
investment from the national point of view'.

The idea that rural development might provide counterattractions
capable of bringing people back from the towns, or at least, stemming the
flow of migrants to the urban areas, has often proved a vain hope.
However, one project in the hinterland of Bombay provides a small but
successful example. Known as the Gram Gourav Pratisthan, meaning
Village Pride Trust, its location is indicated on Fig. 2.3. The basic principle
is that households owning very small areas of land — some as little as 0.2ha
— can come together to manage a water source and use it for irrigation.
This makes it possible to grow two crops each year instead of one, and the
results have been sufficiently impressive for recent migrants to Bombay
with land rights in the area to join the water management groups and
subscribe their share of the cost. In one village, some 25 families out of 100
were living in Bombay or other towns, and the project leader estimated that
15 would shortly return 'for a better life than in the slums'. In another
village, 7 out of 35 families in a water management group had returned to
the countryside from an urban existence in Sholapur (Chambers 1981;
Paralkar 1982).

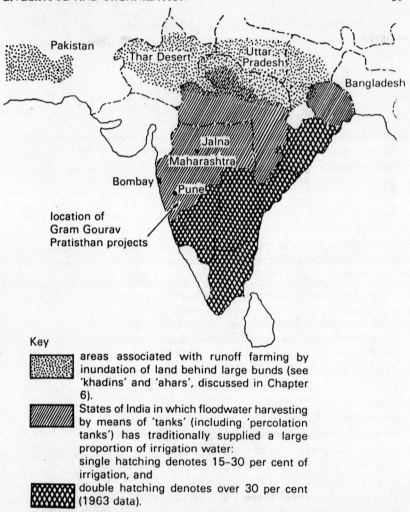

Key

areas associated with runoff farming by inundation of land behind large bunds (see 'khadins' and 'ahars', discussed in Chapter 6).

States of India in which floodwater harvesting by means of 'tanks' (including 'percolation tanks') has traditionally supplied a large proportion of irrigation water:
single hatching denotes 15–30 per cent of irrigation, and

double hatching denotes over 30 per cent (1963 data).

Fig. 2.3   Location of the Gram Gourav Pratisthan (GGP) projects in India, and the background of contrasting water harvesting traditions. The GGP projects make use of water from percolation 'tanks'. (Prasad 1979; UNEP 1983)

This programme is based on floodwater harvesting by check dams and percolation tanks built across small streams. A percolation tank is, in effect, a dam built on permeable ground so that floodwater is held back long enough to percolate into the ground and raise water levels in wells further down the valley (Fig. 2.4). Thus the water is stored underground as much as behind the dam (where evaporation losses are high), but a pump is then required to draw water from the well and irrigate cultivated land. The problem for the owners of the very small plots is that although the percolation tanks and wells exist, the cost of the pump (usually electrically

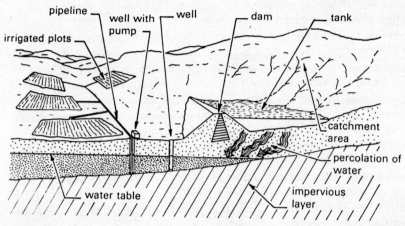

Fig. 2.4   Schematic view of the operation of a percolation tank which retains floodwater and recharges an aquifer so that land may be irrigated by pumping from wells. Percolation tanks are usually formed by building dams or bunds across natural drainage channels. They fall into the general category of 'water harvesting', or 'floodwater harvesting', but depend on channel flow and are usually on a larger scale than 'rainwater collection' in its most specific sense.

powered) and the necessary pipes is more than they can afford and greater than can be justified by their own fraction of a hectare. It is only if 30 or 40 families with adjacent plots share a pump that a scheme becomes viable.

In fact, the programme now consists of 52 water management groups in which there are a total of 1,725 families with 1,333ha of land to irrigate (Ray 1984). The success of the scheme depends on its parent organization (known as the Pani Panchayat) which sponsors the water management groups, offering soft loans, negotiating grants and establishing legal title to water rights at wells. Each group has its own leader and a paid field assistant whose job is to keep a log book of irrigations requested and carried out, and of loan repayments. Fortnightly meetings are held for group leaders and assistants where problems are discussed and information from the official agricultural extension service is circulated.

As with the pastoral groups in Africa mentioned earlier, there is the prospect here that water technologies can raise the level of livelihood for the rural poor provided that the scale is right for a group of families to work together. The organisational factor is crucial. There is a need to avoid the inefficiencies of large co-operatives, but yet to overcome the disadvantages of extreme small scale which the individual low income family will otherwise face.

It is tempting to assume that villages, where they exist, provide the right size of unit. But villages may be divided, sometimes bitterly, by conflicts of interest, and in India by caste. In African countries as well as in India, bland assumptions about community participation in water developments can be entirely invalidated by such problems. In several instances in South

India, for 'historical and economic reasons, the sense of being one village community does not exist' (Chauhan and Gopalakrishnan 1983). However, some sections of a village may be united by common interests, by common problems of poverty or poor housing, as well as by networks of extended family relationships. It is groups based on such bonds that may have the best chance of success in the 'participatory' schemes for management of agricultural or water resources (UNRISD 1974).

In the Gram Gourav Pratisthan most water management groups appear to have been formed on the initiative of their own members, many of whom do have family links or share common problems. One group includes a number of widows farming their own land. Once groups are formed, representative members attend regular meetings of the Pani Panchayat to request recognition of their project. Small groups such as this obviously need some such parent organization to provide technical advice, to co-ordinate purchases of equipment, and so on.

The importance of effective organization is also emphasized by the fate of many traditional rainwater or floodwater harvesting systems under modern conditions. Often the labour to build and maintain dams, tanks and runoff collecting channels was organized under a degree of pressure from authoritarian social structures. Sometimes these were relatively paternalistic and fostered a sense of village solidarity and co-operation; sometimes, as in parts of West Africa (as well as Asia), water resources were developed under systems of caste-work and even slavery. With the decline of such institutions, maintenance of old earthworks has often been neglected and the construction of new ones has ceased.

For example, the decline in the efficiency and use of floodwater harvesting in India by means of tanks and contour bunds (*ahars*) has been attributed to the disappearance of *zamindar* landlords who owned large tracts of land and could require tenants to remove silt from tanks or build new bunds. Ray (1984) confirms that the 'broader context' of rainwater harvesting in India is dominated by 'the decline of traditional authority' and the parallel loss of 'village concensus' and communal effort. The new atmosphere is one in which opportunity for individual gain has been greatly enhanced.

Experience in other countries underlines this point. In North Yemen, the ancient feudal system in which less than 10 per cent of the population controlled 90 per cent of the land was also highly successful in sustaining agricultural production through water conservation. But recently, with tenants gaining more independence by taking up temporary industrial employment outside the country, runoff farms and terraced cultivation have been neglected.

In the very different conditions of Mao's China, major water conservation works — including much floodwater harvesting — were constructed by large labour forces organized by the communes. But with the more individualistic type of farming recently introduced — the so-called 'responsibility system' — it is suggested that the maintenance and extension of these works will become much more difficult (Hinton 1984).

One cannot envisage the return of autocratic landlords, or even a new development of large communes, and questions may therefore be raised about the continuing relevance or applicability of some forms of water harvesting. The value of the Pani Panchayat programme in India is that it demonstrates a form of organization for water management which does not depend on authoritarian structures but on voluntary co-operation. However, it may also be that the smaller scale of rainwater collection as compared with floodwater harvesting will eventually provide a better fit with the new kinds of organization which are emerging.

3. DATA COLLECTION AND DESIGN CRITERIA

TECHNICAL AND SOCIAL ASSESSMENTS

The essence of appropriate technology is that equipment and techniques should be relevant to local resources and needs, to feasible patterns of organization, and to the local environment. It is easy to talk generally about these things, as in the previous chapter, but the design of rainwater tanks or runoff farming systems for a specific area requires a much more detailed analysis. Information will be needed about rainfall, existing water sources, availability of materials, housing and roof types, and the people's means of livelihood. However, there are likely to be different points of view about local needs and how the project may affect them — as was also seen in the previous chapter. Experts on water supply, local residents and government officials may all have different views about what should be the goals of the project. One essential task, therefore, is to collect information which clarifies these different views and seeks common ground between them.

It may appear that the more technical aspects of a cistern or ground surface catchment will have to be designed by trained personnel without reference to local views. However, design decisions made this way are often compromised by site conditions, or negated by the purposes for which people actually use rainwater. One might make a precise technical calculation about the optimum size of tank only to find that a different size is built in order to make construction easier, or to cut costs. Even if the tank is built to specification, its size may prove to be wrong because its users draw water from it in different quantities or at different intervals from those assumed, or use it in unexpected ways, such as to store water brought from other sources (as in Botswana and Indonesia: Latham 1984b; Gould 1983). In other words, innovations concerning the use of tanks are likely to be made after the design process, as conventionally understood, has been completed.

Thus the development of an appropriate technology for rainwater collection (or for anything else) cannot be achieved by the simple process of collecting information and using it to formulate an optimum design. It is necessary instead to think in terms of an 'innovative dialogue' in which information, opinion and innovation come from users of the system as well as designers. A more conventional term for this process is 'adaptive research', which usefully denotes the need to modify techniques to suit local conditions but which does not sufficiently acknowledge the input which must come from local informants. If an introduced technology is to take root in a particular locality what is needed, in addition to research as a specialist activity carried out by experts, is a dialogue — such as that described by Payne (1985) as 'interactive research'. He argues that the impact of technical expertise on human welfare is limited by 'how well we make the connection between professionalism and the problems experienced and perceived by the majority of the population'. In the context of rural society, an approach is required in which professionals interact with local people, 'not merely to study them but to listen and learn from them'.

One example concerns experts on crop storage who recommended a range of metal grain bins for use in Andhra Pradesh (in India) on the basis of conventional engineering criteria. They ignored existing grain storage methods in the area, assuming them to be inefficient and wasteful without making any measurements that could provide a check. But their recommended grain bins were found to be costly and inappropriate, and no progress was made until another research team began again, this time with a study of the traditional storage techniques already in use, and devised improvements of them based on discussion with local craftsmen (Greeley 1978). The same contrast is to be seen in technical reports on rainwater collection. All too often such reports discuss hydrology in terms of computer runs on rainfall records, but offer only the barest comment on whether local people already collect rainwater from roofs (perhaps in portable containers) or whether they already cultivate small plots by runoff farming methods. Indeed one has to turn to the work of social anthropologists (e.g. Bradfield 1971, Morgan 1974) to find out about such things.

Yet if water specialists were better prepared to observe traditional water catchment arrangements, they could gather many general clues about the hydrology of the area and the kinds of technique likely to work well, as will be shown in Chapter 6. If they were prepared to 'interact' more directly and talk to local farmers, they could learn about dates when the soil is moist enough for planting, frequency of crop failures, and many other matters. Moreover, awareness of traditional techniques might suggest how modern equipment could be used to build on existing practices rather than displacing them.

One manual on the training of fieldworkers for rainwater tank construction projects which recognizes these points is the *Training Guide* of the American WASH programme. This suggests that the initial compilation of information for planning a rainwater project in a particular village should be subdivided between a 'social assessment' and a 'technical assessment'. Both are conceived in terms of dialogue — that is, interactive research.

The technical assessment begins by seeking out formal rainfall records from weather stations near the project area. Frequently, the figures obtained will be unreliable, or will come from places that seem unrepresentative of the project site. Fieldworkers must then necessarily turn to the 'oral, qualitative data base', asking people about wet and dry seasons, observing visual impressions of rainfall intensity, and noting folklore about droughts (Kay 1983). Thus the WASH *Training Guide* advises that if amounts of rainfall have to be guessed using records from some rather distant weather station and a map showing isohyets, villagers can provide a check on the adequacy of the estimates so obtained. By contrast, the *social* assessment suggested is concerned with collecting information on:

- existing rainwater catchment practices;
- opinions of local people about the usefulness and quality of water collected from roofs — what type of water use would have highest priority: drinking, cooking, washing, livestock or garden?
- opinions as to whether shared or individually owned rainwater tanks would be best;
- views of people interested in acquiring rainwater cisterns as to how much time and money they would wish to expend.

Information should also be collected on the chief means of livelihood in the village and on time and resource constraints affecting these. Some preliminary views can be formed as to whether, and how, rainwater collection could make a contribution to local livelihoods. It is important that this be done searchingly and frankly because there is always a danger that a project team aiming to build rainwater cisterns will press ahead towards construction without being sure that the cisterns can really meet a need, or that people want them and can afford them.

If technical and social assessments lead to the conclusion that it would be desirable to construct cisterns in a particular locality there would then be need for further data collection, this time to compile what the *Training Guide* calls an 'inventory of local skills, materials and experience.' The importance of this is that if one can devise rainwater collection equipment based on materials which people know how to use, it will be easier and cheaper to build and maintain. Data included in the inventory would cover costs and wages, as well as dealing with available materials and identifying local craftsmen (especially masons, basket-makers, or people capable of making large pots).

In countries such as Thailand and Indonesia, to which the *Training Guide* is closely related, it may seem obvious that local skills of this sort should be fully used. But in Africa, where local skills may be less clearly compatible with western techniques, project planners have often ignored them completely. Many development programmes fail, and much environmental degradation and soil erosion occur because local construction techniques are ignored or undervalued.

THE SIGNIFICANCE OF HOUSING

In nearly all technical and social assessments, and in most inventories of materials and skills, considerable attention must necessarily be devoted to housing conditions. If collecting of rainwater from roofs is envisaged there is an obvious requirement for information about the materials of which roofs are made. Enquiries should also be made about whether any gutters have been fitted, and whether households already collect rainwater — even if from only small lengths of roof (Fig. 3.1).

If surveys extend to other aspects of housing, and also to ancillary buildings, they can yield useful information about local building materials and methods. It may be especially instructive to examine grain storage bins, since these are often roughly the same size and shape as rainwater cisterns. Thus, in the past, disused rainwater tanks have been re-used as granaries (in Botswana for example) and conversely several innovations in cistern design have originated from traditional types of food store. For example, the *Ghala* tank which is built in Kenya is made by modifying a traditional granary basket or Ghala and plastering it inside and out with a 2:1 sand/cement mixture (see Box 3.1) This technique also owes a good deal to reports of traditional water jars in Thailand. Another example is the large adobe (mud-walled) grain bins used by the Dogon people of Mali, West Africa, which were adapted as water tanks by the addition of wire reinforcement and a plastered cement lining (Watt 1978).

Examination of local buildings and their surroundings may reveal other techniques which are relevant. The Botswana house compounds and threshing floors which are surfaced with a clay/cow dung plaster and can be used very effectively as rainwater catchments were mentioned in Chapter 1, whilst in Asia, the use of bamboo in construction is another local technique from which much has been learned (Kaufman 1983)

However, a housing survey may be valuable as much for its social as for its technological implications. One point to notice is whether houses are being extended or rebuilt, or whether many are in disrepair. Experience in several countries is that where houses are being actively improved, it is relatively easy to arouse people's interest in such things as latrines, rainwater tanks or new types of cooking stove — items which can all be perceived as desirable additions to the home. On the other hand, if housing is seriously overcrowded or poorly constructed and people cannot afford any improvement, they will not be able to afford rainwater tanks either.

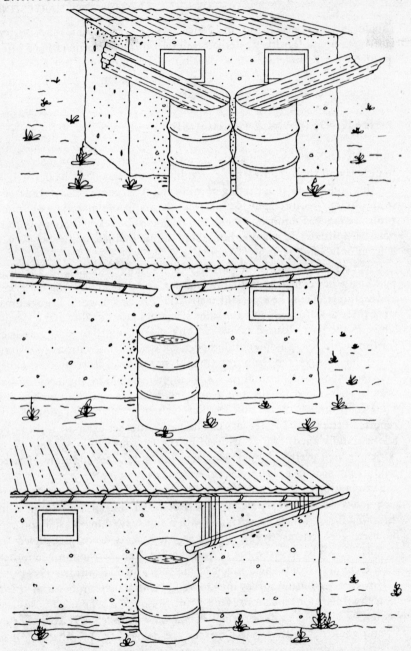

Fig. 3.1   Improvised rainwater collection with 200 litre oil drums used for storage (after Hofkes, 1981 and White et al., 1972). A survey in Kisii, Kenya, revealed that 33 per cent of households collected water in oil drums compared with 17 per cent which had permanent tanks. Most of the remaining families collected some runoff from roofs in pots, pans or buckets placed under eaves during storms. (Omwenga 1984)

Box 3.1 Construction of a plastered basket or 'Ghala' tank of 2.3m³ capacity. (UNICEF, 1982)

Materials See Table 5.3

Construction of basket A 'Ghala' or granary basket is made without a base as in Diagram 1. In Kenya, the basket frame is made from sticks from a woody shrub which grows country-wide. In Rwanda and Burundi, the frame is made from bamboo. Provided that the material is strong, the basket could conceivably be made from any number of shrubs or sticks which can be woven into basket form.

The actual shape does not seem very important, but it is recommended that the bottom be omitted so that the sides can bond with the base.

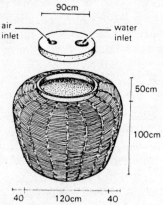

Diagram 1

Method of construction

1a. Construct a foundation of rocks 200cm diameter, 20cm deep.

b. Spread murram on the rocks and stamp down to a 1-5cm thickness. (Murram is a naturally occurring mix of sands, clays and pebbles commonly used in road surfaces.)

c. Lay a 2.5cm layer of concrete 1:2:4 on the foundation.

d. Place the water pipe with socket and tap fitted in position as shown in Diagram 2.

e. Place a 5cm layer of concrete 1:2:4 on the foundation.
Immediately place the basket centrally on the foundation and work it into the concrete.

g. Add concrete as necessary around the base of the basket to ensure that it is firm within the foundation (see Diagram 2).

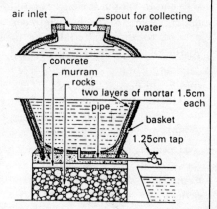

Diagram 2

2a. After the base has set, a mason should begin plastering the inside from the bottom up. Careful attention must be given to bond the sides with the base, adding a little cement to give a smooth curve.

b. Plaster the inside of the basket with two layers of plaster. The first layer should be a 1.5cm thick 1:3 cement and sand mixture and the second 1.5 cm thick 1:2 cement and sand mixture.

c. Apply the plaster with a trowel, first by throwing the cement on to the weave and then smearing it on and smoothing it in. The outside of the tank is plastered in a similar fashion.

d. Cure the plaster by draping the tank with wet sacking as soon as the cement has set. After 12 hours, fill the tank to a quarter capacity—this greatly helps the curing process. Keep the sacking wet for a minimum of seven days.

Note: poor curing has been the major cause of tanks cracking and the correct use of the procedure should be strongly emphasised. It should also be pointed out that curing cement can be assisted by immersing water up to 45 days.

e. Construct a lid on the ground using reinforced cement (see Diagram 2). A suitable form can easily be cut out in the earth. Lids are usually between 3-5 cm thick, depending on the tank opening.

One way of checking on how realistic a proposed cistern design might be is to enquire about the cost of building a house in the locality concerned. If materials needed for the cistern cost more than 10 or 15 per cent of what is needed to buy materials for a house, the cistern is probably too costly. The Ghala tank in Kenya, and cisterns built in Indonesia and Thailand using bamboo reinforcement instead of metal, have been highly significant in enabling low-cost tanks to be made, though there is still some way to go in ensuring their durability. Another way of keeping costs down — which is used in many projects — is to construct smaller tanks than would otherwise be desirable.

However, the point of a survey of housing conditions goes deeper than seeking clues to what people can afford. It can also be a useful starting point for discussion with local people about their most urgent needs. What people say they want will often be quite different from what the professional thinks they need. And while the professional may validly provide information to encourage people to see their needs in a different light, this should be in the context of a dialogue, not pressurized forms of health education designed to change views at all costs. What professionals ought to recognize is that however great their sense of mission and however justifiable their views about water, local householders will see their inadequate supply as just one of a whole range of problems, others being connected with housing, food, low income, family relationships and so on — all the problems of poverty and of the human condition. A particular improvement in water supply, attractive in isolation, may not fit well with a strategy for coping with other problems, and in any case, the poorest people may see their most urgent needs in terms of food and housing, not water and health (Chauhan and Gopalakrishnan 1983).

What water-supply professionals need to do in such circumstances is to look for common ground where their own goals and those of the people overlap. If they aim only to build a certain type of rainwater cistern, and it is clear that the people have other priorities, there may be no basis for a project. However, it is unlikely that the issue will be posed as starkly as this. More probably, the survey of housing will identify some groups of homes with tiled or metal roofs in good repair and evidence of recent improvements and extensions, and it will be tempting to feel that these would provide the best starting point for a rainwater programme. In other areas, by contrast, houses may be in poor repair, with no recent building work done, and roofs so roughly thatched that collection of rainwater from them is hardly feasible.

It has often been commented that quick visual surveys of housing provide one of the easiest methods of identifying places where the low-income groups are to be found, and for advocates of rainwater harvesting this is likely to expose a particularly critical dilemma. Having found the groups of people likely to be most in need of a better water supply, one may then find that a rainwater system is almost impossible for them because of its cost and/or their inadequate roofs. One may then learn from the people that they want better housing far more urgently than they want water tanks.

At this point, the rainwater advocates will need seriously to consider where their priorities lie. Is their commitment and that of the funding agency to a specific technology, or to seeking to improve the livelihoods of the poor? To use the jargon of more sophisticated policy debates, is the priority 'technology push' or 'response to need'?

If the primary commitment is to demonstrate rainwater technology, the best chance of a successful project will be in the areas where houses already have good roofs and active home improvements are evident. On the other hand, if there is a commitment to working in the poor areas, various other possibilities ought to be considered. Firstly, there is the option of postponing rainwater collection as an immediate aim and initiating a housing improvement programme instead. This is more likely to accord with the people's own sense of priorities than is a specialist form of development which would leave the worst of their living conditions untouched. Sometimes, work with the very poor will mean accepting the continued use of traditional roofing materials and tackling the problems of collecting rainwater from thatch (Fig. 1.8). More often, perhaps, a housing improvement programme will lead to the installation of new types of roofing. Then, very simple forms of rainwater collection could be introduced almost immediately, perhaps using containers people already possess (Fig. 3.1), with short lengths of modern guttering, or if they can afford it, Ghala tanks (Box 3.1) or a local equivalent.

Better housing materials may be a particularly urgent need in the shanty towns which fringe many urban areas, where materials for thatched roofs may be almost unobtainable and corrugated iron expensive. Locally made tiles may be available or possibly wooden shingles — which can be made from coconut tree trunks that have been split. There are also new materials such as fibre reinforced cement, made into tiles. These have sisal or coconut-coir reinforcement and are potentially very cheap in regions where sisal or coconuts are grown (and where cement is available) (Parry 1981). In India, corrugated fibre sheeting made from waste paper has been successfully used, with impregnated asphalt for waterproofing and durability (Rao 1975).

A second option for advocates of rainwater collection who also feel a commitment to working with the poorest social groups is to try and understand why people in the project area are so poor. This would mean extending the data gathering exercise to seek extra information on local means of livelihood, and to gain insights into whether water resource development might contribute in any way. If the people have access to land, would extra water allow more crops to be grown? Or could it extend the growing season? If rainwater collection from roofs is not feasible, are there ground catchments that could be used — or even opportunities to collect runoff from road surfaces?

A third strategy, and the one most usually suggested for areas of poor housing, is to promote a communal rainwater system using the roof of some large public building as a catchment, such as a school or a church. Alternatively, where people cannot afford their own cisterns, but their house roofs are suitable for rainwater collection, shared tanks are a possibility. In Indonesia, for example, large tanks ($9m^3$ capacity) are sometimes shared by four families, and smaller tanks ($4.5m^3$) by two. Such arrangements may often be necessary, but there are difficulties in allocating responsibilities for maintenance of shared facilities and in ensuring that individual users do not take disproportionate amounts of water. Although there are generally doubts about the merits of communal as opposed to individual catchment tanks, where discussions have been held with local people, it is usually possible to state quite clearly which approach is preferred. Molvaer (1982) and Sinclair (1983) report 'a preference for individual household tanks in the Kitui District of Kenya', whereas Swift (1984) indicated 'the suitability of communal ground catchment systems' in some pastoral areas of West Africa where 'communal decision-making is a traditional practice'.

Clearly, then, information collection about housing is not simply a matter of observing and mapping roof types and building materials, but has implications which must lead on to discussion with local people about their preferences regarding house improvement, shared facilities, and several other matters.

THE HYDROLOGY OF RAINWATER SYSTEMS

With the data requirements of rainwater projects set in their wider context, it is now important to consider the more technical kinds of information that are essential for planning, especially those concerning rainfall. A first and vital point to notice is that the hydrology of rainwater collection needs to be approached differently according to whether one is dealing with runoff farming or the collection of water from roofs. With the latter, projects can be successfully initiated using very uncertain knowledge of rainfall amounts, but in runoff farming, a detailed appreciation of rainfall intensity and runoff is essential from the start. Many hours of labour may be required to construct bunds, channels and terraces to control the flow of runoff on cultivated land. If these are inadequate for the volume of runoff which actually occurs, and are destroyed or seriously damaged in the first major storm, the demonstration effect of the project will be extremely negative. The cultivators affected by such an experience may never try again.

Therefore, in areas where there is no prior experience of runoff farming,

Shanan and Tadmor, speaking about winter rainfall conditions (1979), advise that *at least* two years should be spent collecting rainfall and runoff data on site before any large-scale construction begins. There may be some traditional runoff farming in the area, study of whose performance can allow cultivation on new sites to begin earlier, and Chapter 7 indicates approaches based on this which differ markedly from what Shanan and Tadmor advise, particularly with reference to summer rainfall. However, it will always be desirable to identify a weather station in the region where records can be used as a guide to long-term minimum and average rainfalls. To check whether its data correlate with weather at the project site, daily records from the weather station should be compared with both quantities and timing of rainfall observed on site during the two year preliminary period.

Information to be sought from a weather station might also include data on temperatures and evaporation rates, especially for the season when the rain is recorded. This is because runoff farming must be carried out in a different way if the growing crop has to cope with the heavy evaporation losses of a hot summer, or alternatively, if it can benefit from the cooler growing conditions of a winter rainfall regime (see Chapter 6).

Information on rainfall intensities is especially important in the context of soil erosion. Storms in which intensities exceed 25mm/hour are very likely to cause erosion on exposed ground surfaces. In most temperate regions, only 5 per cent of rain comes into this category, but in the tropics, it can be up to 40 per cent.

For the design of microcatchments or runoff farming systems, then, we need a considerable amount of hydrological information, as summarized in Box 3.2. For example, during the nine growing seasons which occurred at Lokitaung in north-east Kenya between the years 1975-83, the average rainfall was 218mm. The following simple calculation was made to estimate the catchment: cultivation ratio for a sorghum crop:

Turkana sorghum requires 400mm of rain within the growing season, but the average rainfall is 218mm. Rain falling on the cultivated plot is therefore deficient by an average of 182mm, and an equivalent amount of water is the *minimum* which must be supplied in the form of runoff from the catchment area. However, it will be desirable to supply much more runoff than this since the actual rainfall will frequently be less than average. In this instance, experience suggested that if runoff equivalent to 400mm of rain on the cultivated area could be achieved in an 'average' season, providing the crop with 618mm in total, then the minimum requirement would be achieved in many drier years.

If the area of the cultivated plot in m^2 is represented by B, then runoff equivalent to an extra 400mm of rain amounts to a volume of 400 × B litres of water.

Box 3.2 Summary of measurements needed for design of microcatchments and runoff farming systems.

DATA REQUIRED

1. Daily rainfall measurements over 2–3 years from rain gauges about 2km apart on the project area.

2. Estimates of average and minimum monthly and annual rainfall.

3. Measurements of rainfall intensity and *runoff* in individual storms so that earthworks can be designed to cope with maximum water flows. Textbooks on runoff farming (Shanan and Tadmor 1979) and soil conservation (Hudson 1971) give details.

4. Estimates of total runoff in months prior to and during the growing season in order to calculate the catchment area needed to provide sufficient water for the crop. Ratios of *cultivated to catchment areas* vary from 1:2 or 1:5 in Texas and Arizona (Fangmeier, 1975; Jones and Hauser, 1975) to 1:20 or 1:30 in the Negev Desert (Evenari *et al.*, 1982).

5. Measurements of open pan evaporation and of *soil moisture* may be useful in refining calculations of necessary catchment areas, optimum planting dates, etc.

To measure RAINFALL INTENSITY, it is best to use a continuously recording rain gauge with a pen trace. It is also possible to time the lengths of individual storms, note rainfall, and calculate average intensity in mm/hour. (Peak intensity may be estimated from the average values by methods given in the aforementioned textbooks.)

To measure RUNOFF, small runoff plots can be laid out on proposed catchment area, (see diagram). Sites should be chosen with surface conditions and slopes that are typical. Allowance must be made for the fact that runoff is a much greater proportion of rainfall on small catchments as compared with large ones (Chapter 1).

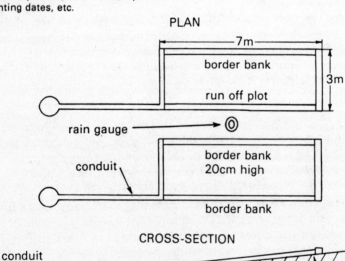

PLAN

CROSS-SECTION

The amount of runoff actually obtained from the catchment was estimated by the method described in Box 3.2, and was found to be 30 per cent of the rainfall, that is:

$$\frac{30}{100} \times 218\text{mm in an average year.}$$

If the area of the catchment is A, the actual volume of water running off it is then:

$$\frac{30}{100} \times 218 \times A \text{ litres,}$$

which must provide the requirement of $400 \times B$ litres previously specified. Equating these two quantities, we can then calculate the necessary ratio of catchment area to cultivated area, A:B.

$$\text{Thus A:B} = \frac{400}{218} \times \frac{100}{30} = 6.1:1$$

Despite the allowances made in this calculation for drier seasons than average, a greater margin of safety is actually sought in this part of Kenya, and the ratio of catchment to cultivated area normally used is about 10:1.

By contrast, when rainwater is to be collected from house roofs, much more approximate data is usually sufficient. The main question hydrologists need to ask is 'how big should the storage tank or cistern be?' This breaks down into three subsidiary problems:

1. matching the capacity of the tank to the area of the roof;
2. matching the capacity of the tank to the quantities of water required by its users;
3. choosing a tank size that is appropriate in terms of costs, resources and construction methods.

Some researchers have devoted considerable attention to calculating answers for the first two questions, using computers to process long runs of rainfall records where these are available (see Fujimura 1982), or even to simulate data where records are missing. This may be appropriate in some richer countries where the usual approach is to start with the second question above, specifying a desirable level of consumption and then designing catchment areas and storage tanks so that this can be provided. By contrast, in poorer countries much greater weight has to be placed on cost, and hence on the third question. It also makes sense to take account of what resources are available — roofs as they already exist, local materials, and labour. One can then work out a plan for expending these resources in a way that comes as close as possible to a target for water consumption (Keller 1982). In practice, costs and construction methods tend to limit tanks to smaller capacities than would otherwise be justified by roof areas or likely needs of consumers.

For this reason, elaborate calculations aimed at matching tank capacity to roof area and consumption are usually unnecessary. However, a simplified calculation of this form can give a rough idea of the potential for rainwater collection in a particular region. The starting point is data for average monthly rainfall, expressed in millimetres, and measurements of the roof from which rain is to be collected — its length and *horizontal* width. The volume of water (in litres) likely to be collected each month is then found by multiplying the average monthly rainfall by the horizontal area covered by the roof (in square metres), and then multiplying by 0.8.

The latter figure is the runoff coefficient, and allows for the fact that some rainfall will be lost from the roof by evaporation and in other ways. While 0.8 is typical for a hard roof, the number to adopt here would be better chosen in the light of the roofing material actually used, for which some rough figures are given in Table 3.1.

Table 3.1   Runoff coefficients. (Hofkes, 1981; UNEP, 1983; Frasier, 1975 and Gould, 1983)

Type of catchment	Coefficients
Roof catchments	
— tiles	0.8 - 0.9
— corrugated metal sheet	0.7 - 0.9
Ground surface coverings	
— concrete	0.6 - 0.8
— plastic sheeting (gravel covered)	0.7 - 0.8
— butyl rubber	0.8 - 0.9
— brick pavement	0.5 - 0.6
Treated ground catchments	
— compacted and smoothed soil	0.3 - 0.5
— clay/cow-dung threshing floors (Botswana; Gould 1983)	0.5 - 0.6
— silicone-treated soil	0.5 - 0.8
— soil treated with sodium salts	0.4 - 0.7
— soil treated with paraffin wax	0.6 - 0.9
Untreated ground catchments	
— soil on slopes less than 10 per cent	0.0 - 0.3[*]
— rocky natural catchments	0.2 - 0.5

[*] *Figures for specific sites should be determined using runoff plots as in Box 3.2.*

When expected monthly volumes of water have been estimated in this way, the figures are plotted on a diagram such as Figure 3.2. In this diagram, each calculated monthly total is added to the total for previous months so as to represent, by an approximate, stepped form of graph, the way in which water levels in a cistern would rise through the year if none were drawn off and used. In Figure 3.2, the dry season is from May to September. Very little water enters the tank then, so the line on the diagram remains almost horizontal.

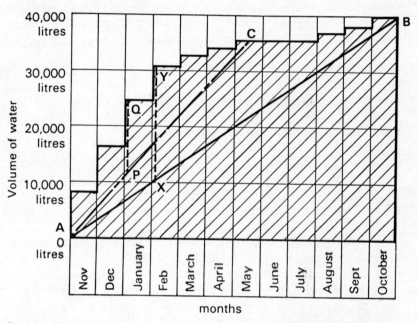

*Fig. 3.2   Diagram representing volumes of water collected from a roof (stepped line), and the consumption of water by users of a rainwater tank filled from that roof (sloping lines **AB** or **AC**). Each step in the line representing water collected indicates the contribution made by one month's rainfall. The diagram is drawn so that its left hand side corresponds to the month in which the tank is most likely to be empty. The steps thus represent the gradual filling of the tank during the rainy season.*

When plotting graphs of this kind, it is important to start at the left hand side with the beginning of the rainy season, when the tank is assumed to be empty, so that the way in which the water level rises during the rains is clearly illustrated. In Figure 3.2, the graph begins in November, which is the first month of really heavy rainfall.

Usually it is assumed that people will take the same amount of water from the tank each day throughout the year. This is unrealistic because consumption varies greatly with the seasons, and according to whether water from other sources is being used. However, by assuming a constant rate of consumption, we get a rough indication of the system's capabilities.

Again referring to Figure 3.2, the total amount of water running off the roof in a year of average rainfall is recorded as about 40,000 litres. So theoretically, if their cistern is of adequate size, the owners of the roof could ration themselves so as to use all this water in 365 daily withdrawals of 112 litres each. This steady rate of use is represented by the straight upward sloping line AB. At point B, where this line meets the stepped line representing rain water entering the system, the tank has been emptied, though it should be filled again almost immediately with the onset of the new rainy season. However, at point X, where the two lines are farthest apart, the tank is fuller than at any other time. The distance separating the two lines, XY, then represents a volume of 20,000 litres, which is thus an estimate of the capacity the tank should have — 20 m³ — if it is to provide the 112 litre daily ration.

Although it is unlikely that any household would draw exactly the same ration from the tank on every day of the year, it is possible to think of this as one method of using a rainwater tank. It might be called the 'rationing method'. By contrast, Parker (1973) working in Ghana, regarded it as more realistic to think of people using their tanks according to a 'rapid depletion method'. This envisaged that members of the household take all the water they require from the rainwater tank for as long as it contains water, and then turn to an alternative source. They will especially tend to do this if the alternative source is a long way from the house, or if they are working hard in the fields during the season when the tank is full, because the tank is so much more convenient.

In Figure 3.2, the steep line AC represents use of the tank by the 'rapid depletion' method, with point C indicating the date when the tank is empty. This is in May, and the maximum amount of water stored, represented by line PQ, is about 15,000 litres. So a tank of this latter size — 15m³ — would meet the rate of consumption shown as AC for about six months in the year: November to May.

This illustrates the paradoxical choice which often has to be made between a *large* tank capable of meeting a rationed rate of consumption over a whole year, or a *small* tank capable of providing for greater consumption on a rapid depletion basis. For most households, the latter will be the more realistic option.

Hafirs and excavated cisterns on arid grazing lands will have to meet a very different pattern of demand. During the brief rainy season, when animals can drink at natural water holes, there may be no withdrawals of water from a cistern or small hafir, only losses due to evaporation and perhaps leakage (Fig. 3.3, line AB). Then, when the water holes have dried up, herds will be moved so that they can graze within each reach of the hafir, and will be watered there regularly — perhaps daily, or perhaps on alternate days. Withdrawals will be very heavy — cattle drink between 20 and 100 litres per day depending on their breed and size, and varying with

ambient temperatures, but camels, goats and sheep require much less
(usually less than 5 litres). As water levels in the cistern or hafir get low, the
herdsmen will find out which other water points in the region can still
provide for their livestock, and will then move on. Figure 3.3 illustrates a
location with a short July-August rainy season, and indicates schematically
the likely consumption of 200 cattle for a 6 week period in the dry season.
Once again, the stepped line shows inflows to the cistern, and the straight
lines **ABC** show consumption. The cistern is empty at point C, and the
maximum storage required is indicated by **PX**.

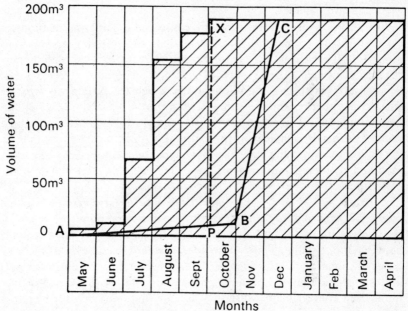

*Fig. 3.3   Volumes of water flowing into, and being consumed from a cistern (or very small hafir)
in an arid pastoral region. The rains come mainly in July and August. The cistern is used to provide
drinking water for livestock which graze in the area during November and early December. The
cistern is empty during mid-December until early May.*

AB *represents loss of water by evaporation while the cistern is not being used;*
BC *is the consumption of 200 cattle during 6 weeks, at the rate of 20 litres/head/day (approximately);*
PX *is the storage capacity required to meet this demand, which in this case is very slightly more
than the volume of water consumed by the animals.*

In designing a cistern or hafir for use in these circumstances, the starting
point should probably be an examination of how much grazing local
grasslands and forage shrubs can withstand. Cattle will graze within a day's
walk of the water point. If it is thought that the area defined by this can only
safely feed 200 cattle for six weeks, care should be taken to limit the
capacity **PX** to their likely requirements, so that lack of water forces the
herd to move on in due time, and allows the vegetation to recover.

TANK CAPACITIES IN PRACTICE

Reverting to the question of how large *household* water tanks should be, we have seen that it is unrealistic to assume that people will ration themselves precisely when using rainwater. However, lessons can still be learned by gathering together some of the varied recommendations for tank sizes which have been based on the idea of rationing. Thus in Table 3.2, the data given by a number of authors have been recalculated to provide information in a standard format relevant to roofs of revatively small houses, 30m² in extent. Where the original authors emphasize figures for much larger roofs, these are also included.

Not all the figures in this table are comparable. Differing methods of calculation (or estimation) have been used, and differing assumptions about runoff coefficients. More fundamentally, divergent views about how reliable rainwater systems should be are incorporated in the figures. Several authors specify conditions under which the system will operate with 95 per cent reliability — that is, with the tank containing water and maintaining the daily ration for 95 per cent of the time, but with supply failures during drought leaving the tank empty for 5 per cent of the time. As the figures for Botswana and Java show, recommendations may be greatly modified if altered requirements regarding reliability are fed into the calculation.

A surprising feature of Table 3.2 is that despite the large variations which might be expected to arise from different assumptions of this sort, recommendations for tank capacities mostly lie in a rather small range between 3m³ and 8m³. This is particularly remarkable in view of the wide range of climatic conditions represented. However, information from Java indicates that, in high-rainfall regions, authors may be suggesting smaller tanks than are feasible because they assume that households will restrict themselves to a rather limited daily ration. So even if local rainfall could provide a larger ration — say 60 litres per day in Java — tank capacities are specified for half this, presumably because that is consistent with a tank capacity which people can afford. Only for the two most prosperous countries represented, Australia and Bermuda, are significantly larger tanks recommended with a view to maximizing the daily ration.

This may seem to confirm the unreality of sophisticated hydrological calculations. Not only is the idea of a strict daily ration at variance with normal human behaviour, but many calculations are not entirely objective — they incorporate assumptions about how big the daily ration should be based on economic criteria. Observations of how much water people use for drinking and cooking can, of course, provide a rough guide, and a ration of 5 litres per person daily seems to accord with conditions in Indonesia (Kerkvoorden 1982) With typical families of between four and six individuals, it is thus tempting to design for 30 litres per household

Table 3.2   Some recommended rainwater tank capacities based on the assumption that water consumption is rationed to ensure an all-year supply (Water Panel, 1974 and data from the authors cited) (rel. = reliability)

REGION AND DATA SOURCE	MEAN ANNUAL RAINFALL* (mm)	SAMPLE ROOF AREA* (m²)	RECOMMEN- DED TANK CAPACITY (m³)	THEORETICAL DAILY RATION FOR RELIABLE ALL-YEAR SUPPLY (litres)
AFRICA				
Ghana, N.E. region (Parker 1973)	800 in two wet seasons;	30	7.5	66 (a)
Swaziland, Lowveld (Farrar 1974)	635 with 6 dry months;	30	5.0	37 (a)
Botswana, Francistown (Gould 1983)	470 with 7-9 dry months;	30	{ 4.5 / 4.5 / 8.0	31 (80% rel.) / 22 (95% rel.) / 31 (95% rel.)
INDONESIA				
Java, Jakarta area (Irish et al 1982)	1800 no really dry months;	30	{ 1.2 / 5.0 / 3.6 / 7.8	30 (80% rel.) / 60 (80% rel.) / 30 (99% rel.) / 60 (99% rel.)
Madura (Irish et al 1982)	1500 with 5 dry months;	30	5.1	30 (99% rel.)
Java, Yogyakarta area (Latham 1984)	1800 with 6 dry months;	(b)	5.0	30 (c)
THAILAND				
Khon Kaen area (Nopmongcol et al 1981)	1300 with 4 dry months;	60 / 30	11.5 / 5.8	90 (95% rel.) / 45 (95% rel.)
AUSTRALIA				
Sydney (Perrens 1982)	1210 no dry months;	320 / 30	126 / 11.8	800 (d) / 74 (d)
Griffith, New South Wales (Perrens 1982)	390 with no defined wet season;	965 / 30	336 / 10.5	800 (d) / 25 (d)
BERMUDA				
(Waller 1982)	1500 no dry months;	30	11.7	— (e)

* Most authors do not state recommendations for 30m² roofs but give graphs or tables from which these can be read off; the term 'dry month' is relative and does not imply total lack of rain.
(a) no statement of reliability (rel.) in these instances
(b) Latham quotes actual roof areas from which rainwater is collected ranging from 12 to 31m² with 62m² available in the latter case.
(c) recommendations based on experience, not exact calculation.
(d) average probability of failure once in 5 years
(e) figures based on local regulations, not exact calculation

daily. If the recommendations of Table 3.2 are followed, this would suggest tanks of 3.6m³ capacity for households in the Jakarta area.

In practice, however, tanks are constructed according to a smaller number of standard sizes: 2.5m³ and 10m³ in West Java, and 4.5m³ and 9m³ in the Yogyakarta area. So even if the recommendations concerning the most appropriate capacity could be regarded as precise and realistic, a tank could not be provided to match it. Many programmes standardize tank sizes and cannot tailor capacities to suit the rainfall of a particular area nor the number of consumers in a particular household, so on these grounds also, sophisticated calculation is unnecessary.

Commenting on tank capacities in the Yogyakarta region, Latham (1984b) concludes that they are 'determined by cost and ease of construction' more than by hydrological theory. On the basis of experience he suggests that the minimum storage volume per family which can supply *only drinking water* (5 litres/person/day) is about 5m³ for Yogyakarta. 'If any other use is to be satisfied by rainwater, each family should have 10m³ of storage.' As it is, 4.5m³ tanks are usually shared between pairs of families. They are used on a rapid depletion basis, and often go dry 'in as little as one month'.

Having commented that most of the recommended tank sizes in Table 3.2 are in the range 3-8m³ for a 30m² roof area, we may add that the standard sizes adopted in programmes operating in Africa and Asia represent a somewhat larger range: 2-12m³. One reason, of course, is variation in roof area. Although 30m² is a fairly typical catchment size (e.g. in Kenya and Indonesia), Latham (1984b) points out that many tanks collect water from only half a roof. In Indonesia and Thailand, 60m² or even 100m² could be used, justifying much larger tanks. By contrast, in Africa, many houses will have roofs of less than 30m².

However, tank capacities are in practice usually determined by what people can afford. The choice of a tank may also depend on what contribution it makes to people's livelihoods. If a tank is used by rapid depletion and only provides water for a few months each year, it is worth asking in what season will that water benefit livelihoods most?

Ray (1983) comments on the use of rainwater in gardens to extend the cropping season by a few weeks and allow a supplementary crop to be grown. If this relatively modest, seasonal use of water provides a major increment to livelihoods, either through sales or nutritional value, it may be optimal for a project to install tanks of only 3m³ capacity (which local people might say are too small), even though the unit costs of such tanks are greater than for tanks of 10m³ capacity. The economies of scale arising from the larger tank will be wasted if the extra water is unproductively used.

More typically, if the supply of drinking water from a tank is most significant in saving time spent carrying water during a busy season, the best size of tank will be the one which provides all the water needed during that season, but no more. However, where the problem a community faces is one of resource constraints — an absolute shortage of water at some time in the year, or a serious problem of water quality — it is less easy to suggest solutions for which small tanks will be adequate. The time when water is most needed may be the end of the dry season, yet this is when a small tank is almost certain to be empty. Noting this problem in Indonesia, Ray suggests that households might ultimately be advised to acquire two small tanks, one for use on a rapid depletion basis, the other to be held in reserve and not used at all until other sources have dried up. By contrast, in Kenya, Ray notes that when Ghala tanks were first introduced, the size was usually 1.1m^3, but these were felt to be rather small, and 2.2m^3 tanks are now most popular. In this context, village-level research by UNICEF concluded that rainwater collection can form a valuable *wet season* supply for the household, and that small containers suited to this limited function do make an impact on the household (Molvaer 1982).

Thus development workers are slowly accepting the seasonal value of tanks used on a rapid depletion basis, and have moved away from emphasis on rainwater for all-year supply, necessitating large and costly storage systems. Moreover, experience in Kenya is that once tanks of about 2 or 3m^3 are made available, they are in high demand. Agencies concerned to help the rural poor might perhaps do best by concentrating on this relatively small size of tank, in Kenya at any rate, since those who can afford larger tanks buy them on their own initiative. Many houses belonging to better-off farmers may be observed to possess 5-10m^3 tanks, made locally from corrugated galvanized iron, or from fired bricks (with cement lining and wire reinforcement).

In Indonesia, the preferred type of tank is one built of ferrocement with 9 or 10m^3 capacity. However, in order to provide a low-cost alternative for poor families, much work has been done on a tank in which bamboo is used in place of metal to reinforce the plastered cement walls. With this method of construction, the maximum size for a satisfactory tank is felt to be 4.5m^3 and several hundred tanks of this size have been built (O'Reilley 1984). As with Ghala tanks, there are still doubts about how long-lasting they will be. If the bamboo reinforcement is left exposed at any point, it deteriorates rapidly. In Thailand, bamboo is used to reinforce relatively thick-walled tanks built of concrete (rather than cement). There seem to be fewer problems with this method of construction, and tanks of just under 12m^3 capacity are regularly made (Fricke 1982).

It is construction methods such as these, and what can be afforded, which determine most choices of tank capacity, not hydrology. Data such as those of Table 3.2 are marginally useful mainly as a check on the tanks' theoretical capability.

WATER QUALITY AND HEALTH

A major advantage of rainwater collected from house roofs is that it is usually much cleaner than water from other sources (apart from boreholes and springs), and thus may offer a considerable advantage if reserved for drinking and cooking. However, it should not be assumed that water from roofs is totally free from contamination. Birds, small animals and wind-blown dirt may all contribute some pollution. Moreover, the water is usually lacking in mineral salts (including fluorides and calcium salts) whose presence in other water supplies is regarded as beneficial in appropriate proportions.

Wherever water quality tests have been carried out, some bacteriological contamination of water from roofs has been found. Often it is very slight, but one outbreak of diarrhoea on a Caribbean island was traced to bird excreta on a roof. On Belau, a Pacific island, water from 60 per cent of roofs was free of contamination, but samples from 25 per cent showed high total counts of coliform bacteria, and included some faecal coliforms (Romeo 1982). Experience in Bermuda seems to reflect a more consistently high rainwater quality, with no faecal coliforms detected and a maximum of 2 or 3 total coliforms per 100ml (Waller 1982).

Such findings may not always be very significant because conditions in the storage tank or cistern are more critical than conditions on the roof. A cistern formed by excavation below ground level, and any tank without a cover , is very much at risk. On the other hand, if a tank is completely covered, and if organic debris is prevented from entering with the water by means of a suitable strainer or filter, any bacteria or parasites carried by water flowing into the tank will tend to die off. Thus water drawn from tanks several days after the last rainfall will usually be of better bacteriological quality than the fresh rainwater.

When rain falls after a long dry period, water collected from a roof may carry noticeable amounts of debris arising from dust and leaves which have accumulated on the roofs and in gutters. Many authorities therefore recommended that water running off the roof during the first 10-20 minutes of a storm should be discarded, and many devices have been suggested for diverting this initial 'foul flush' away from storage tanks. The simplest method is to have flexible joints in the pipes conveying water from gutters to tanks (Fig. 3.4), or gadgets which automatically hold back or discard a certain volume of water before allowing any to enter the tank have also been designed. The simplest is a 10-litre receptacle through which rainwater passes on its way to the tank (Fig. 3.5).

Few devices for foul flush rejection seem likely to be used or maintained consistently in village conditions, so it is worth noticing that although they are valuable in preventing visible debris from entering a tank, such devices have less effect on bacteriological pollution. Contrary to former belief,

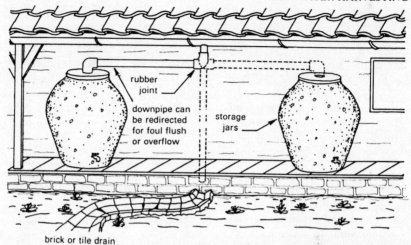

brick or tile drain

Fig. 3.4   Jointed downpipes enable the first flush of rainwater after a long dry period to be diverted away from storage jars. (Institute for Rural Water 1982)

recent tests suggest that bacteria are likely to be present in runoff from a roof throughout a storm, increasing as rainfall intensity increases (Wheeler and Lloyd 1983). Thus the omission of a foul flush deflector may not be crucial. However, the material which would then be washed into the tank may affect the appearance and taste of the water; it will mean that the tank needs to be cleaned out more often; and more importantly, there is every chance that organic debris in the tank will enable bacteria and other organisms to survive longer, with the result that the usual improvement in water quality during a period of storage does not occur. Thus it is still strongly advised that for any catchment surface, the first 15-20 minutes of rain should be diverted away from drinking water tanks if at all possible, perhaps using jointed downpipes as in Figure 3.4.

However, in view of the difficulties which may make the rejection of first flush water impracticable, it is important to note the more basic precautions for ensuring that rainwater is of good quality. The roof and gutters should be accessible for cleaning, which should be done at the beginning of every rainy season, and their regular maintenance is also very important. On Bermuda, roofs are whitewashed for greater cleanliness. There should also be some form of coarse screening between guttering and the delivery pipe, and a finer screen or filter at the point where water enters the tank. Even with the simplest screens, though, maintenance in village conditions is poor (Latham 1984b). Another maintenance task which should be carried out annually or when the tank becomes empty is to clean it out, removing sediments and if possible disinfecting it. If water quality is still regarded as suspect it may be necessary to advise filtering water through a ceramic filter or boiling it before drinking. The worst fouling of roofs by birds and insects as well as by debris occurs under trees, and roofs in such situations ought not to be used for rainwater collection if alternatives exist.

Ground surface catchments and excavated tanks are particularly vulnerable to contamination. In Botswana, excavated tanks covered with corrugated metal roofs become a habitat for frogs and other small animals, and the water shows a high level of bacteriological pollution. In Swaziland, excavated tanks were built in the early 1970s whose storage space was totally enclosed, and into which water flowed via a layer of sand. Water from these was of consistently high quality, though a frog gained access to the pump shaft of one (Farrar 1974).

Controversy sometimes arises as to whether rainwater tanks should be advocated for drinking water supply if freedom from contamination cannot be guaranteed. It is suggested that engineers should not advocate use of a water source from which they themselves are not prepared to drink. However, the question that might be better asked is whether the rainwater system leads to an improvement in people's livelihoods, not whether it meets some idealized standard. If the water provided is of a better standard than would otherwise be used, or if it is of the same standard but more readily available, livelihoods may benefit. What one needs to beware of are systems which look good to the engineer but which would actually tend to erode livelihoods, either because the costs involved are too great, or even because health hazards are worsened. The greatest danger of the latter arises where tanks and gutters become mosquito breeding sites. Thus in areas where malaria is endemic, the most important health precautions are not those aimed at preventing contamination, but precautions against mosquitoes. These include ensuring that gutters do not contain depressions in which water is left standing, and fitting a fine gauze on all openings to the tank, such as overflow pipes. Maintenance is again crucial. A report from Indonesia notes that gauze on overflow pipes had been damaged, perhaps by children, and suggested that it should be fitted on the inside of the opening where it would be less vulnerable (Latham 1984b).

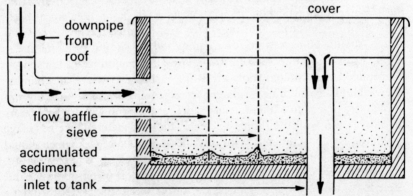

Fig. 3.5   Baffle tank designed to hold back sediments, leaves and other debris before rainwater from a roof enters storage. (UNEP 1983)

It is of course true that ordinary people who are not biochemists judge the purity of water by taste, colour and smell — and women in South India judge it by how long pulses take to cook (Chauhan 1983). One should therefore not be surprised if in some countries, such as Bangladesh (Ahmed 1972) people prefer dirty pond water to tubewell water because of the taste. Similarly, a report from Indonesia mentions that mud is sometimes mixed with rainwater to give it the required local flavour (Soedjarwo 1981).

Following the injunction that engineers drink the water they expect others to imbibe, one of the present authors spent a week in Swaziland drinking water (after boiling) obtained at dams where cattle had stirred up a heavy suspension of colloidal clay. This gave the water a sickly-sweet taste, acceptable to the author in soup and coffee but not in tea, and it was easy to appreciate that people accustomed to this would find pure water excessively bland. Technical and social assessments in a village should therefore include assessment of water quality from existing sources and enquire which sources people prefer. Effective health education may, of course, persuade people to accept a blander taste, but it may also be worth experimenting with recipes in which rainwater confers better flavours. During surveys, enquiry might also be made about traditional methods for improving water quality. In parts of South America, crushed bark from certain trees is added to water. Elsewhere, various seeds are used, or curd from sour milk, and in parts of India, leaves from the neem tree. The use of such substances with rainwater could be helpful in providing a familiar taste.

STRATEGIES FOR DATA COLLECTION

This discussion of two specialist areas, hydrology and health, has shown that the information required for planning a rainwater project does not only consist of data which need specialist expertise for their collection and analysis, but also involves much more general information, for example about existing water sources and how they are used, or local experience of the effects of drought. Such information, often looked down on as 'anecdotal', may be useful for filling gaps in the technical data, and in showing whether rainwater collection can make a contribution to improved livelihoods, and if so, for whom and in what form.

In order to collect this information, people who speak the local language need to visit villages where projects are envisaged and carry out surveys like the social and technical assessments discussed earlier. The individuals who do this may be community workers or health workers already employed in the area; they may be agricultural extension workers, and they may include residents elected by the villages concerned. In a large programme, community workers may need to carry out surveys in a considerable number of villages, and any local residents who take part will clearly need careful briefing. Thus it is desirable to provide some formal training for the survey teams, and the WASH *Training Guide* quoted earlier envisages an intensive course lasting a week (5½ working days).

During such a course the community workers (as we shall now describe them), need to be told not only why the information is needed, but also how to collect it systematically. To this end, it may be useful to provide them with *checklists* of points which can be learned by *observation* (for example, concerning building materials, roof types, and roofs overhung by trees) at the same time, giving them *questionnaires* covering points about which local people should be asked. Such checklists and questionnaires might be compiled in a preliminary way by picking out the main points made in each of the previous sections of this chapter, though they will also need to be refined in the light of local experience. The important point to remember is that the technical assessment should principally be seeking answers to the question 'is a rainwater project technically feasible in this village?' Meanwhile, the social assessment seeks to know whether there would be active support for such a project from the people. The relationship of these questions to the later survey of skills, materials and resources, is illustrated by a 'decision tree' in Figure 3.6.

One important point about decision trees is that they pose questions which must be answered 'yes' or 'no', and so therefore the decision about whether a rainwater project should go ahead can be answered in the negative. It is important that surveys are carried out in a way which leaves this option open. Where advocates of rainwater collection are over-keen on their favoured technology, there is a danger that they will compile questionnaires on the assumption that the project will go ahead and only its details can be modified. As Chauhan (1983) puts it, surveys of this kind tend to be 'treated like market research for a new consumer product. If the community is indifferent to the product, it is assumed that the answer is to advertise the benefits more widely and educate the 'target population' that this is what they *should* want. The designers of programmes and technology will rarely admit that the "products" themselves may be inappropriate.'

To guard against this danger, it first needs to be recognized that although the use of checklists and questionnaires is almost inevitable if information is to be systematically obtained, over-use of them can have the effect of excluding real dialogue with the local people and preventing them from 'participating' in anything but a formal sense. A questionnaire may allow us to find out what we want to know, but nothing more — it will tend to exclude ideas and information volunteered by local people.

It is therefore strongly advised that questionnaires used when interviewing householders should be brief and confined to essentials. The interview should be open-ended, and the community workers should be prepared to listen for perspectives on local problems which the project organizers may not have considered. Often such insights are best generated if people are

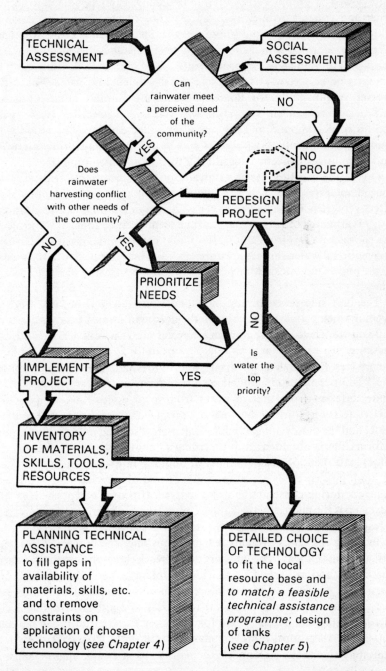

Fig. 3.6   'Decision tree' representing successive phases in the planning of a village rainwater collection project.

interviewed in groups rather than individually. For example, a group of older and younger women with a female interviewer may express views which a mixed group would not, and the age difference could stimulate comparisons which would show which recent changes in housing or water supplies are valued as 'improvements'. It is particularly important to obtain women's views, as it is, of course, women who usually have the greater responsibility for domestic water use — and often for home improvements and gardens also. Apart from informal interviews with groups of neighbours, or members of extended families, discussion with people attending village gatherings may be useful, as may formal meetings and committees convened specifically to discuss water supplies.

One of the two Indonesian rainwater programmes mentioned earlier in this chapter (e.g. in Table 3.2) illustrates many of these points very effectively. It is run by a local agency, Yayasan Dian Desa (YDD) in the Yogyakarta area of Java. Villages which seem likely candidates for projects are chosen by YDD from among the poorer communities in a district where conventional water sources are unreliable and inadequate due to the nature of the underlying rocks. Many of the villages are critically short of water at times.

The first step taken in any individual community is to visit it on an evening when people are meeting in the headman's house (maybe to watch a favourite television programme). Several YDD people will go to these sessions, just to meet people, talk about family affairs, and to introduce themselves. Eventually, conversation turns to water, and when tea is made, the YDD people produce their own containers of fresh water. Its taste is quite different from that of water from local ponds, and villagers are invited to try it. Further meetings are arranged where the benefits of good water and the disadvantages of local water are discussed more fully and more information is obtained from the villagers about local needs. Finally the YDD staff mention the possibility of building rainwater tanks. The basic technology is carefully explained and the demands which would be made of villagers during construction are discussed. If people accept the idea, the next step is the choice by the village committee of a local person (known as a 'cadre') to be trained in the construction technique.

Building the tanks presents few problems once the procedure has been discussed in this way. The villagers do the work themselves with the help of the cadre, and are asked to provide the bamboo required. Indeed, one advantage of using bamboo reinforcement in the tanks is that it increases the villagers' input and makes the tanks less of a gift. Where people can afford it, they are asked to pay for the other materials also — many are too poor. All groups, however, make a sufficiently large contribution to feel that the tanks belong to them and, as a result, maintenance is generally good.

TAKING TIME

If building tanks in Indonesia presents few difficulties, effective use of the water they contain seems more problematic. It has been found that for as much as a year after they acquire a tank, some householders are doubtful about the water it provides. They are unaccustomed to its taste, and are unfamiliar with water that looks so clear. Some fear that chemicals in the tank (perhaps detergents) are the cause of its strange appearance. A good deal of reassurance is required about this, and YDD staff make frequent informal visits on their way to other projects in the area. In addition, they organize educational activities aimed at ensuring prudent use of the water, care of the tanks, and confidence that the water is safe. The taste problem takes a long time to overcome, but easy availability of the water helps persuade owners to use it for drinking and cooking.

Latham (1984b) comments that: 'All this is time-consuming but YDD see it as a necessary part of introducing the tanks', and as a major factor making for the sucess of their programme. Provision of water is regarded as a starting point for village development, and YDD link it to additional programmes of animal and crop improvement. Many hundreds of tanks have been built, but more important than numbers is the willingness of YDD personnel to spend time in the villages alongside the people concerned listening to local views and working out solutions to water supply problems.

In other countries, also, and in other aspects of rural development, it is noticeable that the most effective fieldworkers and agencies are usually those which are prepared to spend time with the people they attempt to help. In Kenya, one project which was building excavated rainwater-tanks and latrines grew up through a long period during which a lone fieldworker got to know local families, built up 'an accurate picture of people's problems', and gave encouragement to 'decision-making mechanisms' based on village meetings. Indeed, so much time was spent on these activities that funds from America were in danger of being cut off due to 'lack of results'. Commenting on this, Batchelor (1985) notes that although most agencies realise that a period of assessment and 'familiarization' is required in any project, 'pressure from performance-orientated donors often cuts this short or . . . at least combines it with a prototype project'.

Occasionally, programmes seem to run smoothly without the preliminaries advocated here, but, when that occurs it is usually because people have been prepared for the new technology by other experiences. Subsequent chapters discuss a rainwater tank programme in part of Thailand where some people were already using large jars to collect water from their roofs. Thus the taste of the water and the method of collecting it did not seem so alien as it did in the YDD region. However, one result of there being shorter periods of assessment and discussion is that the Thai programme is now criticized for being too construction-orientated and for paying too little attention to maintenance and local-level organization (Fricke 1982).

All these issues do not just apply to tanks collecting runoff from roofs, but also to other forms of rainwater collection. Obviously, though, social and technical assessments and subsequent discussion are very different in detail if a runoff farming project or a communal effect to exploit a rock catchment is planned — or if nomadic herdsmen are being approached about renovating cisterns or building new livestock watering points. However, it has not been possible to describe a rock catchment project here, nor any programme concerned with pastoralists, largely because of the lack of documentation. In the latter case this is because the orientation of the book is towards the work of non-government organizations, most of which have left the problems of pastoralists to government.

Therefore, although provision of water for livestock in arid and semi-arid areas is potentially one of the most appropriate of all applications of rainwater collection, little more will be said about it here. Instead, the remainder of the book will discuss firstly, rainwater tanks used to provide domestic water, and then later, attempts to apply the same concepts about the organization of programmes to some recent work on runoff farming.

4. RAINWATER TANKS AND TECHNICAL ASSISTANCE

TECHNICAL ASSISTANCE PACKAGES

Development workers have frequently been perplexed at the slow rate with which applications of rainwater technologies have spread. In one village in Lesotho, 63 per cent of houses have iron roofs, but less than 2 per cent have gutters (Feacham *et al.* 1978). In Ghana, a similar reluctance of house-owners with metal roofs to install gutters has also been noticed (Parker 1973). In both countries, women face long walks to fetch water, and people appreciate the value of rainwater and place containers under their eaves when it rains. So their lack of interest in gutters and permanent storage containers is not due to any ignorance of the value of rainwater.

Even where organized programmes have built significant numbers of roof catchment tanks within limited districts, one can rarely report that the techniques they introduce are being actively replicated in surrounding areas. Nor can one often say that local builders, craftsmen or businessmen have copied the programme's construction methods and are promoting the techniques on their own account.

Some general reasons for this disappointing situation have already been discussed, and others, some of them specific to particular areas, may be identified during social assessments. In both Lesotho and Ghana, one constraint could be that the installation of gutters would be a job for the man of the household, and it is usually the women who carry water and who put out small containers to collect rainwater during storms. If rainwater tanks were promoted as improvements to the appearance and structure of a house rather than simply as a means of saving time spent carrying water, they might appeal more strongly to the men. Thus rainwater technologies may fail to spread because they are not perceived in the same way by all villagers, and water supply experts rarely take enough trouble to find out how different groups do perceive them.

Another constraint, however, is that in the past there has been no real concept of technical assistance at village level. If Lesotho villagers can obtain gutters, downpipes and brackets as cheaply as Feacham *et al* claim, and money is not an obstacle, do the villagers actually have the tools necessary to fix them? If it is the women who would have to do the fixing while men are absent in urban employment, do they have the skill, and if not, is anyone trying to assist them?

One mistake made in the early days of the Appropriate Technology movement was to think that small-scale technologies could be disseminated around the world merely by publishing relevant information and making it widely available. Clearly, the availability of information is essential, and we should take a comprehensive view of how it may be spread — through advertising, the printed word, the broadcast media, talks and demonstrations, advisory services and extension work. But it is wrong to assume that if a book or even a demonstration project can show that a new technique is of potential benefit to people, that technique will be quickly taken up by them without further promotion. As Whitcombe (1983) puts it, the replication of any 'appropriate' technology is a highly complex process, and few agencies have been able to develop a 'methodology to go beyond prototype development'. If a 'truly appropriate technology' is developed its originators often assume that 'it will sell itself'.

Tanks and large jars for collecting rainwater from roofs do sell themselves in a few places, and there are also one or two agencies which have reasonably effective methodologies for replication. Table 4.1 lists examples of such agencies, and by implication, suggests that their success may be attributable to the comprehensiveness of their technical assistance activities within village communitites. None of them limits itself to demonstration projects, or to providing information via educational or extension work.

Compared with the examples in Table 4.1, the technical assistance methodologies of many agencies tend to be deficient in some of the following ways:

- fully comprehensive packages of help with information, skills, materials and money are rarely developed;
- there is a lack of commercial involvement, e.g. with builders interested in constructing rainwater tanks as a business venture (in contrast, see Layton 1984);
- there is inflexibility and lack of dialogue with potential users of rainwater because of over-commitment to one specific technique;
- there may not be sufficient attention to local organization, especially in relation to maintenance;
- follow-up and monitoring of completed tanks or other works may be neglected.

It was suggested in the previous chapter that village surveys could culminate in the compilation of an inventory of local materials, tools, skills and resources (Fig. 3.6). This inventory can be helpful in identifying technology which matches the resources of the village; it is also a starting point for developing the necessary technical assistance package. However

Table 4.1 Technical assistance in four roof catchment programmes

COUNTRY and area	ZIMBABWE Bulawayo area	KENYA Karai loc-ation, Kiambu	INDONESIA Gunung Kidul near Yogya-karta	THAILAND Khon Kaen Province
AGENCY and source	Friends' Training Centre (Hlekweni 1975)	UNICEF (Molvaer 1982)	YDD* (Winarto 1981; Latham 1984)	CBATDS† (Fricke 1982; Power 1983)
OPTIONS OFFERED TO VILLAGERS				
rainwater tanks	ferro-cement 9m³ (later brick)	Ghala tanks 1.1, 2.2 and 4.5m³	ferro-cement 9m³; bamboo cement 4.5m³	bamboo concrete, 6–11m³
roofing materials	experi-mental	NO	NO	NO
guttering	metal type supplied	n.d.‡	metal or bamboo	n.d.
complementary programmes	agricul-tural	cooking stoves	agricul-tural	varied; fam-ily planning
COMPONENTS OF TECHNICAL ASSISTANCE PACKAGES				
training specialist craftsmen	YES	YES	NO	NO
or community-worker technicians . . .	NO	NO	'cadres'	'village technicians'
bulk purchase & transport of materials	YES	YES	YES	YES
loan of formwork	YES	formwork not needed	formwork of local material	YES
financial help: payment by instal-ments . . .	NO	n.d.	YES	YES
subsidies . . .	YES	YES	YES	slight
printed leaflets, instructions on construction	YES	n.d.	YES	YES
follow-up work on maintenance, health education	slight	YES	strongly developed	YES

* YDD is the local Indonesian agency Yayasan Dian Desa.
† CBATDS is the Community Based Appropriate Technology and Development Service of the Thai agency PDA.
‡ n.d. denotes no data available

good the match between the chosen technology and local resources, there will always be some constraints on the use of that technology, such as a lack of certain skills, or the high costs of cement and transport of materials, or the need for a particular tool. The aim of technical assistance is of course to reduce the effect of these constraints by the various means listed in Table 4.1. Training is probably most universally important, but bulk purchases and transport of materials aimed at reducing costs are often necessary, as is the loan of tools, or some sort of financial help for householders acquiring rainwater tanks. Helping people to organize themselves for carrying out the work and perhaps for following it with other changes in village conditions is also important, though it is too big an issue to analyse within the confines of Table 4.1 (however, for a comparison see Table 7.2).

The cost of rainwater systems may seem to demand particular attention from those who plan technical assistance activities. Very small rainwater tanks or jars will often be used because that is all that people can afford, and sometimes shared tanks are proposed in order to reduce the cost falling on each household. However, a good deal can be learned from regions where significant numbers of households are prosperous enough to afford the full cost of individually owned roof catchment-tanks. In the Khon Kaen province of Thailand, for example, many people have well-constructed timber houses built on platforms (Fig. 4.1) with corrugated iron roofs. They already collect rainwater, and even in the poor villages, 30 per cent of households have some guttering. Elsewhere, as many as 60 per cent do. Roof areas are large, often exceeding 100m², though guttering may only be installed on half the area (Nopmongcol *et al.* 1981). Hemispherical ferrocement jars up to 2m³ in capacity are available commercially and are purchased by some households.

Such an area is clearly ripe for a programme aiming to build larger tanks, and one need not be too surprised at the success of the agency represented in Table 4.1 which has completed 6,500 tanks in four years (Nation 1984). The tanks range in size up to 11.3m³ but are typically 9.4m³; they are made of bamboo-reinforced concrete.

With housing standards in this area so high, it may be appropriate to draw comparisons with technical assistance offered in a much more prosperous country. The South Australian government initiated a 'rainwater tank promotion campaign' in the Adelaide area during 1981, based mainly on advertising and the provision of information. According to Hoey and West (1982), this led to many new tanks being purchased by householders. The main features of the scheme were:

- a booklet written for householders giving advice about the installation and maintenance of gutters and tanks;
- an advisory service (by telephone);

*Fig. 4.1   Raised wooden platform houses with corrugated iron roofs in Khon Kaen Province,
Thailand. Gutters are usually attached to only one slope of the roofs. The houses have bamboo-
reinforced concrete rainwater tanks such as those built within the programme described in the
text. See also Table 4.1. This illustration is from a booklet distributed in Thailand by UNICEF.
(UNICEF and Fricke 1982)*

- a major newspaper publicity campaign which stimulated advertising
  by local manufacturers of tanks; but
- no financial incentives or subsidies.

In poorer communities, financial help is often essential and advisory
services need to be more personal and practical. But in countries where
better-off families purchase rainwater tanks on their own initiative, such as
Thailand and parts of Kenya, and where tanks are available on the market,
local versions of this sort of campaign could be very effective. They could lead
to existing tanks being better used as well as new ones being installed, and
could encourage better maintenance. One should not be squeamish about
'social marketing' of this kind. It can contribute to development by

encouraging the constructive use of private resources and by reducing demand on stretched public water supplies. It can also confer 'status' and improve the 'image' of the technology concerned, which is a more important factor in arousing enthusiasm than most health educators and extension workers care to admit. Moreover, such campaigns aimed at better-off groups may indirectly widen political support for subsidized projects in poorer areas.

In Thailand, although the prior existence of gutters and some small rainwater jars made it easy to arouse interest in the larger tanks, a considerable amount of technical assistance has still been necessary. Householders work together in loosely organized mutual-help groups with 10 or 15 people in each, but they still need help from a 'village technician'. This is a local person recruited to attend special training sessions. Technical assistance also includes the loan of metal formwork and tools, bulk purchases of cement, and a scheme whereby householders can pay for the materials by instalments. The initial payment is equivalent to US$22, and subsequent monthly payments are in the range $6 to $10. The option of payment by instalments has been crucial. The total cost to a householder of a large (11.3m^3) tank was $175 in 1982 when the 1.4m^3 ferrocement jar — which is all most people could otherwise afford — would have a market price of only $25 (Fricke 1982).

Taking a general view of costs and methods of payment, strategies likely to be helpful include use of low-cost, local materials wherever possible; bulk purchasing (e.g. of cement) as a means of negotiating lower prices; credit or saving schemes to make payment easier; and of course, outright subsidies.

Small mutual-help groups may have a part to play in enabling people to cope with costs as well as in practical construction. For example, savings clubs oriented towards bulk purchasing have been successful in parts of Africa. They usually consist of neighbours, or groups of families with similar interests and existing ties of friendship, and they agree a common goal for which all members wish to save over a specified period of time (up to a year). Savings clubs of this type hold weekly meetings for members at which they pay a fixed contribution and have a stamp stuck on their cards. When sufficient money has been accumulated, the materials which club members have agreed to buy are purchased in bulk and shared among them. This system has been successfully used in Zambia for the purchase of corrugated iron roofing sheets for home improvements.

Such schemes work well if there is an agreed objective in which people can sustain a shared interest. The best examples have been in Zimbabwe where farming families have saved to make bulk purchases of fertilizer. With such things as rainwater tanks it is usually better if the desired improvement comes much sooner, and if the saving is done retrospectively when the benefits of the project are apparent. This is what happens in

Thailand when people pay for tanks in instalments. The scheme is made possible by the operation of a 'revolving loan fund'. Under this system, the agency responsible for the rainwater programme sets aside a fixed sum of money from which the cost of each family's tank is paid. This constitutes a loan to the family, and as they pay back the money month by month, the fund is replenished and new tanks can be financed for other households. People should be encouraged to regard loan funds as money belonging to the community as a whole and not to an impersonal body such as a bank. They will then be aware that delaying repayment of their loan will postpone the day when a neighbour can borrow money for his own rainwater system.

TRAINING VILLAGERS AND CRAFTSMEN

When householders acquire rainwater tanks on their own initiative, this is most often by purchasing them ready-made from a factory (as is possible with small cement mortar jars in Thailand). Galvanized corrugated iron tanks are available for purchase ready-made in many countries in a range of sizes up to about 10m³.

Few organized programmes which promote rainwater collection use factory-made tanks, often because of a self-help emphasis within the village, but also because of transport difficulties and the high cost of these sorts of tanks — especially the metal ones. However, since tank construction is a skilled task, any self-help effort must involve specially trained individuals, even if most of the more basic tasks are left to the householders themselves. Indeed, the provision of skilled help needs to be linked in a co-ordinated way to the help given with supplies of materials (such as cement), and the help, just discussed, with payment. As we have seen, village-level technical assistance must go far beyond providing information and education if it is to cater for the needs of low-income communities. Assistance with *skills*, *supplies* and *payment* are three of its most important practical ingredients, and there is also the question of organization.

Several approaches to the development of necessary skills have been used in rainwater projects. Training may be offered to village craftsmen (as in Kenya), or to community workers or individuals chosen at village meetings who are given special training as 'village technicians' (in Thailand) or construction 'cadres' (Indonesia).

There is a sharp distinction to be noticed here between the 'community-worker technicians' and the specialist craftsman (Table 4.1). If a village technician is thought of as a community worker, his role will be seen as assisting and supervising householders who build their own tanks. In Thailand, where groups of householders help each other, a group usually finds that after relying heavily on the village technician in building their first one or two tanks, they are able to construct others without further help. Thus skills become widely diffused in the village. By contrast, the village craftsmen trained in Kenya carry out the whole construction task for householders. They do not assist others to acquire building skills but function as specialists, potentially able to work as commercial tank-building contractors.

The WASH *Training Guide* (see Chapter 3) envisages that the skills of tank-building should be taught to 'masons' at the same time as community social workers are trained to carry out surveys, social assessments and related educational work. This implies a non-commercial view of the mason's role, and aims to provide a basis for co-operation between masons and community workers. If community workers are to explain the rainwater tanks adequately to people, they must know how they are built. At the same time, masons may co-operate in much of the survey work, particularly in technical assessments and in compiling inventories of materials and resources. The WASH *Guide* assumes that masons can be trained in the same one-week course as the community workers, if it is organized with separate sessions for practical work. However, time-tabling tank construction exercises in such a course may be difficult because of the time required for cement or concrete to set. Layton (1984) is probably more realistic when he describes three-week courses for training young men to build ferrocement tanks on a commercial basis in the North Solomons (Papua New Guinea). Business development officers take part in the training in an effort to teach entrepreneurial as well as technical skills.

Much pioneer work on rainwater tanks has taken place in Zimbabwe under the aegis both of Young Farmers' Clubs and of church organizations. One starting point was the high costs and corrosion problems associated with the galvanized iron rainwater tanks which were already widely used in Zimbabwe. Efforts to produce cheaper and more durable tanks mostly involved ferrocement construction.

The Young Farmers' groups put their main efforts into large circular tanks with domed tops. Some were built to collect water from roofs and rock catchments. Others, constructed in exactly the same way, were built in excavations in order to collect water from ground catchments with smooth, cemented surfaces (Fig. 4.2) and with chicken wire reinforcement (e.g. at Rowa).

By contrast, a church group based at Hlekweni, near Bulawayo in the south-west of Zimbabwe, concentrated on a smaller ferrocement tank for collecting water from roofs. Its size was standardized (at 9m³) so that many tanks could be built by repeatedly using the formwork. The method of construction is explained by Watt (1978) and more briefly in Box 4.1. Of particular interest here is the technical assistance which enabled householders to acquire the tanks, and the distinctive approach to the transfer of skills which was developed. Whilst individuals were trained as specialist craftsmen, they were encouraged to work *with* householders, and

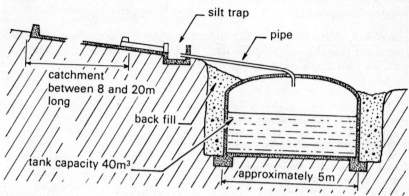

Fig. 4.2   A ferrocement rainwater tank in Zimbabwe built in an excavation so as to collect water from a smooth, cemented catchment. Withdrawal of water from the tank is by means of a hand-pump (not shown). A tank of this size (40m³) would normally require a catchment measuring about 20m × 10m, i.e. larger than the example shown. (Hall 1975; see also Watt 1978)

the latter for their part were asked to provide sand for mixing the cement plaster, and to contribute their labour where unskilled work was required. This helped to hold down costs, but also meant that householders learned more about tank construction on the job, and thus might be better able to maintain their tanks subsequently.

The technical assistance package also involved a subsidy on costs and the supply of metal guttering (which was specially made at Hlekweni) as well as the loan of formwork and tools. At first, some tanks were built without payment from the householder, the cost being born by drought relief funds. However, villagers were sceptical, expecting that money would be demanded at some later stage. From 1970, it was decided to charge a nominal amount (equivalent to US$12) and the tanks were then in such demand that four builders trained at the centre were kept constantly busy. But it was noticed that only the better-off families with good houses were acquiring the tanks, which could not easily be fitted to traditional thatched houses with curving eaves, so it was decided to phase out the subsidy. There were hopes that it would be possible for the builders to continue work on a commercial basis. However, although the tanks were cheaper than the competing galvanized iron ones, they were still too costly for most villagers. Thus the effect of rising cement prices and the withdrawal of subsidy was that fewer tanks were built.*

Reports from the area ten years later suggest that many of these tanks are still in use. However, since 1977, Hlekweni has been building rainwater

*The eventual record was (Hlekweni 1975): 1971: 73 tanks at nominal charge equivalent to US$12; 1972: 59 tanks costing householders $30 each; 1973: 55 tanks at $30; 1974: 12 tanks at full commercial price, i.e. about US$75 (Keller, 1982, quotes material costs as $62.50 in 1973, and via Watt, 1978, quotes $150 for 1982 price levels).

Box 4.1 Procedure for building a 9m³ tank of the type developed at the Friends' Training Centre, Hlekweni, Zimbabwe. (Hlekweni, 1975; Watt, 1978)

1. The formwork needed to build this tank can be used repeatedly for construction of many tanks. It is made from sheets of corrugated iron curved to a radius of 1.25m and is in four sections, each quarter of a circle in plan, and equal to the full height of the tank. Each section has angle iron riveted to the vertical edges. When the formwork is assembled, the angle iron flanges face up to one another and have holes which allow them to be bolted together through a wooden wedge (Diagram 1).

2. A circular foundation 2.8m in diameter is dug out on site and a concrete floor 80mm thick is laid. A 20mm bore pipe bent to a U-curve is concreted into the floor in such a position that one end will project upwards in the finished tank 80mm above the floor and the other end will be outside and can be fitted with a tap.

3. Erection of the formwork follows when the floor slab has hardened. After oiling the formwork, wire netting of 50mm mesh is wrapped round it and tucked under it at the bottom (Diagram 2). Then a length of 2.5mm plain wire is pulled round each corrugation and the ends are twisted together until the wire is taut. (Two wires are used in the four bottom corrugations and in the topmost one.)

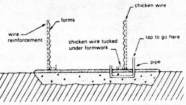

Diagram 2

4. Plastering of the outside then begins, first with a thin layer of 1:3 cement/sand, then two hours later with a second layer to a depth of 15mm. This should be finished smooth with a float, entirely hiding the corrugations.

5. The formwork is unbolted some 48 hours after the second plastering. Ladders used for climbing into the tank are leaned against the house, not against the incomplete tank. An overflow pipe with mosquito screen on its inner end is built into the top of the tank wall. Then a 50mm layer of concrete is laid on the floor.

6. The inside walls are plastered once the floor has set. Two layers of 1:3 cement/sand are applied to fill up the corrugations. The inside walls and floor are finished off with a thick cement slurry to render the tank water-tight.

7. Curing. Water to a depth of 50mm is poured in and the walls are periodically moistened or otherwise kept wet for seven days.

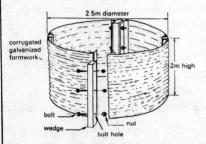

Diagram 1

tanks of brick with wire reinforcement and cement linings, because the availability of broken bricks (or bricks made on site) makes these cheaper (Gould 1983).

Experiences of this sort show that the design of a rainwater tank is not merely an abstract problem in engineering, but is crucially related to the type of technical assistance that can be organized, and the sort of materials and other resources which are available in the locality. (This is why technical assistance has been discussed in this book before the chapter on tank design.) Both the planning of technical assistance and the design of hardware depend on establishing what materials, labour, and financial contribution it is reasonable to ask householders to provide. Careful thought will also be necessary about the provision of guttering and downpipes, although this is a striking omission in many reports on rainwater collection programmes. It may be that guttering is considered to be simpler than tank construction and is taken for granted – which presumably means that householders must supply their own. But for some people installation of a gutter may seem a formidable task, and it has sometimes been said that inadequate guttering is a major constraint, discouraging some householders from acquiring tanks at all.

In places where satisfactory rainwater jars or tanks are available on the market, technical assistance should perhaps aim mainly to provide guttering and offer advice as to which type of tank to buy, with possibly some help from a revolving loan fund to pay for it. Some programmes may make their task over-complicated by concentrating too much effort on building tanks independently of the market. Their task might be simpler if they exploited the existence of the commercially available tanks and concentrated on the constraints which prevent low-income groups from acquiring them.

SELF-SUSTAINING PROGRAMMES

It should be the ultimate aim of every programme that its work will become self-sustaining, and independent of external subsidy. This means that tank construction must be incorporated into the normal production system of the country, whatever that might be — individual craftsmen with their own businesses, larger commercial organizations, local collectives or publicly-owned factories. In many countries, the long-term future of household rainwater collection will depend on what the individual family can obtain on the market, and on what craftsmen and commercial outlets have to offer. The public service traditions of many aid agencies make them reluctant either to form a relationship with local commerce or to teach entrepreneurial skills to the craftsmen they train. Yet these things may be necessary if rainwater techniques are to take root and continue to develop in a region. Indeed, it may be desirable to offer training to people who explicitly wish to exploit the techniques for commercial profit, charging them an appropriate fee for the training. This happens in principle with the three-week courses on ferrocement tank construction in the North Solomons. However, instead of paying cash, 'would-be entrepreneurs' are merely asked to provide food and accommodation for the Training Unit staff (Layton 1984).

The Zimbabwe project referred to earlier was probably right to envisage that the builders it trained should ultimately operate independently with their own tank construction businesses, though the tanks being built proved too large and expensive for this goal to be achieved. A programme in Karai Location, Kenya, organized by UNICEF (Table 4.1) seems to have come nearer to success in this respect. One reason is probably that it started with much smaller tanks of the Ghala type (described in Box 3.1), with correspondingly lower costs.

At first, the people trained in the Ghala technique were young men who had not yet settled down. When some left the area, training was offered to established local craftsmen who already had skills as basket makers or masons. At first they were sceptical and did not think the tanks would become popular, but after a year or so, demand increased rapidly. However, UNICEF had asked that a committee of local people be set up to organize the project. Orders for tanks were channelled through the committee, so the craftsmen could not promote their business independently. Molvaer (1982) implies that this has inhibited technical initiative. Some craftsmen have thought it best to merely do 'what they were told' since that is what they were paid for. However, some owners of tanks have had ideas for improvements, and a couple of ideas did also come from craftsmen. The main change which resulted was that concerning the basket-work frame of the tanks which was not initially plastered on the outside. Tanks made this way were found not to be durable, and so now plaster is always applied both inside and outside.

This programme has developed considerable momentum and one sign that it might become self-sustaining is that craftsmen now recruit and train apprentices on their own initiative. UNICEF therefore no longer has to train each new craftsman, as they did with the first two groups of tank builders. However, 'without orders — and orders are due to acceptance by the committee — the craftsmen would go idle' (Molvaer 1982), and the idea of a craftsman himself seeking orders seems to have been very slow to develop. Householders are showing initiative in acquiring rainwater tanks, including some from outside the area officially covered by the programme, but the committee is still in charge.

Molvaer comments that a change in approach would help craftsmen to acquire 'a bit of the entrepreneurial spirit', but adds that individuals whose enterprise is encouraged ought to be those with roots in the local community. A man who has close ties with the people for whom he works is more likely to conduct his business in a manner combining a sense of service with the necessary entrepreneurial skills. Besides these attributes, craftsmen also need to be more open to innovation. Molvaer suggests creating a 'climate of change' by disseminating information about rainwater techniques in other areas. In Karai, basket-framed Ghala tanks were adopted after some failures of *unreinforced* cement jars. But in other parts of Kenya, there have been unhappy experiences with Ghala tanks (Sinclair 1983), and despite the 300 or more built at Karai, they are still regarded as unproven. Thus a programme supported by the Diocese of Machakos encouraged a more robust technology, in *concrete ring* tanks, whilst *brick* is used by some private contractors and *metal* tanks are available commercially. In one area, some 150 *ferrocement* jars of 5m³ capacity have been built to a UNICEF design (Byrne 1983). It is suggested, then, that a more innovative spirit would develop if there were active exchanges of experience between the craftsmen who build these varied types of tank.

A different model of what constitutes a self-sustaining programme is needed when rainwater techniques are implemented by mutual-help groups of neighbours without the involvement of specialist craftsmen. This applies both to rainwater tank construction, and to the co-operative groups of up to forty families practising small-scale irrigation of the kind discussed in Chapter 2. Neither mutual-help groups nor community workers can usually be 'self-sustaining' in isolation. They need encouragement, advice and technical support on a continuing basis, as well as help in negotiating with commercial suppliers and government departments. Some kind of 'parent' organization for the small groups is therefore necessary, and we may consider three ways in which it may operate.

Firstly, there may be a regional or national federation of local mutual-help groups with administrative officers elected by its members. Secondly, the parent body may be officially organized. Many governments operate services to support farmers' co-operatives, and the same framework — or a more flexible version capable of dealing with smaller groups — could be adapted for this purpose.

Thirdly, however, the 'parent' role may be undertaken by a voluntary agency or non-government organization. All the examples cited so far are of this type. They include the Pani Panchayat organization linking groups of small-scale irrigators in India (Chapter 2) and the roof catchment programmes in Thailand and Indonesia (Table 4.1). For the activities of such bodies to have a permanent effect and to be self-sustaining, it is important that agencies undertaking this role have deep roots within the countries concerned. Few foreign or international agencies have a sufficiently strong commitment to very long-term support of specific projects. However, any agency of this kind could make its programmes increasingly self-sustaining by encouraging an evolution toward a federal organization in which the mutual-help groups it supports eventually assume control and manage the parent body themselves.

One function of the parent organization will be to sustain technical assistance activities so that the replication of rainwater tanks continues. However, it must also support villages which have already built rainwater tanks but are encountering problems in their operation. An indication of what may be needed in this respect can be seen from the activities of the Indonesian agency Yayasan Dian Desa (YDD). Its routine technical assistance activities are summarized in Table 4.1. They centre on the training of village construction supervisors or 'cadres' to assist in building tanks and to act as contact persons. Some cadres are paid for special tasks but most of their work is voluntary. Materials and transport for tank building are supplied and subsidized by YDD, who also send a staff member to villages where construction is beginning. Even when tanks are completed, staff members visit villages regularly, keeping in contact with cadres, monitoring operation of the tanks, and checking whether rainwater is providing the expected benefits.

An example of the problems discussed by YDD staff during their village visits, is the cost of the ferrocement tanks — which has been a major constraint, as in Zimbabwe. Kaufman (1983) records a discussion about this which took place in a village during 1979. A village headman made the comment that when the reinforcing bars and wires for a ferrocement tank were assembled, they 'resembled his cassava storage bin, except of course this his storage bin was made of woven bamboo'. He wondered whether it would be possible to replace some of the metal reinforcment in the tanks with bamboo. The local cadre then remarked that 'in constructing pit latrines, he often used a cylindrical woven bamboo liner, which he plastered with cement. Such a cylinder could conceivably be built above ground and function as a water tank'.

Kaufman notes that this conversation saw the birth of 'a new hybrid technology: bamboo-cement'. YDD staff who were present were quick to experiment with bamboo in the manner suggested, and made rapid progress with the design of a small (4.5m^3) 'single-family' tank which has since been built in large numbers (Fig. 4.3) It costs considerably less than a ferrocement tank of the same size, but its durability has been disappointing because the smallest accident or defect in the cement plaster can lead to rapid decay of the bamboo which is exposed. Initially, however, bamboo-cement seemed a real break-through. Trained cadres were often the chief means by which villagers learned the method of construction and sometimes one cadre would train another (Kaufman 1983). Although this points to a self-sustaining pattern of development, it seems unlikely that volunteer cadres could, or would, function successfully for long without support from YDD.

The continued contact of YDD with villages also led to recognition that

Fig. 4.3 Three stages in the construction of a bamboo-cement rainwater tank in Indonesia. In the final diagram, cement plaster is being applied to the bamboo reinforcement whose assembly is seen in the other two diagrams. (Kaufman 1983)

many tanks were not achieving 'their intended effect on the local water situation'. Instead of being used to provide emergency water in the dry season, it was found that tanks were being most fully used in the rainy season and were often empty long before the 'critical period' of water scarcity toward the end of the dry season. Noting this, YDD staff also observed rainwater being drawn from tanks for 'non-essential' purposes as well as contaminated water from ponds being poured into the tanks on occasion. In other words, the long-term commitment of YDD led them to *monitor* the operation of the completed tanks and so to discover these apparent eccentricities in usage. That in turn led them to suggest an improved and expanded educational effort to help people become 'better managers' of water resources.

MAINTENANCE, MONITORING AND INNOVATIVE DIALOGUE

For a programme to be self-sustaining, it is not enough for rainwater systems to be replicated effectively — they should also be well maintained so that their benefits are permanent. Their operation should be carefully monitored by the parent organization with particular attention to deficiencies in maintenance, and to any defects in tanks which develop over time, so that the long-term technical assistance provided can adapt to problems as they arise.

Where rainwater tanks have been acquired through commercial transactions between householders and craftsmen, if the craftsman is a local person who has close links with his customers, he will quickly be alerted if tanks crack or start to leak, even if this is after a long period of use. His training should cover the repair and maintenance of tanks as well as their construction. Indeed, he might be encouraged to visit customers periodically during the rainy season to inspect tanks when they are full and look for wet spots and cracks. Those whose tanks show evidence of faults could then be revisited in a season when tanks are empty, so that necessary repairs can be carried out.

Many maintenance tasks are simply a matter of keeping gutters, screens and filters clear of debris, as discussed in Chapter 3. These are matters for which householders must be responsible. In some areas, it will be especially important that mosquito net or gauze on overflow pipes and other apertures is always in good condition. Householders should be encouraged to check on this regularly, but it should also be seen as a responsibility of craftsmen doing other repairs that they also check mosquito protection. Project organizers may also find it useful to draw up a schedule, such as that given in Box 4.2 to ensure that all the maintenance tasks listed are covered in the training of craftsmen and in the educational work they undertake within the villages. Good maintenance is often difficult to achieve, and the

Box 4.2 A schedule of operation and maintenance tasks for concrete and ferrocement rainwater tanks and associated roofs and gutters. (IWACO, 1982-considerably modified)

TASKS NEEDING FREQUENT ATTENTION FROM HOUSEHOLDERS

1. Roof surfaces and gutters to be kept free of bird droppings. Gutters and inflow filters must be regularly cleared of leaves and other rubbish.
2. The mosquito net on the overflow pipe should be checked regularly, and renewed if necessary.
3. Unless there is some automatic means of diverting the first flush of water in a storm away from the tank, the inflow pipe should be disconnected from the tank during dry periods. Then 15-20 minutes after rain begins, it can be moved back into position so that water flows into the tank.
4. The water level in the tank may be measured once a week using a graduated stick (which should be kept in a clean place and not used for any other purpose). During dry periods, the drop in water level should correspond approximately with consumption. If this is not the case, the tank is leaking, and wet spots on its walls should be carefully looked for.

ANNUAL OR INFREQUENT TASKS FOR WHICH TECHNICAL ASSISTANCE MAY BE REQUIRED

1. At the end of the dry season, when the tank is empty, any leaks that have been noticed should be repaired. Where there have been wet spots on the walls,

a cement/water mixture is applied on the inside and finished off with a layer of plaster. If there has been evidence of leakage but no wet spots have been discovered on the walls, the floor should be treated with a cement/water mixture and then finished off with a layer of plaster.
2. The roof surface, gutters, supporting brackets and inflow pipes need to be checked and repaired if necessary.
3. If a sand filter is incorporated, the filter sand should be washed with clean water or renewed. Other types of strainer, filter or screen must be checked and repaired as necessary.
4. The mosquito net on the overflow pipe should be checked and if necessary renewed.
5. Removal of deposits from the bottom of the tank is periodically necessary. Depending on local conditions, this may be desirable annually (IWACO 1982) or only once in 3-5 years.
6. After repairs have been carried out inside a tank, after deposits have been cleaned out, and after a new tank has been completed, the interior should be scrubbed down with a solution of one of the following: *3 parts vinegar to one of water, OR 1 kg baking powder to 9 litres of water, OR ¼ cup (75ml) of 5% chlorine bleach to 45 litres of water.* After scrubbing, the tank should be left for 36 hours and finally washed down with clean water.

subject should appear prominently on the agenda of all monitoring and evaluation activities.

In the Indonesian work, maintenance problems reported include failure to clean and repair inlet filters on tanks and damage to mosquito screens (Latham 1984b). However, maintenance has largely been left in the hands of householders and village 'cadres' and is generally thought to be good. The main problem to emerge has been the deterioration of some bamboo-cement tanks, which illustrates the importance of monitoring for design policy and future choice of technology, as well as for planning technical support.

In discussing these issues, general comment on the desirability of 'participation' has been avoided because of the often misplaced ideological connotations of this over-used word. The case studies have indicated ways in which villagers have participated more or less actively in rainwater projects, although the technical assistance provided from outside their communities has usually been more crucial.

'Dialogue' or 'partnership' (Drucker 1985) are other equally over-used words, but ones which may have a rather more important meaning to convey. In Indonesia, we have seen that an exchange of ideas between villagers and professional staff led to the invention of bamboo-cement construction, and in Kenya, exchanges between craftsmen were seen as offering potential for innovation. When YDD staff in Indonesia observed how villagers were using rainwater, and planned an educational programme to improve water management, this was dialogue of another kind. It was a response to what people were doing rather than what they were saying, and it led to innovation in the 'software' element of the programme. To install hardware and then not to monitor its utilization and performance is to ignore a dialogue which could lead either to improvements in hardware, or to recognition of unforeseen maintenance or training needs.

Innovative dialogue and partnership is necessary at every stage in the development of a rainwater programme (or indeed any other kind of water supply). It should begin whenever an outside agency arrives in an area with new ideas, and should continue through construction and monitoring until, perhaps many years later, some of the original ideas in modified form have become part of the local culture and are being implemented in a self-sustaining manner. The beginning of the dialogue might be a social assessment in which it emerges that local people have a view of their most urgent needs and goals which differs significantly from outsiders' expectations. In a survey in Guinea-Bissau, villagers were found to identify their most urgent needs with food supplies. Asked about improved water provision, they spoke of water for rice-growing and for irrigating vegetables (Chauhan 1983).

A project which sets out to build rainwater tanks cannot usually be so responsive to local needs that it can divert its energies to irrigating ricefields. It should not, however, insist that rainwater be used only for drinking if the people feel their greatest need is water for a small vegetable plot. Where people use rainwater tanks in unexpected ways, it is nearly always a mistake to see this as simply 'misuse'. The villagers may well be bad at managing water resources, but an agency which is open to dialogue will also wish to consider that apparent misuse is really a reflection of some unmet, unarticulated need. Rather than misusing tanks, the people may be innovating intelligently to cope with the unrecognized need. The biggest exceptions to this may concern health aspects of water quality and contamination which are not obvious to the layman, and where 'misuse' may well reflect a requirement for information and 'education'.

Very occasionally a new technique will be so well suited to what people want, and so well marketed, that it seems to catch on overnight without adaptation. More usually, however, innovative dialogue is a slow process in which hardware and patterns of maintenance and use are gradually modified. Even in Thailand, where small pottery rainwater jars were already in widespread use and people were receptive to suggestions about larger containers, quite a number of tanks had to be built before the new technique crossed the 'threshold of popularization' (Fricke 1982). In the Kenya programme already quoted, only a few people, mostly from better-off households, took advantage of the water jars being offered when they first appeared, and it was twelve months before the threshold of popularization was crossed. Yet these are programmes in which progress has been unusually good.

Innovative dialogue requires patience and a long-term commitment. It is not something to which experts flown in from overseas can contribute greatly during brief consultancies. Significantly, two of the agencies represented in Table 4.1 are local ones with roots in the areas where they work; in addition the Zimbabwe programme has been experimenting with rainwater collection for around fifteen years. It is not unusual for innovative dialogue to extend over long periods such as this. Another example is in Botswana, where experiments with excavated rainwater catchment tanks have been undertaken at intervals since 1966, but without widespread construction of such tanks until the early 1980s. Slow progress has been attributed to an initial lack of government support (Gibberd 1981), but radical modifications of the technique and the purposes for which it was used also seem significant in securing its recent more widespread adoption.

The chief technical problem in the Botswana work was to line excavations so that the stored rainwater would not seep away. Linings made of butyl rubber and PVC sheeting were tried (Gibberd 1969), but the technique selected for development in the early projects was one previously tested in Sudan (Ionides 1966). The basic components were polythene sheeting, mud, and a specially-made building block referred to as a 'sausage'. The latter was a short length of 'lay-flat' polythene tube tied at the ends and filled with a sand and cement mix. The sausages were laid without mortar before the mix set, with 20cm lengths of gauge 8 wire pushed through to hold them together (Fig. 4.4). Being enclosed by polythene, the mix did not dry out quickly, (a perennial problem with the use of mortar in hot climates) and the cement was able to cure fully, achieving high strength with a very lean mixture of 13 parts of sand to 1 part cement. The sausages were laid after the excavation intended for water storage had been lined with two or more alternate layers of polythene sheeting and mud. The function of the sausages was to support

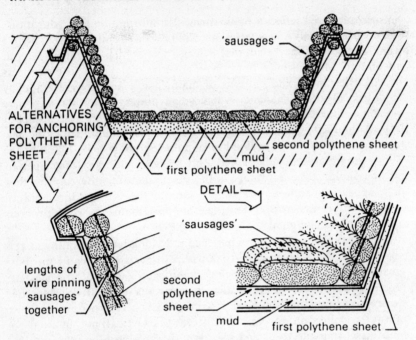

Fig. 4.4 *Simplified diagram illustrating the method of lining an excavated water tank with polythene sheeting and 'sausages' containing a weak cement/sand mix. The diagram is based on tanks built in Francophone West Africa where they are known as 'bassins type Botswana'.*

Note: *The size of the sausages relative to the dimensions of the tank is somewhat exaggerated.*

the sides and protect the sheeting from exposure and damage, whilst the reason for the alternating mud and polythene layers was to create a self-sealing effect should a puncture occur.

Initial trials with this technique in Botswana were carried out by Vernon Gibberd, who subsequently took several initiatives aimed at replicating it. For example, in 1968 he ran a course which attracted a mixed attendance of men and women, village leaders and local staff of the government Community Development Department. This led to the construction of at least two catchment tanks, one at the home of a course participant. The latter (which was privately paid for) had a fault and leaked at first, but after repairs with cement, it has seen fourteen years of continuous use. It is filled by runoff from hard ground immediately surrounding the owner's house, and is complemented by more conventional tanks which collect rainwater from the house roof.

Another initiative in which Gibberd was involved was a programme for building excavated rainwater tanks at primary schools to enable 'micro-irrigation' to be practised in school gardens. Twelve schools took part in the programme, teachers were trained and tanks were built, but as compared with the other projects discussed in this chapter, the technical assistance provided was of a very short-term and limited kind. The Intermediate Technology Development Group (ITDG), based in Britain, recruited an assistant to work with Gibberd, and a grant was obtained to cover the cost of materials. However, there was no parent organization in the region to monitor progress after the tanks were completed, or to provide continuing technical support, and the future of the work was left entirely in the hands of teachers at the schools where tanks were built.

Unfortunately, many of the teachers were transferred to other schools quite soon after the catchment systems were completed. Had there been adequate monitoring and follow-up the new teachers replacing them could have been encouraged to maintain and use the catchments. As it was, however, Gibberd had other responsibilities and his ITDG assistant had left the country. Neither was immediately aware of the altered staffing at the schools. Thus the new teachers were given no help in continuing with rainwater collection and in most cases it was entirely abandoned.

There is much parallel experience in other countries where attempts to develop rainwater systems or gardens at schools have been disappointing. Ghala tanks at schools in Kenya have been far less successful than those at private homes (Sinclair 1983), and the same may prove true of excavated catchment tanks at schools in a neighbouring area (Childers 1984). Similarly, ITDG's second project in southern Africa, at schools in Swaziland, did not achieve all that was expected of it. This again entailed the construction of excavated tanks utilizing playgrounds for rainwater catchment, but this time — with the aim of providing water for drinking — domed 'beehive' structures were built inside the tanks to enclose the stored water (as advocated by Ionides 1966). Sand spread on top of the 'beehives' then ensured that water was filtered as it entered the tank, and a small hand-pump was installed for withdrawing water.

A mismatch between these tanks and the schools is suggested by a generally gloomy picture of slow construction, incomplete tanks and broken pumps (Moody 1972), but the occasional successful example emphasizes the role an enthusiastic teacher can play. One such in Swaziland was the headmistress of Secusha School who ensured that her school's tank was properly completed, took trouble over maintenance of the pump, and made good use of water from the tank in cooking school meals.

Teachers in Botswana also included occasional enthusiasts. Tamasane School had a well-run garden even before its catchment system was built (Moody 1969). With the aid of water from the tank, it was providing vegetables for 200 meals per week by July 1968. When visited by one of the present authors in 1972, the garden and tank were in full use, and the whole school seemed impressively well run, with models and pottery made by the children on display. Ten years later, Gould (1983) reported that the tank was still being used (though it had needed repair by cementing over most of the lining), water being drawn for washing clothes as well as for growing tomatoes. It seems that many of the schools projects that fail do so because they are based on the assumption that all the teachers involved will be as committed as were those in the successful project. The reality is that most teachers, like most community workers, most village technicians, and most mutual-help groups, need continuing support from a locally-based technical assistance organisation.

VILLAGE ROLES IN REPLICATION AND INNOVATION

The conventional view of 'participation' in water programmes tends to envisage considerable responsibility and voluntary effort being undertaken by community workers, teachers, and village people in general. The concept of a practical or innovative dialogue between a technical assistance organization and villagers may be more realistic because it does not presuppose anything final about allocation of responsibilities. Rather, it stresses the monitoring of practical experience and the exchange of views with the aim of detecting problems as they arise, and modifying organization (and hence responsibilities) or hardware accordingly.

Many people are inclined to see the Botswana schools project as a 'total failure' but Gould (1983) takes a more positive view, arguing that there was some replication of the catchment systems elsewhere, and that the Botswana work may have had 'influence . . . on later developments of the technology'. If it had influence, then on some level there must have been dialogue, even if the absence of effective monitoring and the lack of help with immediate problems at the schools indicates that the dialogue was incomplete.

In order to work out what sort of dialogue took place and whether it influenced innovation or replication, some of the oranizations and individuals connected with rainwater development in Botswana have been identified and are indicated by the marked(°) names in Figure 4.5. This diagram summarizes a great deal of research into the contributions of the various groups, and seeks to show not only the slow and sometimes unexpected ways in which innovations arise, but also the occasionally crucial role played by highly motivated individuals. Reviewing water supplies in several African and Asian countries, Chauhan (1983) concludes that the 'key agents of development' are often exceptionally dedicated professionals, sometimes unidentified staff members in a voluntary agency or government ministry, but sometimes playing a more conspicuous part, as Vernon Gibberd did in this instance. Other individuals with more modest but still significant roles were the Morwa school teacher and members of the Zimbabwe programme quoted earlier. The latter kept in

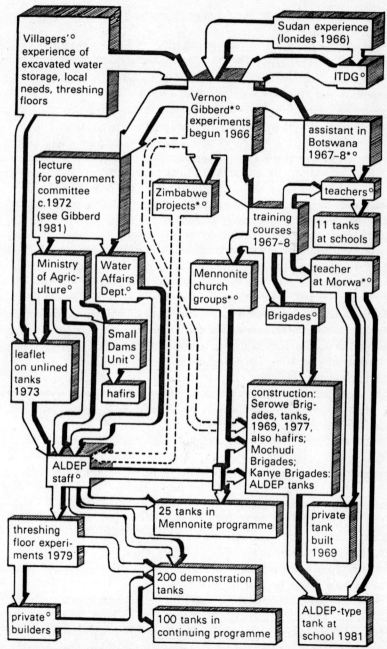

Fig. 4.5 A representation of the development of rainwater collection techniques in Botswana between 1966 and 1981, showing the main flows of ideas and information (arrows), and identifying some key participants in the innovative dialogue (°). (Sources for developments prior to 1972: personal interviews (*) by one of the authors; for later developments, Gould 1983 and Cullis 1984). ALDEP is the Arable Lands Development Programme.

regular contact with the Botswana work and built their own trial tanks with polythene sausages.

Figure 4.5 also mentions village people, some of whose children attended the schools where tanks were built. Their voluntary labour was called on during construction, but not enough attention was paid to their experience, opinions and priorities. For example, water for school gardens was not a priority for them, but water at arable lands distant from the villages was of greater concern. Moreover, rainwater collection in excavated 'tanks' was not something entirely new in which people needed instruction from an outside agency. Many farmers already made excavations for rainwater collection near to their arable land (Gibberd 1969). These excavations were unlined, and so were only feasible on clay soils, but they retained rainwater during the short period in each year when people were living on their lands. For this particular application, then, the seasonal availability. of rainwater was well matched to a specific need.

Government initiatives in rainwater collection were slow to develop (despite Gibberd's urgent advocacy of them (1981)), but appear to have taken more account of villagers' experience than did the ITDG work. For example, in 1973, the Ministry of Agriculture issued a well-illustrated leaflet advising farmers on the construction of unlined 'water catchment tanks' on their arable land. Though reflecting influence from the earlier programme, the leaflet also gave formal recognition to the traditional practice of excavating small rainwater ponds, recommending dimensions and promising help from extension officers in assessing soil conditions. At the same time, the Ministry was using earth-moving machinery to construct 'hafirs' (Classen 1980), which were much larger, unlined excavations designed to provide water for livestock.

Another direction in which the Botswana tradition of excavated drainage storage could develop was indicated by a footnote in the Ministry's 1973 leaflet. This said that if a farmer's unlined excavation did not hold water, it 'could be lined with plastic sheeting or cement — seek advice from your District Agricultural Officer'. The idea of a cement lining was taken further in 1979 when chicken wire was pegged to the sides of experimental excavated tanks and cement was plastered onto it; the resulting ferrocement lining was highly effective, and produced what amounted to a new type of tank in this region. Strikingly similar rainwater tanks have since been built in Kenya (Batchelor 1985; Childers 1984), probably with knowledge of the Botswana experiments derived from Maikano and Nyberg (1980). In a leaflet describing the Kenyan design, UNICEF advocates a hemispherical excavation rather than the shape indicated in Figure 4.6, and refinements in the method of covering the tank and the inlet filter.

The Botswana tanks were developed as part of the Ministry of Agriculture's Arable Lands Development Programme (ALDEP), and are also notable for the way in which threshing floors of traditional

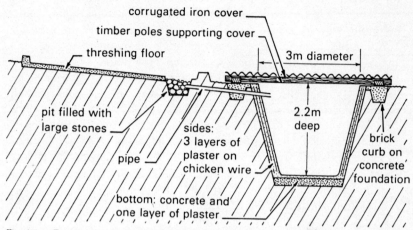

Fig. 4.6   Excavated rainwater tank in Botswana with ferrocement lining. The catchment area is a threshing floor surfaced with a clay/cow dung mixture which is worked to a smooth, hard finish. (Whiteside 1982; Gould 1983)

Note: Vertical dimensions have been exaggerated.

construction were adapted as catchment surfaces (Maikano and Nyberg 1980). Here again it seems that government water experts were learning from villagers, and especially from the occasional farmer who diverted drainage water from a threshing floor to fill his excavated storage. Another source of ideas, possibly indirect, was experience in Zimbabwe with cement-surfaced catchments of about the same size and shape as threshing floors (Fig. 4.2). The Zimbabwe installations also included ferrocement tanks, though information about simpler methods of lining excavations with ferrocement seems also to have reached the ALDEP workers from ITDG.

Thus, a very diverse range of exchanges of information involving government staff, farmers, and outside agencies all played a part in the innovative dialogue which led to the development of the ALDEP rainwater collection tank (Fig. 4.5). Following the success of the initial experiments, a nationwide pilot project was launched in which 200 demonstration tanks were built for farmers in a wide scatter of locations. This can be seen as a way of extending the dialogue by seeking to encourage additional farmers to acquire tanks, thereby spreading knowledge of the tanks and at the same time gaining experience of their use under a greater variety of conditions. This extended dialogue has included other people also: a Mennonite church community has begun building tanks for farmers in its area, usually of 40-50m³ capacity, and young men in the artisan training 'brigades' have been involved in tank construction. The teacher at Kurwa whose private tank was mentioned earlier arranged for a large 40m³ tank on the ALDEP model to be made at the school of which she is headmistress. I was informed

for watering a vegetable garden (Gould 1983). In addition, one local community development trust has produced its own instruction booklet describing how excavated tanks of this sort are made (Whiteside 1982).

Alongside these voluntary contributions to 'dialogue' and replication, the official ALDEP technical assistance programme offers loans and subsidies for farmers wishing to acquire tanks, and has trained local builders to make the ferrocement linings, with the intention that they should undertake the work on a commercial basis. The builders, however, complain that the officially fixed price is too low for them to make a profit.

A conventional perspective on the development of rainwater catchment in Botswana would tend to stress only *formal* arrangements for technical assistance, noting the short-term nature of ITDG's initial commitment and the much more substantial ALDEP programme. The exchange of information which contributed to innovation would also be seen in formal terms, and would include evaluations commissioned by ITDG and consultants' reports to government departments (e.g. Classen 1980). The conventional perspective would thus ignore or under-state informal learning processes — the information picked up from villagers, and the role of individuals whose private use of rainwater tanks and personal initiatives have spread ideas even when official bodies seemed to lack interest.

It is probably true that informal processes of dialogue always play some part in filling gaps in organized technical assistance programmes and help to keep them in touch with local realities. They are an essential accompaniment to more formal research effort and to technical assistance if the replication and improvement of a technology is to proceed at all vigorously. Examples have been cited from Indonesia as well as Botswana in which knowledge of existing village techniques contributed to significant innovations, and parallel experiences have been noted in other technologies (Pacey 1983).

Agencies must operate in an organized way, however, and cannot simply leave informal exchanges of information to proceed at their own pace. Thus organized *assessment, monitoring* and *evaluation* are important elements in the planned component of innovative dialogue. Evaluation usually refers to a longer-term perspective than is dealt with by the monitoring activities described so far. Rather than looking for immediate problems of operation or maintenance, evaluation tends to ask broader questions of a water supply: 'is it being fully used?' 'Is it achieving its intended benefits for health or livelihoods?' The World Health Organization (1983) has developed a 'minimum evaluation procedure' (MEP) which allows such questions to be investigated without excessively time-consuming research. Survey procedures are similar to those used in the social and technical assessments described in Chapter 3, but now they apply to completed rainwater systems or other supplies and adopt specific criteria of function and use. These latter include the quantity of water supplied, its quality, the reliability of supply, and the alternative sources which are used when the supply fails.

But however thoroughly an agency learns from such evaluations, replication of the technology it promotes will not come about solely as a result of formal knowledge and official schemes of technical assistance. The crossing of 'thresholds of popularization' depends also on the inter-actions between individuals and local organizations which generate enthusiasm and stimulate ideas — inter-actions between householders and builders who construct tanks; between farmers and extension officers; between commercial and public sectors in the economy. The role of villagers in this process should not be misrepresented by exaggerated claims about participation, but neither should it be under-estimated.

5. DESIGN FOR DRINKING WATER SYSTEMS

CONSTRAINTS ON ROOF CATCHMENTS

The design and construction of storage tanks is technically the most interesting and difficult aspect of rainwater collection, and it is perhaps inevitable that a discussion of design should focus on that. However, in Chapter 1 it was suggested that rainwater collection should be thought of as involving a *system* whose components were identified as including catchment surfaces, gutters, and some aspects of the end-use of the water, as well as storage tanks. Moreover, it was observed that most components in these systems have associated means of protection against such hazards as contamination of water, mosquito breeding, and animals falling into tanks.

In subsequent chapters, an even broader view of rainwater systems has been suggested, embracing the livelihoods of people who use rainwater, the organization of groups of users, and constraints limiting the replication of techniques. These are all things which may influence the detailed design of tanks and gutters. In Chapter 3, for example, we observed that the capacity of the storage tank a family requires might vary according to whether the family needs an all-year supply, or whether its livelihood depends on work done during an especially critical season when a convenient source of water has particularly high value in time-saving or for growing a vital crop.

Constraints affecting the replication of rainwater techniques — high costs, inadequate guttering, unsuitability of local roofing materials — clearly require close attention during the design stage of any project. In practice, most rainwater programmes do not tackle major problems of repair and reconstruction of roofs, but install tanks only where roofs are judged adequate as catchment surfaces. However, the point has been made that if a programme gives priority to low-income groups, the bad state of their housing, including roofs, should receive attention. Technical support for roof repair or replacement might then become part of the programme. This might involve introducing and testing new low-cost materials such as sisal-cement roofing tiles; it might include training builders in a new technique or paying them to assist householders who cannot carry out their own repairs; or it might entail setting up a revolving loan fund or savings scheme so that a householder can pay for corrugated iron sheeting in easy stages (Chapter 4).

Guttering seems to be a difficulty for many householders, yet it is rarely mentioned in reports from technical assistance programmes. Where there are practical obstacles to installing conventional gutters, one option may be to devise ways of collecting water from roofs without them. In Bermuda, this is achieved by means of slanting ridges on the roof surface known as 'glides' (Fig. 5.1). They are formed of lengths of stone cut to a triangular shape, or else are precast in concrete, and are bedded on the limestone roof slates with cement mortar. This method is only practicable where roof surfaces are smooth, and it would not be satisfactory with corrugated iron. Elsewhere, troughing below the eaves but near to ground level has been used to collect rainwater in small containers. Such troughing may be particularly appropriate for thatched roofs (Fig. 5.1) and could be used to fill a larger permanent tank or jar at a low level, perhaps constructed in a shallow excavation.

The cost of conventional guttering is often said to be small compared with the cost of a tank. In the Zimbabwe work discussed in the previous chapter, metal guttering was made by the technical assistance organization in its own workshop. When the total cost of a ferrocement tank installation was quoted as roughly equivalent to US$75, this included $6 for gutters and a further $6 for fixing them. The latter was a labour cost which could be saved by householders able to fix the gutters themselves. But since lack of the necessary skills appears to be a constraint in itself, the cost of guttering in this instance should be reckoned as $12 or 16 per cent of the total.

The conveyance of water from eaves gutters to the inlet of a storage tank can be via an extra length of guttering (Fig. 5.2), or it can involve a complex array of downpipes (Fig. 5.3). In view of the need to keep costs low and avoid maintenance problems, the simpler approach is clearly preferable. However, when a large tank is filled from gutters on both sides of a house, it may not be easy to have extension gutters bridging across from the eaves to the tank. In that case, to avoid the complications illustrated by Fig. 5.3, two small tanks may be better, each filled by one side of the roof. Despite the diseconomies of scale which make two small tanks considerably more expensive than a single large one, the saving on downpipes can lead to a cheaper installation, or at least to no greater expense (see Table 5.1). In many countries, including Thailand, Indonesia and Kenya, many low-income households can only afford small tanks collecting water from one side of the roof, in any case. A second tank on the other side is therefore an option for future improvements rather than an immediate possibility.

In tropical areas, the high intensity of rainfall in some of the heavy downpours that occur means that gutters must be larger than in temperate regions if they are not to overflow. In general, gutters with a cross-sectional area of 200cm^2 will be able to cope with all but the heaviest rain when

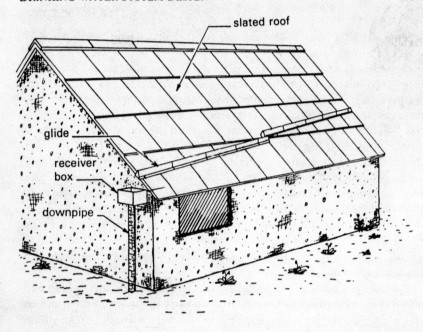

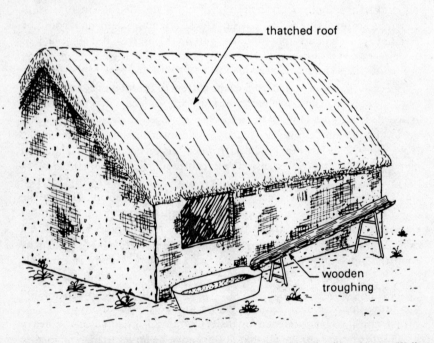

Fig. 5.1   Alternatives to guttering: glides (Bermuda) and low-level troughing (Ghana). (Waller 1982 (Bermuda) and Novieku 1980 (Ghana))

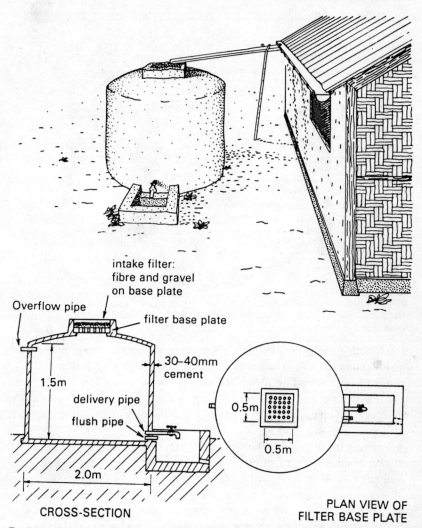

intake filter:
fibre and gravel
on base plate

Overflow pipe

filter base plate

30–40mm
cement

1.5m

delivery pipe

flush pipe

0.5m

0.5m

2.0m

CROSS-SECTION

PLAN VIEW OF
FILTER BASE PLATE

*Fig. 5.2   A bamboo-cement rainwater tank in Indonesia with a short length of guttering making
the connection between the eaves gutter and the inlet filter on the tank. The guttering can be
temporarily moved to divert 'first flush' water away from the tank. The section and plan show
details of the inlet filter. (Kaufman 1983)*

attached to a small roof, which implies approximately 200mm width for
gutters of semicircular section (Figure 5.4). However, where local materials
such as bamboo are used, sizes will have to depend mainly on what is
available.

Another problem is simply the weight of the gutter when loaded with
water. Gutters will need to be well supported so that they cannot sag or be
pulled away from their supports. They must be carefully positioned to

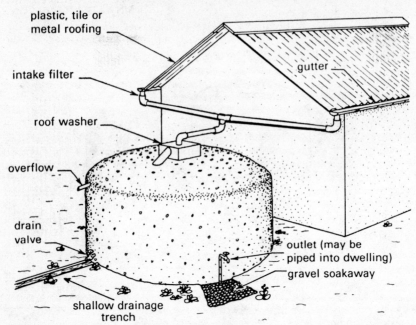

Fig. 5.3   Downpipes for collecting water from both sides of a pitched roof. (Institute for Rural Water 1982)

catch both gushing flow from the roof and also drips. In addition, they need an adequate slope for their entire flow length so that stagnant pools which could provide breeding places for mosquitoes are avoided. For all these reasons, fixing gutters is not a simple task to be left in the hands of inexperienced people, but should be taken seriously in technical assistance programmes.

The way in which gutters are actually supported must depend very much on the construction of the house. Sometimes it is possible to fix iron or timber brackets to walls, but for houses that have wide eaves, some method of attachment to the rafters will be necessary. It may often be easiest to bind gutters to their supports with thick wire, though rope may be used provided that it is replaced regularly, before rotting weakens it. Several techniques for fixing gutters to thatched roofs were illustrated earlier (Fig. 1.8), some of which are applicable for tiled roofs with very little modification, and Figure 5.4 shows other possibilities. It is, of course, impossible to illustrate every feasible method.

As to construction of the gutter itself, one of the simplest methods is to nail cedar or other planks together in a V-shape (Fig. 5.4). The joint is sealed with tar or any suitable, locally available, resinous material (McDowell 1976). Metal gutters can sometimes be made locally, and both metal and plastic (PVC) guttering may be available for purchase. Halved tin cans riveted together have been demonstrated by several appropriate

Table 5.1   **Comparative costs of one large tank collecting water from both sides of a roof as compared with two small tanks*.**

	Large tank collecting from both sides of a roof	Two small tanks, each collecting from one side of the roof
Cost of tanks:		
10m³ size	100	—
5m³ size	—	56
		56
Cost of guttering	17	17
Cost of downpipes	15	3
	132	132

* *Figures are based on experience in Zimbabwe and data on economies of scale indicated by Edwards and Keller, 1984. The notional cost of a large tank is set at $100.00.*

technology centres (e.g. in Nairobi), but no widespread practical applications have been reported. Much the most widely used and important form of guttering produced from local materials is that made from bamboo, for which detail is given in Box 5.1.

Large rainwater tanks may be nearly as high as the eaves of the houses they serve so only short lengths of downpipe are required. Current practice is to connect the downpipe directly to the gutter without a receiver box, and to use a large diameter pipe — 100mm or more — or a length of open gutter. The downpipe should be big enough to carry flows from intensive rainfall and for clogging by leaves to be unlikely. The most important point to consider at this stage is the method that should be adopted to prevent debris from being washed into the tank and to arrange for the dirty 'first flush' rainwater after a dry spell to be discarded. Due to the extra cost of installing any elaborate device and the near impossiblity of maintaining it in rural situations, most programmes do no more than provide a screen or filter at the entry to the tank to prevent the grosser forms of debris from passing. In the Indonesian work quoted earlier, an inlet filter moulded into the tank roof is a prominent feature of the design (Fig. 5.2). No special provision is made for first flush diversion, but the length of guttering which takes the place of the downpipe can be moved during any dry periods and replaced after the first few minutes of rain in a new wet season. Other simple methods of moving downpipe outlets away from tanks during dry

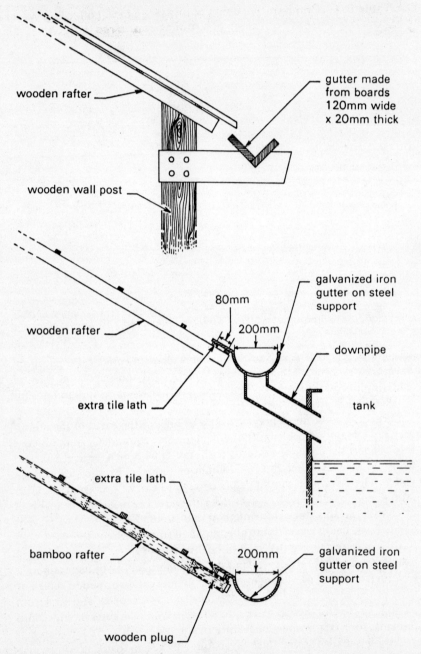

Fig. 5.4   Methods of fixing metal gutters to rafters, and wooden gutters to wall posts. (See Fig. 1.8 for other techniques.) Where rafters are made of bamboo the hollow ends of the rafters need to be plugged with wood before laths are attached to carry the gutter. (For clarity, rafters are shown without the tiles or corrugated iron sheeting they support.)

Box 5.1 Bamboo guttering. (Institute for Rural Water 1982; VITA 1973)

Bamboo gutters are made by splitting bamboo culms (i.e. stems) lengthways down the middle, and removing the partitions inside.

The culms may be split using a sharp knife (Diagram 1) which should have a short handle and a broad blade. Heavy culms can be more easily tackled by mounting an iron wedge on a post (Diagram 2). An axe is then used to make a small breach at the top end of the culm; the wedge is inserted into the breach, and the culm is pushed or pulled toward the wedge until it splits. The edges of the split bamboo are razor-sharp and should be handled with care.

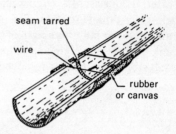

Diagram 3: Joining two pieces of bamboo

Downpipes can also be made from bamboo (Diagram 4). The joints shown have little inherent strength and depend on the gutters and downpipes being securely fixed in position against the walls and roof before the joint is made. Sealing of joints is again done with tar or caulking compound.

Place a small mesh wire screen over the opening of the downpipe so that leaves or other debris which could contaminate the water do not enter the cistern. The mesh should be large enough to catch leaves and debris but allow water to flow through.

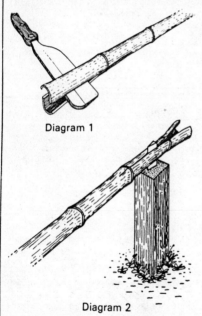

Diagram 1

Diagram 2

Bamboo guttering may be tied to the roof structure with wire at 0.5m intervals. One way of joining lengths of gutter is to use a piece of rubber cut from an old inner tube. The rubber fits under the gutters and is secured to them by wire (Diagram 3). Tar or caulking is then used to make a seal. Ensure that the two pieces of bamboo fit together closely before sealing the joint.

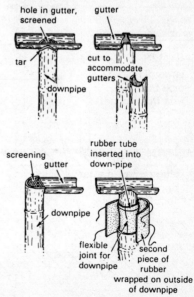

Diagram 4: Joining gutters and downpipes

spells were illustrated in Fig. 3.4. Of all the programmes quoted so far, only the one in Thailand incorporates any device for holding back first flush water. It consists of a length of large diameter pipe suspended alongside the rainwater tank (Fig. 5.5). This is sealed at the bottom with a plug. When rain begins to fall, this length of pipe must fill before any water can enter the tank. It will thus retain any sediments carried by the first flush water. After each storm, the plug is removed and the pipe is drained.

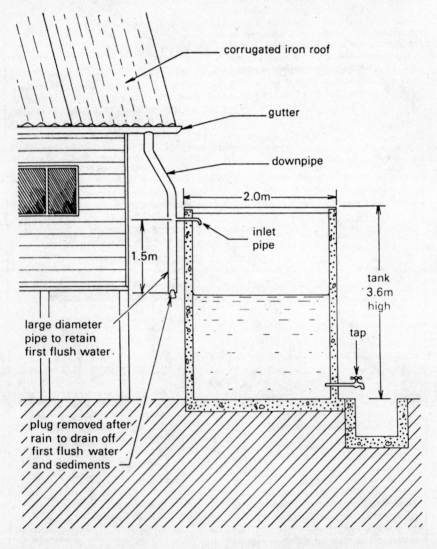

Fig. 5.5   A method of first-flush rejection which is used with bamboo-reinforced concrete tanks in Thailand.

RAINWATER TANK DESIGN

The key decisions that have to be made about tank design relate firstly to materials and methods of construction, and secondly to tank capacity. Both decisions depend critically on costs. Whilst large tanks show economies of scale, so that the cost per cubic metre of water stored may be reduced, with smaller tanks, there is more scope for using local materials and cutting costs that way. Indeed, available choices of materials and methods of construction vary greatly with tank size.

Very small rainwater tanks are often containers made for other purposes which have been pressed into service when the rainy season begins. They include buckets, barrels, bowls, large clay pots, and even tin baths. The ubiquitous oil drum of $0.2m^3$ capacity may be adapted for use as a permanent rainwater tank (Fig. 3.1) and in some countries, large pottery water jars with capacities up to $0.3m^3$ are made for the purpose. However, the development of techniques for manufacturing similar jars from cement mortar is now providing a cheaper alternative to the pottery jar.

Unreinforced cement mortar jars can be made in a range of capacities from $0.3m^3$ upwards. For the smaller sizes, the easiest method of construction is to use sacking stuffed with sand or sawdust as the basic framework onto which cement mortar is plastered (Box 5.2). Like many other techniques for using cement mortar (e.g. for granary bins, NAS 1973), the technique originated in Thailand. However, it has also been used in Kenya notably in the Karai project described in Chapter 4 — but there the sacking/sawdust formwork was found rather cumbersome for large jars, and Ghala tanks were ultimately regarded as more satisfactory. It is of interest, then, that Thai innovators have recently been building cement mortar jars of $1.8m^3$ capacity ('Jumbo jars') using specially made curved bricks or blocks to construct the formwork. These blocks are themselves cast in cement, and are used repeatedly, so that many jars can be made with one set of about 90 of them. Mud is used as a 'temporary mortar' when the formwork is erected. It crumbles away easily when the tank is complete and the blocks are removed (Latham 1984a). This method is used for factory production of Jumbo jars in Thailand. Wire reinforcement is incorporated during construction, so that the jar have sufficient strength to be loaded into lorries for delivery. This makes them comparable to the ferrocement tanks built in many rural programmes.

Many other types of material can be used to make the medium-sized water storage containers suitable for collecting rainwater from the roofs of small houses. However, there has been a striking tendency in the last decade for rural development programmes to opt for cement-based materials. Unreinforced jars (including Ghala tanks) and bamboo-cement tanks have been used for sizes up to about $4.5m^3$, whilst for capacities

Box 5.2 Construction of a cement mortar jar of 1.0m³ capacity. (Institute for Rural Water, 1982)

1. The *mould* or *formwork* for a 1.0m³ jar is made from two pieces of gunny cloth or hessian sacking cut and stitched together with twine as in Diagram 1. After sewing, the resulting bottomless bag is turned inside out.

2. To make the *bottom* of the tank, mark out a circle on the ground 1.0m in diameter and place half bricks or other suitable material around its circumference to act as formwork. Spread paper or plastic sheeting on the ground within the circle to stop the mortar sticking. Mix a 1:2 cement/sand mortar and spread within the circle to a depth of 15mm.

3. When the bottom plate has set, place the sacking bag narrow end down on the plate and begin filling it with sand, sawdust or rice husks. Make sure the mortar base sticks out from under the sack, as in Diagram 2, and tuck the edges of the sacking under the sand or sawdust filling so that the weight of the material holds the sack onto the plate.

4. *Fill the sack,* fold the top and tie it closed. Then smooth and press the sack into a regular shape. Make a circular ring from wood or cement mortar and place this on top as formwork for the opening in the jar. (Diagram 3).

5. *Spray the sacking* with water until it is thoroughly wet. Then plaster on a *first layer of cement mortar* to a thickness of 5–7mm.

6. *Plaster on the second 5mm layer* in the same manner as the first, checking the thickness by pushing a nail in. Build up any thin spots.

7. Remove the sack and its contents 24 hours after plastering is finished. Repair any defects in the jar with mortar, paint the inside with cement slurry. Then *cure* the jar for two weeks protecting it from sun and wind under damp sacking.

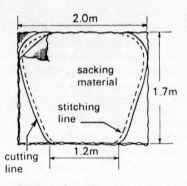

2.0m

sacking material

1.7m

stitching line

1.2m

cutting line

Diagram 1

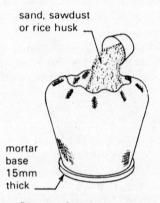

sand, sawdust or rice husk

mortar base 15mm thick

Diagram 2

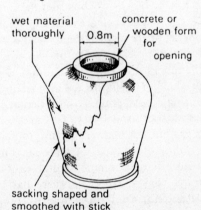

wet material thoroughly

0.8m

concrete or wooden form for opening

sacking shaped and smoothed with stick

Diagram 3

between 5 and 12m³, cylindrical tanks are the norm, and are made of ferrocement or concrete.

Outside rural development work, however, it needs to be remembered that galvanized corrugated iron tanks are often available in this range of sizes and are probably more widely used than any other type. Tanks built of brick are widespread in some countries, and there are also more exotic materials (including fibreglass). In addition, there are butyl rubber liners supported by metal frames or other containers. In Jamaica, for example, metal silos for storage of animal feed are available much more cheaply than metal water tanks, and to provide water storage they can be fitted with a butyl or other plastic lining (Maddocks 1973). In Senegal, similar linings have been used to turn large mud-walled grain bins into water tanks (UNESCO 1981).

Reasons why ferrocement or other cement-based materials are so often preferred include favourable experience of their use in village conditions and with self-help construction. However, costs are also lower and the tanks may last longer than other types. The short life of many corrugated metal tanks is frequently commented on (e.g. by Layton 1984), but the problem is usually one of faulty installation — physical damage to the galvanised surface, lack of a firm and well-drained foundation, and the use of electrolytically incompatible metals for pipes or other fittings. In Kenya, metal tanks last for ten years when properly installed on a raised platform.

Galvanized corrugated iron tanks also have merits when looked at in terms of social benefits and livelihoods. In many areas they are the most readily available tanks for those householders able to purchase at full market prices, and in some places — including parts of Kenya and Papua New Guinea — their construction provides jobs for significant numbers of 'tin-smiths'.

It is impossible to quote cost figures that are applicable to all countries. Cement prices, transport costs and inflation rates vary, and policies for employing craftsmen and/or self-help labour on site also differ from one programme to another. Table 5.2 quotes some figures for West Java (Indonesia) together with some interpolated data from Africa and Thailand which seem very roughly comparable. Cement-based tanks are the cheapest option almost everywhere. The figures for unit storage also indicate economies of scale which will show up in any programme. Where people can only afford relatively small tanks, it makes sense to investigate the costs of bamboo-cement and Ghala tanks. Despite evident low costs in comparison with other 2.5m³ tanks, their unit costs are not especially attractive — big ferrocement tanks may sometimes be cheaper per cubic metre of storage capacity.

The chief exception, where a small tank appears to defeat the scale factor, is the Thai Jumbo jar of 1.8m³ capacity. It is economical in its use of materials, and costs are also kept down by factory methods of construction.

Table 5.2   Comparative costs for different kinds of rainwater tank (1981–2 prices).

The majority of figures are Doelhomid's estimates for West Java, Indonesia (1982), quoted in U.S. dollars and including labour costs. Figures given by Keller (1982) are set in brackets to emphasize that they are not precisely comparable with the West Java data, and brackets are also used for figures from Thailand (Fricke, 1982; Power, 1983)

TYPE OF TANK	Tank capacity 2.3–3m³		Tank capacity 9–10m³	
	total cost	unit cost per m³	total cost	unit cost per m³
Fibreglass	400	160	1800	180
Sheet metal	–	–	900	90
Galvanized corrugated iron	(150)[a]	(60)[a]	(350)[a]	(35)
Ferrocement – West Java type	94	38	200	20
Ferrocement – Zimbabwe type				
materials only	–	–	(150)[b]	(15)[b]
materials & labour	–	–	(220)[a]	(22)[a]
Bamboo-reinforced concrete (Thailand)				
materials only	–	–	(135)[c]	(14)[c]
materials & labour (contractors' price)	–	–	(306)[c]	(32)[c]
Bamboo-cement (West Java type)	70	28	–	–
Ghala tank (Kenya) materials only	(42)[b]	(18)[b]	–	–

[a] authors' estimates
[b] Keller (1982) basing his estimates for the ferrocement tank on Watt (1978) and for Ghala tanks on 2.3m³ capacity
[c] Fricke (1982) and Power (1983) for a 9.4m³ tank

At 1984 price levels, one of these jars would cost the equivalent of US$23, which implies a unit cost of less than $13 per m³ (Latham 1984a). That is lower than any unit cost in Table 5.2, despite the rise in prices since the data for the table were collected. The large bamboo-reinforced concrete tanks which are also built in Thailand have unit costs around twice those of the Jumbo jar yet show some of the lowest costs in Table 5.2. Probably the figures from other countries are not comparable, but details of the Thai bamboo-reinforced tanks to be given later indicate that their low cost is due partly to a relatively small requirement for cement as well as to the absence of metal reinforcement. Rather elaborate formwork is used, however, and so average costs are only low when the formwork is re-used and its cost spread over many tanks.

For tanks with capacities larger than $15m^3$, such as might be needed to collect rainwater from the roof of a large public building, ferrocement remains a possibility (Watt 1978), but brick, stone or cement block construction are also widely used. Such tanks or reservoirs are often built in shallow excavations so that the mass of soil against the tank walls helps withstand the water pressure inside. Where excavation is decided on, however, the cheapest option for a large volume of storage may well be simply to line the sides of a hole with ferrocement, as described previously (see Fig. 4.6). Other forms of excavated storage which might be considered are discussed at the end of this chapter.

Brickwork deserves more detailed consideration not only because of its regular use for building tanks in some countries, but because under certain conditions, it lends itself to very low-cost forms of construction both for small and large tanks. Indeed, costs for brickwork have been omitted from Table 5.2 because of their great variability from place to place. In West Java, a $10m^3$ brick tank costs nearly twice as much as a ferrocement one (Doelhomid 1982), but in Zimbabwe, ferrocement tanks are no longer built by the Hlekweni Training Centre (Table 4.1) because brickwork is cheaper. This is due to the availability of locally fired bricks and cheap broken bricks.

However, trial designs for brickwork tanks have been developed in West Java, and Figure 5.6 shows some structural detail. A quite different type of brick construction which has been used in Zimbabwe is also presented in the same diagram. This latter illustrates the use of steel reinforcing wires to strengthen the tank against the internal water pressure. There is a double skin of brickwork which is built in stages, beginning with three or four courses of the inner skin of bricks. When these are in place, reinforcing wires are drawn tightly round the tank at the points shown, and fixed in place. Then the outer skin is raised by three courses and the space in between is grouted with mortar before the inner brickwork is built up any further. This form of reinforcement is suited to a large tank, in this case of $25m^3$ capacity containing a 2m depth of water. The low-cost brick tanks now being built in Zimbabwe are not identical but they also incorporate wire reinforcement. By contrast, the West Java design in Figure 5.6 is for a much smaller tank ($2.2m^3$) with water depths no greater than 1.2m (though Kerkvoorden quotes 1.5m). There is no wire reinforcement but a fairly substantial foundation helps take up the water pressure. Both tanks are made watertight by applying a cement plaster to the inside of the walls, and when this has set, by brushing it over with a thick cement slurry. However, the floor is dealt with differently in the two instances. The Zimbabwe tank (Fig. 5.6b) has a heavy concrete floor slab which is plastered like the walls

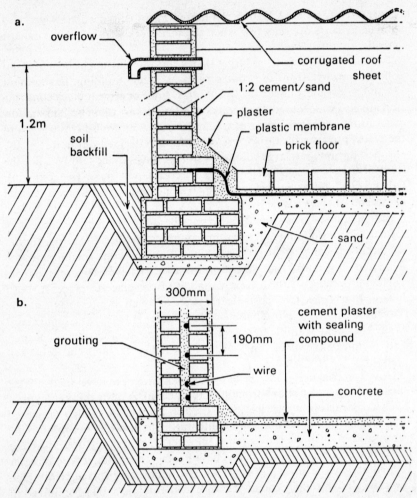

a.

overflow

corrugated roof sheet

1:2 cement/sand

plaster

plastic membrane

brick floor

1.2m

soil backfill

sand

b.

300mm

cement plaster with sealing compound

grouting

190mm

wire

concrete

Fig. 5.6   Contrasting methods of construction for brickwork rainwater tanks. Diagram (a) shows a small tank built in West Java, Indonesia without reinforcement. (Kerkvoorden 1982) The other diagram (b) is a detail of a larger tank designed in Zimbabwe with wire reinforcement between two skins of brickwork. (Hall 1975)

Note: *Bricks are not of standard size.*

and then painted with a proprietary sealing compound. The West Java tank has a brick floor with a plastic membrane below it.

Cylindrical tanks constructed in brick are widely used in East Africa (UNEP 1983), and Nissen-Petersen (1982) describes the use of concrete blocks to build similar tanks in Kenya. Again there are reinforcing wires encircling the tank, this time set in the mortar between the courses of blockwork. More typical of Kenya are *matofali* tanks, that is, made of locally burned brick. They are typically of about 10m³ capacity and are to be seen at the homes of wealthy farmers and in larger sizes are used for collecting water from the roofs of public buildings.

Rainwater tanks built with blocks of coral and lined with locally made cement are to be seen on Wasini Island, off the coast of Kenya (Gould 1983), and tanks with limestone walls are widely used in Jamaica. Despite annual rainfall of 1500mm, parts of Jamaica have a highly permeable limestone such that conventional surface and groundwater sources cannot be developed. Many individual houses have tanks collecting water from roofs, and there are also large public tanks or reservoirs filled from ground surface catchments, some with capacities up to 500m³.

The household tanks are built partly or wholly below ground level and water is drawn from them using buckets or pumps. Because of the permeability of the stone, a waterproof lining of cement or marl is needed. Tanks tend to be large, and Maddocks (1973) quotes costs of construction for one of 27m³ capacity which include a high charge for the labour involved in excavation (US$311 at 1973 prices). After that, construction of the tank itself costs US$989 — which is a large sum even by the standards of the 1981-2 prices in Table 5.2.

DESIGN CRITERIA AND CEMENT-BASED MATERIALS

It is clear from previous paragraphs that a decision about construction methods and materials for any tank-building programme is closely linked to the decision about the capacities required, and that both are closely constrained by cost. It might appear that a choice concerning capacity should be determined by the available catchment area and the rainfall pattern in the area. However, the limitations of hydrological analysis were made clear in Chapter 3. Tanks in low-income communities are nearly always smaller than the hydrological optimum. Therefore, all that is needed from hydrology in most cases is a rough guideline that will prevent money being wasted on an occasional over-large tank that never fills. In Botswana, for example, although Gould (1983) quotes sophisticated hydrological calculations, for many purposes he is content to use a simplified rule to the effect that tank capacity (in m³) should not be more than about 0.2 times the catchment area (in m²). Local experience in other regions will suggest similar rules of thumb, perhaps with larger multipliers where rainfall is higher.

Thus, hydrology merely provides an upper limit on the choice of tank capacities and other criteria are basically more important. They include questions about what people can afford, what employment opportunities are created, and what technical assistance can be provided. Where employment is a consideration and it is intended that tank constructors should run their own business, we have noted that 6m³ ferrocement tanks have been successful in the North Solomons and 2.3m³ Ghala tanks have potential in Kenya; we have also seen that in many countries, there is a place for galvanized iron tanks as well. However, where technical assistance is directed toward training villagers or community workers to help house-holders build their own tanks, it is more important to consider which types of construction are easiest to teach to inexperienced people. In this context, Keller (1982) picks out three types which he regards as especially 'teachable', as follows:

- unreinforced cement mortar jar, $1.0m^3$ capacity (see Box 5.2);
- plastered Ghala basket, $2.3m^3$ (Box 3.1);
- ferrocement tank, $9m^3$ (Box 4.1).

Choice of tanks for their 'teachability' does not, of course, automatically lead to the lowest possible costs. As already noted, brickwork may be a cheaper form of construction than ferrocement where bricks are locally made, or alternatively, bamboo-cement tanks may seem the best low-cost option.

At this point, however, there are other criteria which ought to influence the choice of tank. Bamboo-cement tanks in Indonesia have not proved very durable, and many have lasted for less than five years. Doubts have also been expressed about Ghala tanks. It is probable that much depends on good workmanship with both these types, and on whether adequate curing of the cement mortar is possible. Curing depends on preventing tanks from drying out during a 7-14 day period after construction by pouring some water into the tank, shading it from the sun, and draping damp sacking or cloth over exposed areas. In districts where water is short and people cannot give frequent attention to keeping sacking damp, curing is often poor and tank failures are frequent. In such circumstances, bamboo-cement or Ghala tanks are perhaps inadvisable. Instead, forms of construction should be chosen in which tanks are over-designed and so would be much stronger than necessary if good workmanship and adequate curing could be guaranteed. Tanks which most conspicuously demonstrate tolerance of bad curing are those built of concrete, including bamboo-reinforced types in Thailand and concrete ring tanks in Kenya. However, concrete construction may not be a low-cost option in places where a suitable aggregate cannot be easily obtained.

A final point concerns the type of technical assistance in which some components are supplied to villages from a central depot. Where specially-made formwork is required, as with most concrete tanks, and also with the ferrocement tank described in Box 4.1, this must nearly always be supplied on loan as part of the technical assistance programme. It may also speed up construction if some materials are prepared centrally. For example, chicken wire for ferrocement tanks might be cut to length, or bamboo reinforcement could be prepared this way with benefits for quality control.

In Indonesia, where hundreds of rainwater tanks are now made each year, methods of this sort are being introduced to speed up production. Where tanks are made from pre-cast concrete rings, it will usually be an advantage to establish a central site in a village where rings can be made for households in the immediate vicinity.

To sum up then, criteria influencing the design of tanks for collecting rainwater from house roofs should include the following:

- cost;
- availability of materials (e.g. aggregate, bamboo, local brick);
- employment opportunities;
- 'teachability' and the organization of technical assistance;
- adequate curing of cement mortar;
- design tolerance for bad workmanship;
- possible supply of components from a central depot;
- hydrology as a check on maximum capacities.

Whilst construction procedures for the three most 'teachable' methods of building rainwater tanks have already been described in the information boxes, it remains to list the materials required, which is done in Table 5.3. When tanks are built by their prospective owners, and where suitable sand and aggregate can be obtained locally, the biggest factor in the total cost of a tank is the amount of cement needed, and the metal components such as pipes, taps and wire reinforcement. Table 5.3 quotes the number of 50kg bags of cement required per cubic metre of water storage in the completed tank. The authors of this book have collected data on cement requirements for a much larger range of tank sizes and types, and it is clear that there are some definite economies of scale involved. Whether made of ferrocement or concrete, tanks larger than $7m^3$ in capacity never require more than 1.4 bags of cement per cubic metre of storage, whereas cement mortar jars and Ghala tanks with less than $3m^3$ capacity all require more than 1.7 bags and often as much as 2.0 bags of cement per cubic metre. Among the smaller tanks, the Thai Jumbo jar is exceptionally economical in cement. However, according to Kaufman (1983), the bamboo-cement tanks built in Indonesia require 1.8 bags/m^3, so whilst they economize by using bamboo instead of metal reinforcement, they do not show savings in cement. Concrete often appears to be a costly form of construction (Kerkvoorden 1982), but bamboo-reinforced concrete tanks in Thailand and Kenya require somewhat less cement than ferrocement tanks of similar capacity. The walls of the Thai tanks are three times thicker than the walls of equivalent ferrocement but the extra bulk is accounted for by the gravel aggregate used in the concrete.

It should also be noted that lists of materials required to build a tank include some allowance for wastage. In Thailand, metal boxes were made

Table 5.3 **Materials needed for the construction of some widely used types of rainwater tank.** (Watt, 1978, Fricke, 1982, Keller, 1982, and sources quoted in the information boxes referred to)

	Unreinforced cement mortar jar, as in Box 5.2	Ghala tank, as in Box 3.1	Ferrocement tank, as in Box 4.1	Bamboo reinforced concrete tank as built in Thailand
Capacity	1.0m³	2.3m³	9.0m³	11.3m³
Local materials	rice husks, sawdust or sand to stuff sacking formwork	woven stick granary basket – murram or clay		bamboo
Special requirements	hessian sacking 4m x 1.7m		corrugated iron formwork	metal formwork as in Figure 5.9
Cement (50kg bags)	2 bags	5 bags	12 bags	13 bags
Sand	200kg	500kg	1300kg	1300kg
Gravel, 25mm	–	200kg	500kg	2000kg
Quarry chippings	–	300kg	–	800kg
Chicken wire 50mm mesh	–	–	16m²	–
Straight wire, 2.5mm gauge	–	–	200m	–
Water pipe, 15mm	–	1m	2m	1m
Overflow pipe, 50mm	–	–	0.2m	0.2m
Taps	–	1 no.	1 no.	1 no.
Roof or lid	made of wood or cement mortar	cement mortar	6m² sheet metal	concrete
Bags of cement per m³ storage	2.0	2.2	1.3	1.15

for measuring out materials for bamboo/concrete tanks, to ensure that the required 1:2:3 proportions by volume of cement, sand and gravel were adhered to when the concrete was mixed. Experience shows that this has cut waste so effectively that the cement requirements for an $11.3m^3$ tank has been reduced from 14 to 13 bags (Fricke 1982). In other projects also it may help to use gauging boxes because specific volumes of sand and gravel are difficult to judge by shovelling. For example, if a box is made to the size $0.5 \times 0.5 \times 0.27m$ one box full of sand mixed with a 50kg bag of cement will give a 1:2 cement/sand mortar mix.

Instructions given earlier for building Ghala tanks (Box 3.1) describe how a cover for the tank is made, but similar information is not given for the ferrocement tank described in Box 4.1. In Zimbabwe, where the tanks originated, they were fitted with sheet metal covers. Corrugated iron can also be used if it is firmly fixed in place, and access by mosquitoes is prevented by cementing the spaces under the corrugations. Another technique is to make the framework for a tank roof using chicken wire supported by wooden joists. This is then covered with hessian and painted with a cement slurry. However, the most elegant way of covering a ferrocement tank is to construct the roof in ferrocement also. This may be done by leaving some of the chicken wire reinforcement protruding at the top when the walls of the tank are plastered. Then, after the walls are finished and the formwork is removed, two layers of wire mesh are placed over the tank. They are knitted into the chicken wire at the sides and tied with wire, and a square hole is cut for an access hatch. Then they are firmly supported by props and boards from below to form a shallow, dome-shaped roof, and cement plaster is applied from above. When this has set, the props are removed and the underside of the roof is plastered (Fig. 5.7).

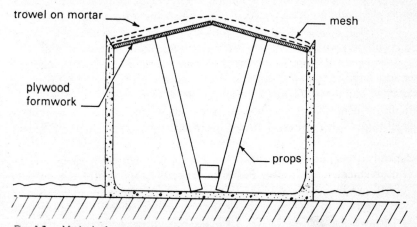

Fig. 5.7   Method of constructing a ferrocement roof for a tank of the same material. The diagram shows trowel on formwork supported by props under the mesh of chicken wire reinforcement. (From 1979)

It is nearly always an advantage to paint exposed water tanks white to reflect the sun's heat, keep the water cool, and reduce evaporation. With ferrocement, and probably other cement mortar tanks, especially those with cemented roofs of the type just described, thermal expansion and contraction entails some risk of cracks developing. If the tank is painted white and as a result does not get so hot in sunlight, this risk will be reduced.

One other way of using ferrocement is to strengthen an existing structure and render it watertight. In Papua New Guinea, galvanized iron tanks are widely used but suffer such serious corrosion that they must often be replaced within two years. However, an alternative to replacement is to use the corroded tank as a permanent formwork within which a new ferrocement lining can be made. Using rather similar techniques, mud-walled grain bins in Mali and Senegal have been lined with ferrocement to convert them into rainwater tanks (Watt 1978; UNESCO 1981). The mud walling not only serves as formwork during construction but is retained as a permanent part of the tank, contributing to its strength and making it possible to use 50 per cent less cement than would otherwise be required in a tank of similar size.

Adobe or mud walling has also been used as purely temporary formwork. In this instance, wire reinforcement is wrapped around a cylinder of mud walling and cement plaster is applied. When the plaster has set, the mud walling is demolished and the structure is plastered from the other side.

This use of mud walling highlights an important issue surrounding the design of all the cement-based types of tank: to what extent can costs be reduced by using local materials for formwork or to replace metal reinforcement? Apart from mud, local wood or fibre may be used. Ghala tanks in Kenya and bamboo-cement tanks in Indonesia are the outstanding examples, though Kerkvoorden (1982) also mentions sisal cement and experiments with palm fibre reinforcement (Ijuk cement).

As already noted, however, there is doubt about the durability of both bamboo-cement and Ghala tanks. This raises a problem of design concerning the relationship between permanent structural reinforcement and the temporary formwork used during construction. The role of any reinforcement in a completed tank is to take up tensile stresses, but not by itself to provide stiffness. During construction, however, when the mortar is wet, the stiffness of the structure and its ability to retain its shape can depend either on the formwork or on the inherent stiffness of the reinforcement, or on both. Ferrocement tanks are sometimes built with very flimsy formwork such as bamboo matting, which has been used in Nepal and Indonesia (Winarto 1981). It is even possible to build them with no formwork at all (Watt 1978). In all these instances, heavy welded mesh is needed for reinforcement, or vertical rebars or angle irons are set in the floor slab so that the reinforcing system will stand up on its own like a cage without formwork. By contrast, the method of ferrocement construction recommended earlier (Box 4.1) depends on rigid formwork, whilst the reinforcement system itself is light and could certainly not stand up on its own.

At first sight, the basket frame of a Ghala tank would appear to be reinforcement of the stiffer kind; cement plaster is applied to it without need for any formwork. However, in some instances, the Ghala basket has been plastered entirely from the inside, leaving the basketwork exposed externally. In the course of time, the basketwork has rotted, and while this appears to have led to some tank failures, in other cases the basketwork has been stripped away leaving an unreinforced cement mortar jar still capable of serving its purpose. It seems, then, that the primary role of the basket frame is to function as formwork by supporting the cement mortar during construction. No doubt it also contributes to the strength of the finished tank, but perhaps only marginally.

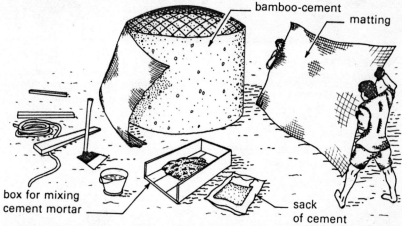

bamboo-cement

matting

box for mixing
cement mortar

sack
of cement

Fig. 5.8   Bamboo matting used as formwork in Indonesia. The tank is initially plastered from inside with the matting wrapped round the outside. The diagram shows the matting being stripped away after the interior plastering has been completed. The next stage is to plaster the exterior of the tank. (Kaufman 1983)

In Indonesia, the mesh of bamboo strips used in bamboo-cement tanks is designed as a true reinforcing system. The tank walls are plastered from both sides so that the bamboo is in the centre of the cement mortar mass. However, it is also clear that the bamboo reinforcement functions as a rigid frame during construction (Fig. 4.3), and the formwork used is a relatively flexible bamboo matting (Fig. 5.8). An inherent disadvantage is that if the bamboo decays, the remaining cement mortar is not a solid mass with considerable strength of its own but has voids at critical points. Because of the need for the reinforcement to stand as a rigid frame during construction the tanks may contain much more reinforcement than necessary. Initially,

Plate 1.   The methodical collection of rainwater in the domestic system of a fairly affluent family in Thailand, showing funnel/filter and a flexible pipe filling the galvanized tank. (Alongside can be seen the traditional decorated clay jars, called 'dragons' fitted with lids.) (John Collett)

Plate 2.   A very basic domestic system in Thailand — a split (halved) bamboo gutter directing runoff from the roof (wooden tiles) into an old oil drum. (John Collett)

Plate 3. A cement jar for rainwater collection at a house near Musani, Kenya, 1983. (John Gould)

Plate 4. A 'Ghala' basket performing the same function at Mwingi, Kenya 1983. (John Gould)

Plate 5.   *An excavated rainwater tank at Tamasane, Botswana, built in 1968, replastered in early 1970s and still operating in 1983. It is used to irrigate a school garden (see pages 92-3). The absence of a fence or cover can be dangerous — even tragic.*

Plate 6.   *An excavated brick-and-cement ground catchment tank of 50 cubic metres at Morwa, near Gabarone, Botswana. (The tank was financed by money raised by the children through the school fund and the free labour of a local builder.) The tank waters the school garden in the dry season. (John Gould)*

Plate 7. A corrugated iron covered rainwater catchment tank at Pelotshetlha, Botswana. The corner of the threshing floor catchment apron can be seen in the foreground. (John Gould)

Plate 8. A brick and cement rainwater catchment tank at Pelotshetla. In the background a woman can be seen smearing the threshing floor catchment apron with a mixture of dung, water and mud. (John Gould)

Plate 11.   Small stone barriers in Burkina Faso roughly comparable to the 'hoops' in Kenya illustrated in Figure 7.3.

Plate 12.   Stone barriers for slowing sheet runoff on very gently sloping land in Burkina Faso.

Plate 13. *One of a series of water-harvesting bunds built with gabion-reinforced spillways, near Lokitaung, Kenya.*

Plate 14. *Detail of gabion spillway construction in a bund system — part of the River Naupwala water harvesting scheme, near Lokitaung, Kenya.*

then, they are stronger than need be, but if the bamboo decays they are more seriously weakened than might otherwise happen.

Many instances of failure in these tanks are attributed to decay resulting from exposure of the bamboo by accident or poor workmanship. Thus improved durability might result from rethinking the role of the bamboo reinforcement. Use of more rigid formwork during construction might open new possibilities for design. Alternatively, small tanks could perhaps be made which, like the Ghala tank, would survive the decay of the bamboo. The latter approach would mean conceiving the bamboo frame primarily as providing support during construction and applying the plaster so that the frame is no longer central to the tank walls. It might also mean modifying the shape of the tank since jar shapes are inherently stronger than cylinders. In cylindrical tanks, the junction between the vertical walls and horizontal floor is a weak point with special need for reinforcement. The benefits to be obtained by any such changes could, of course, only be assessed after observation of kinds of failure in both bamboo-cement and Ghala tanks. Ghala tanks can be and have been made with bamboo basket frames, and it might be particularly instructive to compare their durability with that of bamboo-cement tanks.

Further light on the use of bamboo is shed by experience of bamboo-reinforced *concrete* in Thailand. The concrete consists of a 1:2:3 mix of cement, sand and gravel, and tanks built of this material are set on a 100mm thick concrete foundation slab. Concrete construction is of course based on pouring the mix rather than plastering, and so to make a cylindrical tank, formwork is needed both inside and outside the tank to contain the wet concrete. The metal formwork used in Thailand is illustrated in Figure 5.9, which also shows vertical bamboo culms serving as reinforcement. Horizontal bamboo reinforcement, curving with the tank walls, is also incorporated. The formwork is 0.6m in height, so the walls of the tank are built in stages up to 2.4, 3.0 or 3.6m above the ground. These dimensions correspond to tank capacities of 7.5, 9.4 and 11.3m^3 and suit the high eaves level of Thai platform houses (Figs. 4.1 and 5.5).

The walls of these tanks are 100mm thick as compared with 30mm for most small ferrocement tanks. The extra thickness allows for greater tolerance of poor workmanship such as badly mixed concrete. Fricke (1982) comments that improper curing is also quite often observed but does not usually affect performance. The thick walls and bamboo reinforcement reduce potential for structural defects or load failure. This high degree of tolerance reduces requirements for constant supervision by skilled personnel. Tanks are nearly always watertight so long as the internal plastering is properly done.

Features of design which make construction easy for inexperienced people are obviously important in self-help programmes. Where gravel for making concrete is unavailable on site and a ferrocement tank is chosen as

Fig. 5.9   Two stages in the construction of a bamboo-reinforced rainwater tank in Thailand showing how the concrete is poured between two cylinders of formwork, and how the formwork is raised after each 0.6m high section of the tank is completed. This illustration is from a booklet distributed by UNICEF. (UNICEF and Fricke 1982)

an alternative to concrete, the design illustrated in Box 4.1 is recommended above the many other types of ferrocement tank. This is because the corrugated iron formwork makes it easy for unskilled workers to achieve the correct wall thickness. If two layers of plaster are applied on each side to the point where the corrugations are filled up and a smooth finish is obtained, the tank walls will have a sufficient thickness (at least 30mm) at every point. However, where elaborate types of formwork are required, they must be used repeatedly to justify their cost, and so rapid construction is desirable with the formwork passed on quickly to other households where tanks are to be built.

Tests carried out in Thailand on the bamboo reinforcement confirm some aspects of Indonesian experience. For example, it is found that different species of bamboo vary greatly in strength and durability. Also, when bamboo-reinforced concrete beams were tested under load, failure was found to occur when the bond between the bamboo and the cement gave way. Bond strength could be increased significantly if the bamboo was coated with *dammar* which helps to keep the moisture content of the bamboo low (Nopmongcol *et al.* 1981).

Use of local materials to keep costs down also had implications for the types of cement and sand used. Recommendations given here presuppose that Portland cement is available, but it may often be cheaper to use local types of cement. This may entail problems which first need to be investigated. In Thailand, for example, concrete tanks are made with a local silica cement. This is recognized as a disadvantage but the over-design of the tanks means that local cement has proved satisfactory. On Wasini Island (Kenya) cement made locally from coral lime has for long been used in lining excavated cisterns and tanks built of coral blocks, though commercial cement is now more common (Gould 1983).

As regards sand, the main requirement is that it should be free from organic or chemical impurities. These would tend to weaken the mortar, and indeed, a major reason why mortar should always be mixed on a board or slab, not on the ground, is to keep it free of such impurities. If there is any doubt about local sand, it may be advisable to wash it with a large volume of water (if this can be obtained). Watt (1978) suggests that a moderately coarse sand which makes the mortar more difficult to work has the advantage of better resistance to shrinkage cracks than mortar made with a fine sand.

EXCAVATED RAINWATER TANKS

Excavations used for rainwater storage are of three main types: 'hafirs', catchment tanks and underground cisterns. Hafirs are chiefly used to provide water for livestock (Fig. 2.1), and hence are outside the scope of this chapter on domestic rainwater collection.

Excavated cisterns, often cut in soft rock below harder layers capable of forming a roof, are to be found in large numbers in the Middle East and North Africa, and also in parts of central America (Fig. 1.2). However, most are very old and there are few instances of new construction. In the Negev, excavated cisterns were made under the floors of individual dwellings, both in towns and at isolated farmsteads. These household cisterns were usually of 5-10m³ capacity, that is, of much the same size as many of the domestic rainwater tanks currently built. Much larger cisterns were also excavated for community water supply and for livestock.

Almost the only examples of underground cisterns recently constructed in

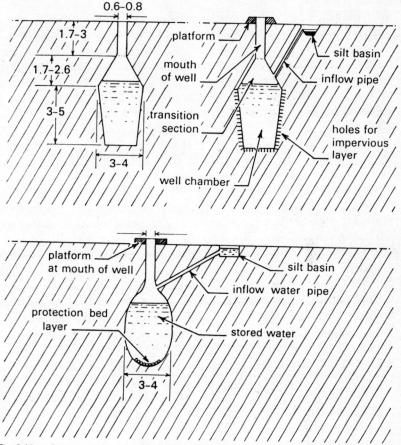

Fig. 5.10   Cross sections of underground rainwater cisterns in the Gansu and Shanxi provinces of China. (Dimensions are in metres.) (UNEP 1983)

large numbers are those reported from China (UNEP 1983) and referred to as 'water storage wells' (Fig. 5.10). These are chiefly confined to loess plateau regions but are very numerous there. In one part of Shanxi Province, 45,000 such cisterns were constructed between 1970 and 1974. In many villages, each household has its own cistern which consists of a jar-shaped or kiln-shaped cavity excavated in the cohesive loess subsoil to a depth of as much as 10m and with a storage capacity around 15m³. The soil has a low permeability, but even so, cisterns are usually plastered inside with a lime-clay mixture to make them watertight. Sites are chosen so that the cistern can be filled by runoff from yards, roads, barren ground surfaces and house roofs. Water flows into the tanks via small silt-trapping basins.

Although well-digging techniques have occasionally been used to construct rainwater cisterns elsewhere, for example in Zimbabwe (See figures in Pacey *et al.* 1977), excavated water storage in the rural development context has nearly always been conceived in terms of relatively shallow catchment tanks, or small dams on rock surfaces or steep slopes. Other types include *nadis*, or artificial ponds in the Rajasthan arid zone in India (Sharma and Joshi 1981) and *telegas* in Indonesia. The latter are constructed in karstic limestone by lining natural sink holes with mud or clay, supported by bamboo framing over large cavities. Water is collected from small areas of unimproved hillside catchment — typically 1000m² in extent — and is used for domestic and livestock purposes. Traditionally there was also some fish farming in these 'tanks'. More recently, telegas have sometimes been deepened, holes in the bottom have been concreted over, and the whole interior lined with clay.

Modern catchment tanks are typically about 2m deep and are used for domestic water supply chiefly where house roofs are either unsuitable for rainwater collection or provide insufficient storage area. An instance which has been given much publicity (UNEP 1983) concerns a purely hypothetical scheme for Manda Island, off the Kenya coast, but more realistic examples are to be found on Wasini island, further south on the same coastline (Grover 1971). This coral island has already been mentioned because of the large number of household rainwater tanks in use there. In addition, however, there are two large excavated catchment tanks which provide public supplies. One has been in continuous use since the early 1950s: it has a ground surface catchment about 1,000m² in extent with a smooth concrete finish. The other excavated tank was completed in 1969 and has a capacity of 300m³ with a lining of butyl rubber sheeting. The catchment was levelled using spoil from the excavation. Its area of 1,500m² was not determined by hydrological calculation but rather by the amount of spoil. The levelled surface was stabilized by mixing cement with topsoil and rolling, and was sealed by spraying asphalt in kerosene (Grover 1971).

The chief technical problems associated with this type of drinking water supply are lining and roofing the tank and protecting the water from contamination. Whilst butyl rubber is frequently used for lining excavated tanks and in some regions may be the cheapest method, the ferrocement lining described in Chapter 4 (Fig. 4.6) is likely to be more durable. The roofing of tanks to reduce evaporation and prevent contamination is a much more intractable problem. On Wasini Island, the tank built in 1969 was provided with a cover of butyl rubber sheet supported by ropes. Holes were made in the cover at intervals so that rainwater would not accumulate on it and weigh it down. However, this did not prove satisfactory. The cover sagged and tore and soon failed completely. Like the older tank on the island, it now has a pitched corrugated iron roof of 18m span (Gould 1983).

The two Wasini tanks differ markedly in the precautions taken to prevent contamination. The catchment area of the older tank is surrounded by a high wall topped by broken glass, and the catchment surface is regularly swept clean. Water from the tank is sampled every two weeks to check on its quality. By contrast, the newer tank, situated in a large village some distance from the main settlement, has no fencing around its catchment and goats wander about at will. The surface is visibly contaminated by goat droppings and other debris. The water from this tank is sampled regularly also, but the results have not yet led to a demand for fencing of the catchment.

In Botswana, ferrocement-lined rainwater tanks have been given flat roofs of corrugated iron supported by poles (Fig. 4.6). This is a durable and effective means of reducing evaporation losses, but the tanks are still open to contamination. More satisfactory, though limited to small tanks of circular shape, is a ferrocement cover reported from the New Hebrides islands in the Pacific. This cover is of a domed shape and is constructed *before* excavation of the tank is begun. First, a circular earth mound is made for use as formwork in constructing the dome. Chicken wire is spread over it and pegged down, then plastered with cement to a thickness of 50mm. Two man-holes of 0.6m diameter are left in the plaster. When the cement has set and cured, excavation begins with men removing spoil through the holes. The excavation is finally lined with ferrocement in the same way as the Botswana tanks (Calvert and Binney 1977). Similar ferrocement linings for excavated tanks have also been used in Kenya (UNICEF 1984).

Whilst there is still much to do in refining designs for rainwater tanks, particularly in reducing costs and devising satisfactory ways of covering them, it is clear from this chapter that a good range of well-tried technical options now exists. The constraints which limit their use in many countries are therefore not strongly related to limitations in the technology — the problem, as we saw in the previous chapter, is more commonly due to inadequate organization and technical assistance.

6. TRADITIONS IN RUNOFF FARMING

CROPPING WITH SUMMER RAINFALL

The World Bank (1984) has commented that none of its economic statistics 'can convey the human misery spreading in sub-Saharan Africa'. Since 1970, food production has stagnated in many areas or has increased only slowly, and grain output per capita has shown a steady downward trend (FAO 1983, World Bank 1984). In 1984, 'abnormal' shortages were reported in 24 countries, with famine conditions attributed to drought in several of them. It is with a considerable sense of urgency, then, that one notes the relevance of rainwater collection techniques in certain limited but significant areas of Africa, both for food production and for the conservation of eroding soils. Kutsch (1982) has reviewed climatic and soil conditions with a view to identifying areas in which the prospects for rainwater concentration and runoff farming seem good, and when his recommendations for Africa are plotted on a map (Fig. 6.1), it is striking that they coincide quite closely with the areas which have experienced food shortages in 1983-4.

However, there has been no serious investigation of the potential of runoff farming in many of these areas. This reflects another of the World Bank's comments, about 'weaknesses of agricultural research'. Information about existing traditions of runoff farming is inadequate nearly everywhere. Sometimes the only well-documented information has been provided by anthropologists and geographers (e.g. Morgan 1974) and agriculturalists have made no contribution at all. By contrast, much more research has been done in India, where some very large runoff farming systems exist (Kolarkar *et al.* 1983), but this is insufficiently appreciated elsewhere. Similar comments can be made about 'micro-irrigation', the range of techniques which allows restricted volumes of water (such as rainwater tanks can provide) to be used for vegetable production (NAS 1974; Gibberd 1969), or for early planting of rain-fed crops (Ray 1983), though it will not be possible to detail these techniques even here.

The use of rainwater in runoff farming is only one of a number of approaches to land and water management which together might contribute to a slow recovery of pastoralism, crop production and forestry in drought-prone areas. Its potential varies according to local climate and

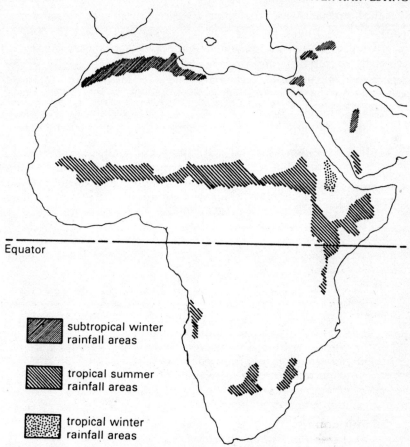

Equator

□ subtropical winter rainfall areas

■ tropical summer rainfall areas

▦ tropical winter rainfall areas

Fig. 6.1   Areas in Africa which Kutsch (1982) identifies as likely to be suitable for runoff farming, together with some adjacent parts of the Middle East. The technique is already used in many of the areas marked which lie north of the equator.

soils (see Table 6.1), and also depends on patterns of social organization. Yet the areas where it might make some contribution contain considerable populations, including many of the 30 million people in the African Sahel.

Potentially, then, rainwater collection in agriculture has a far greater importance — and for more people's livelihoods — than rainwater for domestic supply. But the latter subject has been dealt with first in this book because of better information and clearer evidence of constructive progress. Much of that progress in countries such as Thailand, Indonesia and Kenya is due to local adaptive research or 'innovative dialogue' which has allowed techniques to develop in response to local conditions. Progress is also attributable to the thoroughness with which technical assistance has been planned and provided. Part of the purpose of this section of the book will be to enquire whether any of these lessons about innovation and technical assistance are applicable to agricultural uses of rainwater. Techniques of runoff farming will first be reviewed with the aim of identifying opportunities for innovation, application and development, especially in sub-Saharan Africa and India. Then in Chapter 7, the replication of successful techniques and the planning of technical assistance for runoff farming will be discussed.

Because of the inadequacy of research into runoff farming in many parts of the world, most discussions of the techniques focus on the few areas from

Table 6.1   Environmental conditions and crop characteristics suitable for runoff farming (i.e. farming which makes use of microcatchments, _or_ contour strips/ terraces, _or_ external catchments). (NAS 1974, and data quoted in this chapter)

1. Climatic conditions

   (a) _Winter rainfall areas_
     – minimum average annual rainfall of approximately 100mm can be used (e.g. in the Negev), but 200mm would be more viable.

   (b) _Tropical summer rainfall areas_
     – for small external catchments and within-field catchments, 500–600mm average annual rainfall should generally be regarded as necessary.
     – minimum average rainfall of 150mm can be used when measures are taken to maximize moisture storage (e.g. khadins, Rajasthan).

2. Soil conditions

   (a) _within-field catchment systems_
     – deep soils, clay content, crust-forming capability.

   (b) _external catchments_
     – crust-forming soils or relatively impermeable ground (including rock surfaces).

   (c) _cultivated areas_
     – deep soils (1.5–2.5m), high water-storing capacity;
     – low salinity.

   (d) – _earthworks_ – stable soil types not subject to piping.

3. Crop characteristics

   (a) _perennials, trees_ (e.g. on microcatchments)
     – must be able to withstand long periods of drought.

   (b) _annual crops_
     – short growing season (e.g. quick-maturing millets)
     – deep-rooting habit (e.g. sorghum)
     – tolerance of occasional waterlogging as well as drought.

which detailed studies have been reported — the Negev Desert in Israel (Evenari *et al.* 1968, 1982; Shanan and Tadmor 1979) and the south-western part of North America (Frasier 1975; Dutt *et al.* 1981). It has been tempting to assume that the techniques described in these reports offer the best available demonstration of this type of farming. The Negev example has gained a particular authority not only because of the impressive achievements of desert farming there, and because of the thoroughness of the research work done, but also because of its historical origins. It is a system which has a demonstrable long-term viability. What is too easily forgotten is that other countries, notably India, have equally venerable traditions of runoff farming, some of which may be more relevant to hydrological conditions in the tropical areas.

Kutsch (1982) points out that requirements for runoff farming are very different in regions where rainfall comes in winter, as it does in the Negev and North Africa, as compared with tropical regions where rainfall occurs in summer, at times when evaporation rates are very high. Kutsch identifies many areas in Africa where climates, soils and slopes may in principle be suitable for runoff farming, but is also careful to distinguish areas with summer and winter rainfall, and these are plotted separately on the map in Figure 6.1. Having personally studied traditional runoff farming mainly in Morocco, where the rains come in winter, Kutsch is justifiably cautious about making definite recommendations about arid tropical areas with summer rainfall.

Significantly, the regions which Kutsch tentatively picks out as 'suitable' for runoff farming in the tropics are mostly those with annual average rainfall of at least 300mm, and we would add that the most suitable are areas with 500-600mm.* They are almost never regions where rainfall is as low as in the Negev (100mm). However, he also points out that annual rainfall is not the most important criterion. What matters more is the balance of rainfall and evaporation during the growing season, which is rather favourable in the Negev. By contrast, in summer rainfall areas evaporation rates during the rainy season are very high, and crop water needs are correspondingly greater. A runoff farming system designed for a crop with a 100-day growing season will usually need several storms pro-ducing significant amounts of runoff spaced at regular intervals within the 100-day period if the crop is to do well. In the Negev, a couple of storms within the cool winter growing season can produce sufficient soil moisture on a runoff farm to support a crop. In tropical areas with summer rainfall and high evaporative demand, there is no question of such sparse rains being sufficient.

One limitation of most of the techniques on which detailed research has

---

*The latter is a conservative recommendation because of evidence that *average* rainfall levels in much of Africa are declining (though interpretation of this evidence is controversial).

been done is that because crops are grown during the season when rainfall is expected, it is necessary to avoid collecting too much rainwater on cultivated plots because inundation and waterlogging can kill growing plants, especially seedlings. Thus in American experiments, arrangements have sometimes been made for excess runoff to be diverted away from cultivated plots (Luebs and Laag 1975), and in the Negev, most plots are equipped with spillways of such a height that excessive depths of water on the cropped area are avoided.

In regions with more exacting climatic conditions of limited rainfall in a hot summer season, different strategies are needed, based on storing more water in the soil profile, and sometimes also postponing the planting of the crop until after the season of highest evaporative demand is past. One such strategy involves building high bunds or banks along contours so that extended strips of land may be inundated to a depth of as much as a metre. This water slowly infiltrates the soil or evaporates, and a crop is planted as the water subsides. By this time, the season of highest temperatures may be over, so the crop is able to grow under conditions where evaporative demand is relatively modest.

This technique is used in Sudan, on plains to the east of the Nile where there are large areas of clay soil and gentle slopes. Here embankments are made 'to intercept sheet-wash runoff following heavy storms'. Quick-maturing millet is planted immediately the water left by a storm has subsided. 'The crop grows and matures in 80 days, using the moisture that has been induced to infiltrate the soil behind the bunds' (Wickens and White 1978). According to Kutsch (1982), plots cultivated like this are known as *teras*. He describes them as artificial basins used for cropping on slightly sloping land. The technique conforms with the definition of rainwater collection proposed in Chapter 1 in that the water is sheet flow (not channel flow) on the short and gentle slopes of the Sudan plains.

In North and South Yemen, a similar approach to water storage in the soil is used but in connection with floodwater harvesting rather than rainwater. Indeed, the rainfall from which the floods originate occurs mainly in a nearby mountain area, not in the immediate environs of the cultivated land. It flows in torrents down steep wadis, and where these discharge onto flatter land, the water is diverted from its natural channel by dams or barrages, and is led via canals to innundate large areas of land. There the water is ponded to a considerable depth behind large bunds, sometimes 2-3m in height. Within ten or fifteen days the flooding has subsided and crops can be planted (Clouet 1979; Thomas 1982; Podchivalov 1983).

Similar techniques are used in other tropical arid or semi-arid areas where the rains come in summer, including parts of southern Pakistan (where systems of this kind are known as *sailabas* or *kuskabas*), and northern India (which has *khadins* and *ahars*). In some of these places the source of water is rainfall on a nearby catchment, as in Sudan, but in others, floodwater is used, as in Yemen.

CLASSIFYING RUNOFF FARMING METHODS

The existence of these techniques for using summer rainfall calls for some modification of the classification of rainwater storage methods suggested in Chapter 1. In that discussion, four methods of rainwater storage were compared — tanks above ground, excavated cisterns, small dams and 'soil moisture'. The latter term adequately summarizes how water is stored where runoff farming is practised under winter rainfall conditions, with runoff flowing onto cultivated plots while crops are growing. Although such plots may be temporarily inundated to a depth of 10 or 15cm, this flooding must be very short-lived if the crop is to flourish. Thus the technique presupposes that water will infiltrate quickly and will be stored as soil moisture, leaving ample empty pore space in the soil for aeration of the crop's root zone. The maximum amount of moisture which can be held in soil under these conditions is referred to as the *field capacity* of the soil profile.

The deep inundations practised in summer rainfall areas store more water than this in the soil profile by *saturating* it — that is, by filling up all the pore space so that the soil becomes waterlogged. Because most crops (apart from rice) cannot tolerate this, they are planted after the inundation has subsided but when the water table is still within a few centimetres of the soil surface. Only as the season progresses does the water table fall leaving a steadily larger aerated root zone for the growing crop.

Thus two methods of storing water in the soil need to be distinguished according to whether storage takes place at field capacity (i.e. air in the pore space) or at saturation (i.e. pore space filled with water). In view of this, the comments made in Chapter 1 about moisture storage in soil need the clarification which is provided by Table 6.2. This table, like Table 1.1 in the first chapter, not only classifies techniques according to how water is stored, but also according to the type of catchment from which the runoff comes. Firstly, patches or strips of bare ground *within the fields* being cropped may serve as catchments. Secondly, the water may be sheet flow from *external catchments*, or thirdly, it may be *floodwater* in a stream or channel.

Where moisture storage takes place at field capacity, any of these three catchment types may be used. However, the small-scale option of within-field catchments is not compatible with large bunds and deep inundations, so storage of runoff water in the soil at saturation is usually found only in connection with external catchments or with floodwater utilization. Thus *five* categories of runoff and flood farming are distinguished in Table 6.2, and examples are cited of regions in which they have been used.

Table 6.2   A classification of rainwater and floodwater harvesting systems according to catchment and storage.

Some uses of rainwater also dealt with in Table 1.1 are denoted as follows:

DD - *drinking water and domestic use*
  S - *water for livestock*
  G - *garden irrigation (and micro-irrigation)*
  F - *field irrigation*

	SMALL CATCHMENTS with sheet runoff		LARGE CATCHMENTS with turbulent runoff and/or gullying and channel flow	
	ROOFS of all kinds	GROUND SUR-FACES less than 50-150m length; WITHIN-FIELD CATCHMENTS	SLOPES longer than 50-150m EXTERNAL CATCHMENTS	FLOW in WADIS, GULLIES, RIVERS, and all natural channels FLOODWATER
WATER STORAGE TECHNIQUES				
TANKS ABOVE GROUND	DD	(DD)	n.a.	n.a.
EXCAVATED TANKS	DDSG	DDSG	n.a.	n.a.
SMALL DAMS ("tanks" in INDIA)	n.a.	DDSG	SFDD	SFDD
SOIL AT FIELD CAPACITY	n.a.	contour strips, furrows, bunds and terraces (Morocco, India, North America); microcatchments (Tunisia, Negev);	runoff farms in valley bottoms (Negev, Morocco); bordered gardens (North America); hill terraces with external catchments (Morocco); upland runoff plots (Papago areas, Arizona);	diversion systems (Negev), diversions for water spreading (North America); terraced wadis (Tunisia); check dams for silt trapping (China, North America); warping (China); alluvial fan farms (Hopi areas, Arizona);
SOIL AT SATURATION	n.a.	n.a.	runoff farming by inundation: 'teras' (Sudan) 'ahars' (India) 'khadins' (India)	diversion systems (Yemen, India); river flood-plain farming (Africa);

Source of examples quoted: India and China - UNEP 1983; Sudan - Wickens and White 1978; Tunisia - El Amani 1977; Morocco - Kutsch 1982; Arizona - Bradfield 1971; North America - UNEP 1983.

The focus of this book is on small-scale uses of rainwater and the
localized application of runoff, not on the exploitation of major floodwater
flows, so whilst only three of the five categories are discussed in detail here
the following examples of floodwater utilization are of considerable
interest. Firstly, Figure 6.2a shows one of a number of dams constructed at
regular intervals in the bed of a small valley to conserve both soil and water.

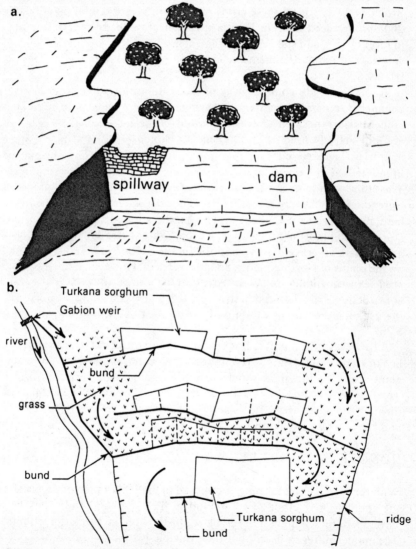

Fig. 6.2   Two forms of floodwater harvesting involving the exploitation of channel flow: (a)
making terraces within the floodwater drainage channel, as exemplified by a terraced wadi in
Tunisia (El Amami 1977); (b) water-spreading illustrated by a pilot project in Kenya; note the
large plots planted with 'Turkana sorghum', a local quick-maturing variety. (Fallon 1963)

These dams function as silt traps, and as soil builds up behind them, fertile plots are formed. Many versions of this technique are to be found — in China, in Mexico (where maize is grown on the accumulated sediments), and in Tunisia. In parts of the latter country, stone dams holding back sediments have the effect of terracing long lengths of wadi, enabling olive, fig and date palm trees to be grown on the terraces, and sometimes cereals also. The natural wadi flow during rains is controlled by spillways and provides water for all these crops in a region where rainfall is only 150-200mm. Terraced wadis in Tunisia have been developed quite considerably in recent years, and state encouragement has led to the systematic design of spillways to standard dimensions (for example, with crests 50cm above the terrace soil level.)

Secondly, a very common way of using flood flows in a wadi or river channel is to construct a dam or barrage to divert water onto cultivated land. Such arrangements have been found on ancient sites in the Negev and are still actively used in South Yemen (Thomas 1982) and many other countries. The diverted water may be used in several ways. The land may be inundated (as in Yemen), or water spreading techniques may be employed. The latter term indicates a flow of diverted floodwater across a prepared 'spreading area' at very low velocities. Thus the water is not ponded on the land, but flows over it. On soils with high infiltration capacities, sufficient is stored as soil moisture to support a crop. Water spreading is particularly appropriate on grassed areas used for forage production, and is practised on the plains of North America and in Australia. However, it has also been used experimentally in West Africa and Kenya. It typically entails constructing a small diversion structure across a seasonal water-course and the use of short lengths of bund to spread the flow without erosion (Fig. 6.2b).

A final way of using river floods where these spread out over a wide river bed or flood plain is simply to wait until floodwaters are subsiding and then plant crops on the areas which have been inundated. This approach is widely used in Africa where major rivers such as the Niger and Senegal pass through semi-arid areas. It is also practised on the margins of Lake Chad and rivers which flow into it.

RUNOFF FARMING BY INUNDATION

With regard to runoff farming as opposed to the exploitation of floodwater, the inundation method used in Sudan, Pakistan and India has been developed to its highest level of sophistication in the latter country. Techniques differ in detail, but the principle is to allow runoff to collect behind a bund and leave the water standing until the planting date for the crop approaches. Then the land is drained and the crop is sown. The area behind the bund is known as a submergence tank, or an *ahar* (in Bihar), or a *khadin* (in Rajasthan), and may cover many hectares (for locations, see Fig. 2.3).

During the period when runoff is ponded behind the bunds, ahars are treated as reservoirs from which water is taken for a number of different purposes. Firstly, overflow via spillways is allowed for; water discharged in this way is often trapped by a second ahar further downslope. There it may be supplemented by water released from sluices in the first ahar when that is drained prior to sowing. Secondly, supplies may be pumped from an ahar to irrigate other land, or may be released for irrigation by gravity flow via pipes passing through the bund. Box 6.1 gives some technical detail and indicates the location of pipes through which irrigation water is released.

A third way of exploiting the water in an ahar, or more particularly, in the very similar khadins of Rajasthan, is to take advantage of infiltration from the inundated land to the water table beyond the bund. Wells are commonly dug downslope from a khadin, and in the Thar Desert (in Rajasthan) such wells are important sources of water for livestock. The wells also help to avoid the build-up of salinity in the khadin soils by increasing the rate of drainage through them. In this area, catchments include large areas of weathered rock which can produce unusually saline runoff.

Cultivation on ahars and khadins is more systematic than in the similar, but much simpler, basins used for runoff farming by inundation in Sudan and elsewhere because the provision of sluices in the bunds allows ponded water to be released in time for the preferred planting date. Thus in Rajasthan, wheat and pulses are sown in November and the main harvest is in April. This very effectively avoids the season when evaporative demands on crops are highest, for during the rainy monsoon season from July to October, potential evapotranspiration is 697mm, whilst during the first half of the growing season, November to February, it is only 106mm (Kolarkar *et al.* 1983). Evaporation rates are highest of all in the hot months of May and June. Some light rain may fall in December, but the majority of the crop's soil moisture requirements are provided by the runoff ponded on the land before planting.

The sharp contrast between this approach to runoff farming and the methods more usual in the Negev, North Africa and America is emphasized in Table 6.3. Here, the American examples show crops benefiting from soil moisture which is present before they are planted, but depending primarily on the rainfall and runoff which occur while the crops are growing. In the contrasting inundation system, almost the whole of the crop's water requirements are met by water present in the soil prior to planting. The table also shows that in areas of reasonably good rainfall, where catchments are relatively small, runoff may contribute much less water than rain falling directly on the cultivated plot. In these circumstances, runoff farming may show little advantage over conventional agriculture in

Box 6.1 Technical details of ahar construction. (Prasad, 1979)

1.   An ahar, made on land with very gentle gradients (so that large areas can be flooded), presupposes clay soils.

2.   The bund, unlike a dam, does not contain a clay core or hearting, nor a cut-off trench. The soil is uniform throughout the section. Upstream and downstream faces usually have slopes of 1:2, although the downstream slope must be adjusted to keep the phreatic line (i.e. the boundary of the saturated zone) within the bund. The height of the bund does not exceed 3m (including a 1m freeboard), and the top width is normally 1m. The upstream face may be pitched with stone.

3.   The length of the bund may vary from 150m to 10km or more. The bund follows the contours as far as possible. However, on very gently sloping land (e.g. a fall of 0.1m in 1km) exact alignment is not important. Where it is desired to terminate the bund it is turned transverse to the contour to meet higher ground.

4.   A long spillway is always incorporated, the crown of which is 1m lower than the top of the bund. It is topped with stone and has a gently graded downstream slope which is paved with stone.

5.   Sluice-gates are set in masonry structures so that the ahar may be emptied quickly in time for sowing. The sluice gates are made of steel plate and are about 1m square; they are operated with a screw. Water discharged from them is led to a local stream, or to another ahar downslope.

6.   Pipes made of stoneware, concrete or cast iron, 150–300mm in diameter, are embedded in the bund at intervals of 50–100m to enable water to be released for irrigation. To prevent erosion around the pipe, small blocks of masonry are built up around it at both ends. When the release of water is to be prevented, the upper ends of the pipes are simply plugged with straw and earth.

PLAN (Not to scale)

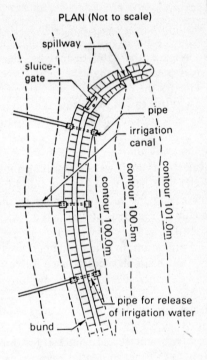

SECTION OF BUND

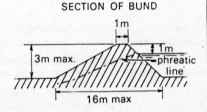

Table 6.3   Sources of soil moisture used by crops under contrasting runoff farming systems.
Data given by the authors cited have been recalculated as percentages of total consumptive use to facilitate comparison. (From Journal of Arid Environments, 'Khadin – a method of harvesting water for agriculture in the Thar desert' by A.S. Kolarkar *et al.*)

	INDIA Runoff farming by inundation (soil initially saturated)	NORTH AMERICA 'Conventional' runoff farming (soil at field capacity or less)	
CROP and district	WHEAT Rajasthan	BARLEY California	SORGHUM Texas
SOURCE	Kolarkar *et al.* 1980	Luebs & Laag 1975	Jones & Hauser 1975
MEAN ANNUAL RAINFALL	200mm	300mm	470mm
RATIO, catchment to cultivated areas	11:1	2:1	2:1
SOURCES OF MOISTURE			
Water and moisture in the soil profile prior to planting: a) due to runoff from the catchment	82%	10%	14%
b) due to rainfall on cultivated plots	15%	12%	18%
Rainfall and runoff during the growing season: a) due to runoff from the catchment	0*	39%	12%
b) due to rainfall on cultivated plots	3%*	39%	56%

* Only occasional light showers during the growing season; no runoff except at margins of cultivated area.

seasons of average rain. The benefits consist chiefly of an improved reliability of yield in poor years because then runoff helps the crop to survive periods of drought (Jones and Hauser 1975).

Whilst the contrast between the inundation system and the North American and Negev methods is clear, different versions of the inundation system ought also to be noticed. In Bihar and adjacent areas of India, as in Sudan, ahars are built on very gently sloping land. During the monsoon rainwater running off the ground above the bund submerges very large areas behind the bund because the ground is so nearly flat. The soil in these regions has a high clay content, which again makes them comparable with

Sudan, so its moisture-retaining capacity is good. Sometimes in India a special variety of rice is sown in the bed of the ahar before it actually fills up. This 'floating rice' can grow in deep water, and although the yield is low, the effort is worthwhile when a second crop, winter wheat, is to be planted once the ahar is drained (Prasad 1979).

Though some ahars may only be 1ha in extent with a bund 100m long, others may be as large as 500ha and the largest of all submerge 4,000ha with bunds wandering along the contours for 10km or more. Large numbers of these systems exist in Bihar state providing about 800,000ha of runoff cultivation, and there are others in Uttar Pradesh (See Fig. 2.3 also).

In Rajasthan, khadins are necessarily rather different because rainfall is less than in Bihar and soils are sandy, so there is almost no runoff from gentle slopes. Instead, khadins are generally located near to low eroded hills and ridges of sandstone and limestone which serve as catchments, generating runoff which flows down to relatively flat valley land. Bunds are constructed in the valleys where they can collect and hold back the runoff water and the sediments it carries (Fig. 6.3).

In this desert area, rainfall is higher than in the Negev, but comes in summer rather than winter. In the Jaisalmer District, where the annual average rainfall is 164mm, many of the older khadins are so constructed

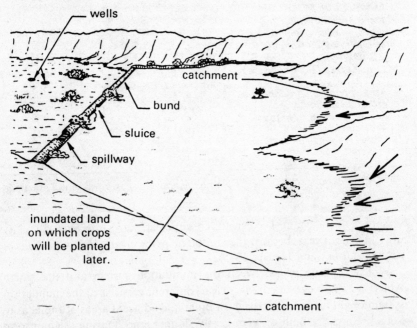

Fig. 6.3   A 'khadin' viewed from the hillside which serves as its catchment, showing an ideal setting for this type of runoff farming – valley land with very gentle slopes adjacent to rocky uplands. (Kolarkar et al. 1983)

that they will fill with a total precipitation of less than 100mm. Water stands in the khadin areas during the whole monsoon period reaching a depth of 0.5 to 1.25m. In November, after the land has been drained via sluices and the crop has been planted, the water table slowly subsides but continues to supply moisture to the growing crop. Typically the depth of the water table at harvest will be about 2m (Kolarkar *et al.* 1983).

Like ahars, individual khadins may be very large. In Jaisalmer District, Kolarkar states that there are over 500 with a total cultivated area of 12,140ha. The first to be made in this area was constructed five centuries ago. Over the years, accumulation of sediments inside a khadin cause a gradual increase in soil level, with fine loam or clay loam soils developing, in contrast to the sandy soils of surrounding areas. The long period for which khadin soils are moist promotes microbial activity and as a result, they contain more humus, are more fertile, and have better moisture-holding characteristics than local desert soils.

It should be noted that while most khadins are true runoff farming systems, filled directly by sheet runoff and from small gullies on immediately adjacent hillsides, there are also some which depend on diverted floodwater. Prasad describes one near Bharatpur which was built in 1895 with a bund 19km long and which is fed by water from a nearby river. It inundates 4,100ha which is later used for winter crops, and water is released from it to allow irrigation of 4,800ha more.

Some western engineers have argued that if techniques of this sort are to be employed in future agricultural development programmes, the land to be inundated ought to be levelled when the bund is constructed. This, they say, would ensure a more even availability of water to crops. But it would add considerably to costs, and the suggestion represents a misunderstanding of the way these systems operate. The build-up of sediments over the years ensures that the land is levelled naturally. Farming methods are slowly modified as soils deepen and the system matures. Artificial land levelling would only offer a temporary advantage in the early stages. Whatever measures are taken, soil and moisture conditions are bound to vary across the width of an ahar due to a varying depth and quality of sediment, and this can be exploited by growing different crops on different parts of the land. Millet may be grown on the margins where there is less moisture while wheat is often the main crop on the deepest soils. Fuelwood trees may also be planted, and date palms can be grown below the bund to make use of seepage water (Ray 1984).

A bigger difficulty confronting any proposals for the extension of this type of runoff farming is the organization involved. With individual ahars or khadins covering several hundred hectares, they are normally divided between many small farmers. Ray quotes a khadin of 150ha cultivated by 25-30 individuals, with some holdings as small as 1ha and the largest around 7ha. In such circumstances, co-ordination of efforts to ensure that bunds are maintained and sluices are opened at mutually beneficial times requires considerable organization. This significantly affects prospects for the perpetuation and replication of these systems as will be discussed in the next chapter.

Runoff farming by inundation can be used on a smaller scale with less massive earthworks in areas where rainfall is higher, and this may offer better prospects for replication. In Rajasthan, Kolarkar *et al.* (1980) point out that while khadins are used particularly in areas with less than 200mm rainfall per year, a different form of inundation is practised in the Siwana area where rainfall is above 250mm. Here, contour bunds only 0.3m high divide low-lying land into strips. Water is led onto the uppermost strip; it gradually flows to lower strips, and is allowed to stand to 0.2m depth. The inundation subsides by November when the crop is sown.

RUNOFF USE ON GROWING CROPS

Runoff farming by inundation works well on clay soils, but on sandy soils, the water table may recede too quickly after the rains cease to support a crop through the whole of its growing season. On the sandy desert soils of Rajasthan, khadins only acquire adequate moisture storage capability after several years of sedimentation. Ray reports on two new khadins which had not yet received their 'optimum load of silt' and so did not retain water into the post-monsoon dry season. Farmers using them planted their land during the summer monsoon rains so that runoff would flow directly onto the cropped plots. Thus structures ultimately intended to make possible the cultivation of winter crops after an earlier deep inundation were initially used for cropping in the more difficult summer conditions, with runoff applied directly to the cropped land.

When used in this way, a khadin works on the same principle as the runoff farms of the Negev and North Africa which have external catchments with bunds and channels to direct water onto growing crops. There are, however, important differences in construction. The relationship of external catchments to cultivated areas is similar, but the size of the bunds required and the methods of water control are very different. A khadin depends on use of a large bund capable of impounding water at a depth of a metre or more. But where water is applied to a growing crop, runoff is not usually impounded at more than 0.1-0.2m. The actual depth of ponded water which can be tolerated by a crop depends on the infiltration capacity of the soil and on how quickly the water will subside. Control of depth depends on dividing up the cultivated area by small bunds built along contours, each of which has a spillway at intervals along its length — every 20m or so. The latter are commonly built of stone with good foundations and an apron on the downstream side to prevent erosion (see Fig. 6:4). Typical dimensions are suggested in Box 6.2, but if experience

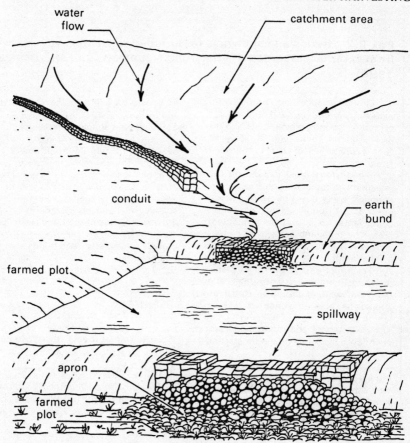

Fig. 6.4 *Components of a typical system for runoff farming with an 'external catchment', including a low bund or wall for collecting runoff on the catchment, and the bunds and spillways necessary for water control on the farmed plot. (Cullis 1984)*

Note: *Diagram is schematic and not to scale.*

shows that the water depths impounded are too great or too little, spillway heights can be modifed by some simple rebuilding.

Water discharged from the spillways on one plot is usually impounded on other plots lower down the field. In a wet year, the uppermost plots may get rather too much water, whereas in drought years the lowest plots may not get enough. At a site in Kenya where this system is the subject of experiment, it is recommended that sorghum should be grown on the upper plots as often as is consistent with crop rotation, since sorghum is tolerant of waterlogging (Critchley 1984). By contrast, it may be advisable to grow drought-resistant millets in the lowest plot.

Yet another way of adjusting to variations in water availability on different plots is to vary the planting density. In a district near Agadir in

Box 6.2 Bunds and spillways for cropped areas receiving runoff from external catchments in the tropics. (Barrow, 1983; Critchley, 1984)

1. On land receiving runoff from *external catchments*, bunds aligned with contours, having spillways at 20m intervals along their lengths serve to control applications of water to cultivated plots.

2. *Dimensions* must depend on the maximum amount of water to be impounded after any one storm. Much depends on rainfall intensities, runoff coefficients, soils, and the catchment area. The following are typical dimension which should be checked against local conditions.

3. For a plot of 0.1ha on a 1% slope, the *bund* might be 0.4m high and 0.5–1.0m wide at the base. One man should be able to construct a 10m length of bund in a day, building it up in 50mm layers of soil, and compacting each layer by trampling before starting the next.

4. Bunds are made at 15–20m intervals down the slope. A farmer may be well advised to build only a couple of bunds in the first year. If these are successful and there are regular over-flows from the spillways, he may wish to add further bunds subsequently.

5. *Spillways* should preferably be built of stone (see diagram) or if this is not available, of termite-proof timber or concrete. The downstream slope should be as gentle as possible with a level area at its foot covered with stones or gravel. Special care is needed at the ends of the spillway to build up a stone shoulder around the ends of the bund and make sure these cannot be eroded. Grass growth on spillways and bunds should be encouraged to stabilize the soil.

6. *Typical dimensions of spillways*:

height, 0.1–0.15m;
width at base, 0.8m;
length, 1.0–2.5m;

7. One rule of thumb is that the total length of spillway needed (in metres) should be 0.5 times the catchment area (in ha). So a 50m length of bund receiving water from 8ha of catchment requires a total spillway length of 4m, either as two 2m spillways, or three 1.35m spillways.

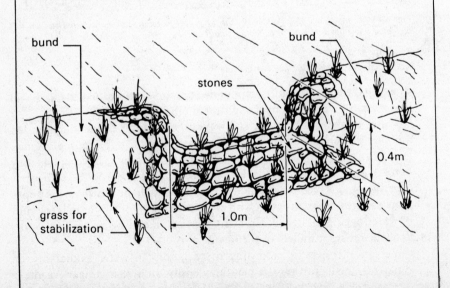

bund

bund

stones

0.4m

grass for stabilization

1.0m

Morocco which receives winter rainfall, Kutsch (1982) has observed that when wheat or barley is grown on plots watered by runoff it is sown to a density of 100 plants per m². By contrast, on plots depending solely on direct rainfall without supplementation by runoff, the planting density is 70 plants per m². Smallholders adapt the weight of seed they use to the average soil moisture situation they expect. The deliberate reduction of plant density results in some sacrifice of yield in seasons of ample rainfall, but it makes for greater certainty that there will be useful grain production in a drought year.

Water availability depends partly on the ratio between areas of catchments and cultivated plots. In desert regions, this ratio may be in the range 10:1 up to 30:1. However, it needs to be stressed repeatedly that runoff farming in areas with average annual rainfall less than 200 to 300mm is only likely to be viable in special circumstances — either when crops can be grown during the coolest time of the year, or when khadins (or something comparable) can be built. For small-scale runoff farming in the tropics, average precipitations in the range 500-600 are suitable (Table 6.1). Then ratios of catchment to cultivated areas may typically be between 20 and 5:1.

WITHIN-FIELD CATCHMENTS

Apart from noticing area ratios, we should also observe how the overall areas of runoff farms vary. Where runoff is applied directly to growing crops without any deep inundation, bunds and spillways are modest in size and can be constructed by an individual farmer on his own land. Thus systems may be quite small, with perhaps 1-10ha of cultivated land. Although this may all be within the holding of one farmer, the external catchment from which he collects runoff may consist of grazing land used by others. An even smaller scale of operation, with greater control by the individual farmer, is possible when runoff is applied to growing crops from within-field catchments. These are of two main types. The catchments may be narrow strips of land from which rainwater runs onto elongated cultivated areas formed by contour ridges or bunds. Alternatively, within-field catchments may consist of a series of roughly square plots like the microcatchments described in Chapter 1.

The strips of catchment area in contour farming are rarely much more than 10m wide, measured downslope, and microcatchments are usually less than 90m long. These modest dimensions offer two technical advantages over the much larger external catchments. Firstly, the problems caused by turbulent, erosive runoff flows from large catchments are avoided, and secondly, with smaller losses from depression storage and infiltration, the proportion of the rainfall which runs onto the cultivated plot is greater. Areas required for use as catchments are therefore less, as typical ratios of

Table 6.4 **Typical ratios of catchment to cultivated areas illustrating the lower ratios characteristic of small 'within-field' catchments**

average annual rainfall	area ratios		source
	within-field catchments	external catchments	
300—600mm			
Kenya, Baringo area	1:1, 2:1	5:1, 20:1	Critchley 1984
Kenya, N. Turkana area		10:1, 20:1	Cullis 1984
Texas, USA	2:1	–	Jones & Hauser 1975
Arizona, USA	3:1, 5:1	–	Fangmeier 1975
150—300mm			
Tunisia*	2:1	10:1	El Amami 1977
Arizona, USA	12:1	33:1	Morin & Matlock 1975
India, Rajasthan	–	11:1, 15:1	Kolarkar et al., 1980, 1983
80—120mm			
Israel, Negev Desert*			
a) runoff farms, range for 100 examples	–	17:1–30:1	Evenari et al., 1982
b) microcatchments	10:1	–	Shanan & Tadmor 1979
c) contour strips	4:1, 20:1	–	

* winter rainfall areas

catchment to cultivated area show (see Table 6.4). Land use can thus be more efficient.

Methods of *contour farming* using runoff from uncultivated strips are very varied, depending on the slope of the land, and on the extent to which farming is mechanized. On flat land, catchment strips can be formed by throwing up low, broad ridges which are sometimes known as 'micro-watersheds'. The troughs intervening between them are then cultivated (Figure 6.5a). On gentle slopes, contour ridges can be used to form strips of cultivation (sometimes referred to as 'desert strips' in American publications: Fig. 6.5b). Finally, on steep slopes, contour bunds may be built to create terraces, often with sloping catchment strips alongside each level terrace (Fig. 6.5c), but sometimes with groups of two or three terraces supplied with runoff from a single catchment.

Although micro-watersheds have been tried experimentally in Botswana and elsewhere (Gibberd 1969), this technique is most easily applied where tractor-drawn equipment allows the watersheds to be evenly graded (Dutt et al. 1981). Contour ridges and bunds are more widely applicable and can be formed using hand tools or animal-drawn equipment. Some African programmes in which contour bunds and barriers have been built will be described in Chapter 7, and details of one type of contour ridge are given in Box 6.3.

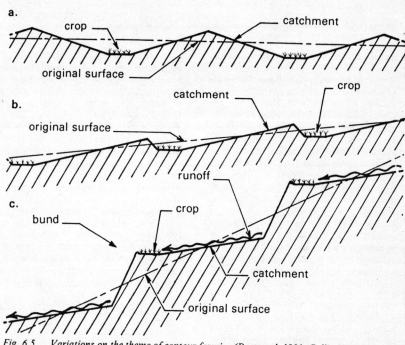

Fig. 6.5   Variations on the theme of contour farming (Dutt et al. 1981; Cullis 1984) (a) micro-watersheds on slopes of less than 1 per cent; (b) contour ridges (desert strips) on slopes of 1–3 per cent; (c) contour bunds forming terraces on slopes steeper than 3 per cent.

Terrace systems for runoff farming on steeper slopes have a long history in many parts of the world, including India, and North Africa. Details vary according to terrain, soils and whether stone is used for building up terrace walls. The width of the cultivated strip depends on local soils and the crops being grown, but in Texas, in a region with 470mm of rain, a catchment to cultivated area ratio of 2:1 has been used for sorghum production. The ridges or bunds defining the outer edge of a terrace are usually about 0.3m above terrace soil level.

In the drought-prone regions of India, contour bunds are fairly widespread as a means of using runoff water to support growing crops (Ray 1984). However, such bunds, which are constructed precisely along the contour in order to *retain* rainwater around the plants, should be distinguished from the graded bunds or furrows, also widespread in India, which are intended to control soil erosion by channelling excess runoff into water-courses and sometimes into 'tanks'. However, Krantz (1981) argues that graded bunds are not always very effective in controlling erosion, and Ray quotes experience of badly constructed bunds which unintentionally depart from the contour. Far from retaining water around plants, the latter become regular streams 'complete with waterfalls'. If catastrophic erosion is to be avoided, then, construction must be adequate

Box 6.3 Forming contour ridges. (Cullis, 1983)

Introduction Closely comparable with the 'desert strips' of Israel and North America, contour ridges have proved an effective means of supporting crop production in semi-arid regions.

Description Runoff is collected behind earth bunds, and therefore concentrated for plant growth. A modification to this system involves the periodic spacing of barriers perpendicular to the flow which prevents the lateral movement of runoff.

Note: A cutoff drain at the top of the site leads all *external* water away from the system.

Design The width of the cropped area in relation to that of the catchment is dependent mainly on hydrological and soil conditions, together with crop water requirements. In a semi-arid part of Kenya with a mean annual rainfall of 600mm, cropped strips of 0.15m width are supplied with adequate runoff from catchments 2 to 3m wide.

Labour Using hand tools, it has been estimated that 0.5ha can be contour-ridged in 16 days, and thereafter maintained with only a few days work per year. The excavation of a cut-off drain, to protect such field systems requires approximately 25–30 person-days to construct. Thus relatively few labour demands are made to reclaim quite large areas.

Note: Hand hoes and shovels may, to some extent, be complemented by draught-animal power to speed up the work or overcome a seasonal labour shortage.

Cropping In the semi-arid sub-tropics of the Sahel, contour ridges have been successfully used for arable cropping of local sorghum and millet varieties. In particularly wet years, the catchment may also be planted with drought resistant legumes such as cowpeas or tepary beans.

In more arid regions, contour ridges can be used to assist the regeneration of forage, grasses and hardy local trees in overgrazed areas. Grass seeds should be spread along the bunds prior to the rains; once established they will spread out onto the catchment area.

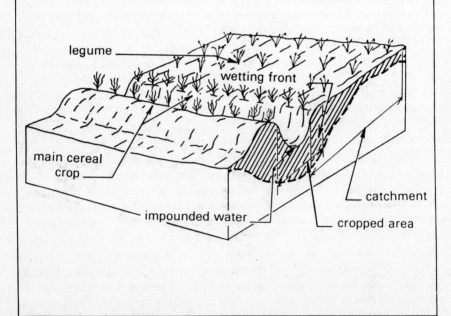

legume — wetting front — main cereal crop — impounded water — catchment — cropped area

both in accuracy of surveying, and in making bunds big enough to cope with the largest likely volumes of water.

On stony slopes in Morocco it is logical that stone is used to build up the bunds or terrace walls, often on very steep slopes. Here there is sometimes little distinction between within-field and external catchment systems. In Figure 6.6a, water from external catchments higher up a steep hillside is controlled by an impediment wall, built without mortar, which holds back debris and gravel and ensures that the runoff is spread evenly along the length of the terraces. In 6.6b, there are within-field catchments above the main terraces, each crossed by three contour ridges. However, the topmost field is also allowed to receive runoff from an external catchment. On contour bench terraces in Texas, extra runoff of this kind is deliberately

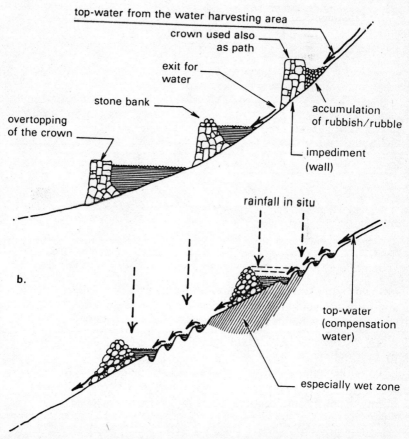

Fig. 6.6   Terraces with stone bunds or walls used on steep slopes in Morocco. (Kutsch 1982) In diagram (a) the terraces receive water from an external catchment; the impediment wall reduces the speed of runoff and spreads it whilst holding back debris; in diagram (b) contour ridges and stone bunds are combined within one system. N.B. The gradients are exaggerated.

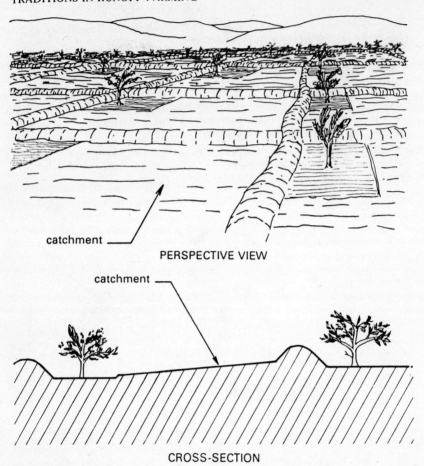

catchment

PERSPECTIVE VIEW

catchment

CROSS-SECTION

Fig. 6.7   Microcatchments in which almond trees are growing in the Negev Desert. The trees are located in a small patch of cultivated soil at the lowest point in each microcatchment.

avoided by making cut-off drains above the upper catchment strips, the aim being to avoid uncontrolled, erosive runoff which could inundate the crop or damage bunds. In Morocco, by contrast, the stone terrace walls allow excess water to pass rapidly, both by infiltrating between stones and by overtopping the walls.

The other main form of within-field catchment, used chiefly for tree crops, was first formally recorded by French travellers in southern Tunisia during the nineteenth century. There, olive trees were being grown within what are now referred to as microcatchments. As the name implies, these are small, often roughly square patches of bare ground which shed runoff into a basin excavated in the lowest corner. Low earth bunds, 0.2-0.3m high, form boundaries to the microcatchment area and direct runoff into this basin where typically a single tree is planted (Fig. 6.7).

Knowledge of the Tunisian version of this technique eventually influenced research in the Negev and led to trials with a range of microcatchment sizes varying from 16m² to 1,000m² (Shanan and Tadmor 1979). Finally, a quadrangular shape was adopted with large microcatchments (up to 250m²) for fruit trees and smaller ones for salt-bushes grown for forage.

Publication of this work has led to further experimentation with microcatchments in North America and Australia, India and Kenya. Dimensions vary with rainfall, soil and the types of trees (or other plants) being grown. In a part of Kenya with rainfall less than 400mm, microcatchment areas measuring 10m × 10m have been successful with planting basins 0.75m deep and 1.25m square. Using hand tools alone, one man might make one or two microcatchments in a day, but ox-ploughs can also be used for making the ridges. The technique is used on very gently sloping land and surveying instruments may be needed to locate the lowest point in each plot.

A hybrid design amalgamating elements of the microcatchment concept with aspects of the contour ridge techniques has been used for establishing grass on bare slopes in Kenya. The system involves constructing ridges in short arcs (see Fig. 7.3). The arcs lie on the contour at their ends, but dip below it at their mid point. These arcs or 'hoops' can be regarded as small microcatchments, open on their upslope side and receiving runoff from outside their immediate area. If grass seed has been broadcast over the area, runoff carries it into the lowest part of each hoop where clumps of grass quickly become established, and from which they spread until the whole slope is covered.

AFRICAN TRADITIONAL SYSTEMS

With these various categories of rainwater and runoff application on cropped land in mind, we can now reconsider traditional African versions of the techniques. A starting point is provided by Kutsch's (1982) account of runoff farming in Morocco, which systematically distinguishes techniques depending on some basic engineering construction (bunds, channels, spillways) from systems which exploit natural runoff flows with little or no construction. Kutsch refers to the latter as 'simple water-concentrating systems', and he calls the former 'improved' systems.

In classifying the many runoff farming methods found in Morocco, Kutsch makes it clear that 'simple' systems are almost always of the external catchment type, and points out that even in the total absence of earthworks to control runoff water, farming methods can be carefully designed to make use of runoff, with tillage and planting density adjusted to exploit the extra water available (Fig. 6.8).

In discussing traditional agriculture south of the Sahara, Kutsch recognizes that while very few 'improved' techniques are used, 'simple' types of runoff farming have been widespread. He cites cultivation in depressions known as *cuvettes* in West Africa, and mentions the *teras* used in Sudan for runoff farming by inundation. The latter, however, do entail the construction of earthworks and might be classified as 'improved'.

It is difficult to carry this analysis very far, however, because there have been very few scientific studies of traditional runoff farming in Africa. Comparable practices used in North America prior to European settlement linger on in a few areas and have been researched in more detail. The results are relevant in showing what features one should look for in traditional runoff agriculture. Some of the best studies describe land occupied by the Hopi and Papago peoples of Arizona. Bradfield (1971) notes that Hopi fields are predominantly on alluvial soils deposited in 'fans' where runoff water flows down the sides of a valley, and gullies carrying flash floods reach gentler slopes, depositing their sediment loads. Much of the runoff infiltrates the soils on these fans and is held as soil moisture. Hopi farmers can identify sites where moisture, drainage and fertility are suitable for agriculture by noticing variations in the natural vegetation. Fields made on such land require only short lengths of bund to spread the water a little more evenly. The sediments and organic debris deposited by floodwater are important in maintaining soil fertility since the fields are not manured. Indeed, commenting on Papago agriculture in the same general region, Nabhan (1984) argues that techniques of this sort are a form of 'nutrient harvesting' as well as water harvesting.

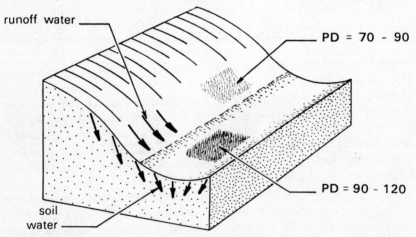

Fig. 6.8 Farmers in Morocco vary the weight of seed sown per unit area of land in order to adapt plant density (PD) to the moisture likely to be available. In this instance, the farmer expects the crop growing in the depression to benefit from runoff and has accordingly aimed for a higher plant density. He has thus planned his cropping as a form of 'simple' runoff farming. (Kutsch 1982)

PD *is expressed in plants/m²*

Earlier, Nabhan (1979) had classified the 'perennially moist microniches' which farmers in arid areas in Arizona have traditionally exploited for growing crops. Some are associated with groundwater and sub-surface moisture, others with floodwater flows, and still others with runoff on upland sites. Many of the techniques employed are 'simple' in Kutsch's terms, but 'improved' systems are also found. Some entail construction of dams or spreader dykes, and some the diversion of water from intermittent or even perennial streams by means of weirs and short lengths of canal. However, the three most basic methods of floodwater and runoff farming which Nabhan observed are:

- upland runoff harvesting before water reaches natural drainage channels;
- exploitation of flash floods by planting on alluvial fans or on the beds of intermittent streams;
- planting on the margins of streams or rivers which flood.

The only study known to us which examines runoff farming in sub-Saharan Africa with comparable detail concerns field systems in the southern part of Turkana District, in northern Kenya (Morgan 1974). Rainfall in this area averages less than 200mm per year, but sorghum is regularly grown by exploiting sites where runoff or floodwater provides sufficient soil moisture. Figure 6.9 maps a small part of the Kerio River valley, and marks the sites of several sorghum 'gardens'. It is noticeable that all three categories of site listed above for Arizona can be identified here also. The use of runoff before water reaches natural drainage channels is demonstrated by the elongated sorghum plot at the foot of the Morulim hill, an outcrop of lava rock. Flash floods water the large fields at Nachor and Kangatet, where dashed lines on the map indicate the route taken by the main flood flows. The third category, planting on streams or river margins, is seen at the bottom of the map at Nagaloki and Lomomuk. As on Hopi and Papago lands, the selection of sites for cultivation is guided by observing the natural vegetation. Waterlogged ground characterized by a particular Acacia species is avoided and plants indicative of better drained soils are looked for. A quick-maturing variety of sorghum is grown which can be harvested within 65 days of planting, and can thus take advantage of very transitory accumulations of moisture.

Cultivation of the crop in south Turkana is undertaken entirely by women. The 5ha field at Nachor was divided into 43 plots in 1967 which were worked by 41 women. Great care was taken of the crop with special platforms erected as vantage points for bird scaring, but the terrain was left in its natural state with no earthworks at all either for water spreading or erosion control. Thus the Nachor field was being eroded by gullying at its downstream end, and land was being lost by deposition of gravel at the upstream end.

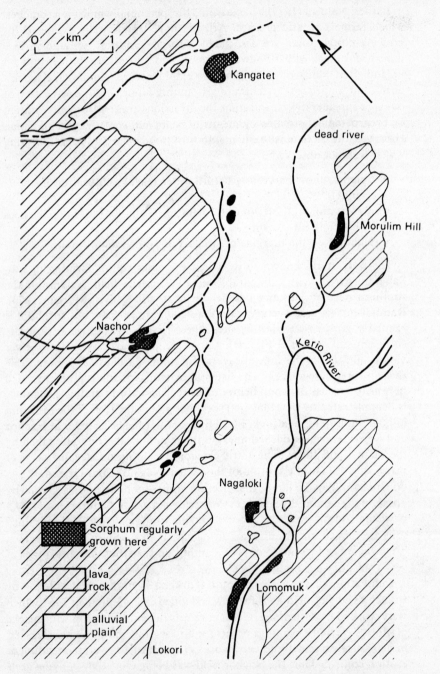

Fig. 6.9 Part of the Kerio River valley in the Turkana area of northern Kenya showing sites where sorghum is regularly grown (dark areas) in relation to natural drainage channels which carry occasional floods (shown by dashed lines). (Morgan 1974)

Despite the fact that runoff and flood farming in Turkana employ only 'simple' techniques, agriculturalists attempting to introduce improved methods in the region have found some aspects of the local tradition highly relevant to their efforts. In one of the earliest of 'improved' schemes, the water-spreading experiment illustrated in Figure 6.2b, the value of the quick-maturing 'Turkana sorghum' was recognized, and seed was brought for planting on the project site from a local woman (Fallon 1963). This project was also influenced by local opinions on planting dates, with the result that there was an October sowing in the first year which the promoters had not planned. Another project in Turkana District, initiated by the Salvation Army, enlisted the support of local people to indentify suitable sites. As in Hopi country and in the Kerio valley, the natural vegetation provided clues. The people were able to point out that the presence of the dwarf shrub *Duosperma* indicated deep loam soils with good potential for runoff farming. One or two of the sites chosen on this basis had previously been used by them for sorghum cultivation (Hillman 1980; Cullis 1984).

'Simple' forms of flood farming and runoff farming exist throughout the semi-arid region immediately south of the Sahara from southern Mauretania and Niger eastwards to Sudan and Somalia. Examples of indigenous 'improved' systems are also to be found, including teras in Sudan and stone barriers across river beds in Somalia. In West Africa, Martin (1979, quoted Cullis 1984) mentions stone bunds used to control runoff in Adar Doutchi (see map, Fig. 7.2). Sorghum is cultivated behind small dams in southern Mauretania, presumably by a version of the inundation method, and natural water spreading sites are exploited in Burkina Faso (ICHS 1972). Wickens and White (1978) comment that: 'these arrested runoff techniques are mostly traditional in origin and aim at increasing the water available to the crop by concentrating local runoff onto particular sites. Simply, the idea is to manipulate the natural accumulation in depressions . . .'

Many of the people in these areas are pastoralists, who may consume relatively small amounts of grain relative to their consumption of animal products, but who yet are often heavily dependent on cereals during certain seasons. Sometimes they obtain this grain by trade, but sometimes they grow it themselves. In that case, the important thing about simple forms of runoff farming is that constant attention to maintenance of terrace walls and bunds is not necessary. Fields can be left for long periods while animals are taken to some more distant area for grazing. Thus Hillman (1980) comments on the difficulty of establishing improved runoff farming among pastoral peoples in the Turkana who are 'unclear' about the aims of such relatively elaborate methods.

Agriculturalists and water conservation engineers working in sub-Saharan Africa often seem unclear in their turn as to how the traditional systems should be regarded. Though some agriculturalists, as we have seen, have learned from the local technology, others ignore it entirely. Small patches of sorghum grown casually by women can too easily be disregarded when experts are oriented towards more formalized systems of farming.

In a valuable account of runoff farming experiments in another part of Kenya, Critchley (1984) well expresses the ambivalent view which is usually taken of existing 'simple' methods. He states that there is 'no long history of runoff harvesting in Kenya', but simultaneously notes that there is a local tradition of cultivating sites 'where there is some inflow from an external catchment'. Moreover, this traditional practice has influenced the work of the programme Critchley describes. Following efforts to introduce within-field catchments in the form of contour ridges, it was found that farmers were reluctant to adopt this approach when their land was already receiving runoff from an external catchment (Fig. 6.10a). It therefore seemed better to assist farmers to improve the efficiency with which they used this existing source of runoff by helping them build bunds and spillways on their fields (Figure 6.10b). If the runoff available from the external catchment proved insufficient, part of the plot could later be re-organized with contour ridges and within-field catchment strips.

Critchley's report presents an excellent example of 'innovative dialogue'. Rather than insisting on the method which seemed technically preferable, his programme was flexible enough to incorporate farmers' preferences based on local traditions. Critchley's report also records suggestions made by the handful of farmers involved in the experiments, such as the 'alternative channel' indicated in Figure 6.10c. It is perhaps worth adding that nearly all 'simple' systems of runoff farming depend on external catchments. Hence wherever 'simple' forms of runoff farming are practised, there may be the same tendency that Critchley observed for farmers to be resistant to alternative within-field systems.

DESIGN PARAMETERS

One difficulty confronting any effort to introduce runoff farming into a new area is that there are a very large number of technical factors which need adjustment if the basic principles are to be adapted to local conditions. The design of a runoff farming system requires a multi-factorial approach — taking account of crop water requirements, tillage, weeding practices and planting densities as well as water management. The latter by itself involves many factors relating to soils, slopes, rainfall intensities, and whether the rain comes in summer or winter. Tillage and weed control both affect moisture loss from the soil, often critically. Limits to what can be achieved by water management can sometimes be balanced by choices concerning crops. The variation in planting density used in Morocco to adjust for different levels of soil moisture is a case in point. The cultivation of quick-maturing varieties of millet (Sudan) and sorghum (Kenya) is another

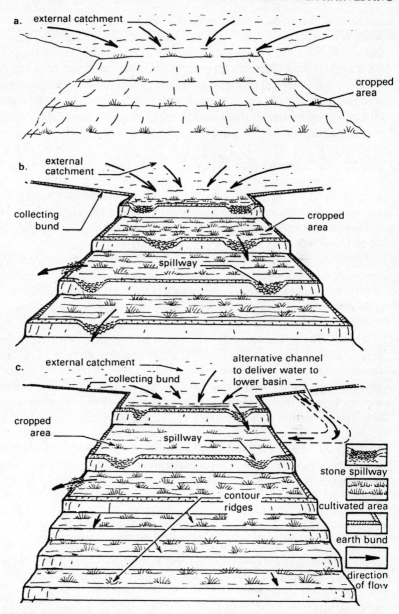

a. external catchment

cropped area

b. external catchment

collecting bund

cropped area

spillway

c. external catchment

collecting bund

alternative channel to deliver water to lower basin

cropped area

spillway

contour ridges

stone spillway

cultivated area

earth bund

direction of flow

Fig. 6.10   Three stages in the development of a runoff farm with an external catchment in the Baringo Pilot Project area, Kenya. (Critchley, 1984 – with modifications) (a) 'simple' runoff farming as practised before the project began – the plot was chosen for cultivation because runoff naturally concentrates there; (b) 'improved' runoff farming with collecting bunds to increase the water available and with bunds and spillways to control water on the cultivated area; (c) a further modification with contour ridges on the lowest plot because insufficient runoff was available from the external catchment. The alternative channel to the middle basin was suggested by one of the farmers in the project.

example, allowing short-lived moisture reserves to be exploited. Sorghum is much favoured as a deeper-rooting crop than, say, maize. It is able to use the whole of the soil profile and has the ability to withstand temporary waterlogging as well as drought.

With a crisis of food production engulfing so much of Africa, reliance on traditional runoff farming is obviously insufficient. Plots of land that chance to receive runoff due to the shape of the terrain are far too limited; they are often vulnerable to erosion, and the flows of runoff they receive are unevenly distributed. But although these systems may be inefficient in these respects, and although they look casual to an engineer, they are based on local environmental knowledge and have been appropriate to the needs and resources of the people who have used them in the past. Such systems are no longer fully appropriate in the context of larger populations and a fundamentally altered economy, but may have continuing value in at least three respects.

Firstly, these systems demonstrate the relevance of runoff farming in many 'drought-prone' areas which are currently experiencing food shortages. Secondly, existing methods exemplify types of runoff manipulation which are compatible with local lifestyles, social systems and patterns of organization.

Thirdly, though, they represent a fund of experience concerning soils, crops, climate and runoff flows. In designing new systems, it is almost impossible to combine the multitude of factors already involved successfully without long and careful trials. On a purely technical level, the benefit of seeking to learn from traditional systems, however apparently 'simple' and insufficient, is that they are likely to include effective choices regarding some of the critical crop or soil factors. Learning from them may thus allow mistakes to be avoided and the development of improved systems to be speeded up. Traditional techniques may also offer clues as to the suitability of inundation as opposed to more conventional methods, as well as influencing choices between within-field and external catchments. In all these respects, traditional methods can provide starting points for adaptive research and innovative dialogue.

The introduction of 'improved' systems of runoff farming cannot, of course, depend entirely on knowledge of traditional systems. It will also be important to collect all the data possible on rainfall and runoff volumes, using the methods outlined earlier in Box 3.2, or at least, simplified versions of those methods. It will be necessary, in addition, to design bunds and spillways on the basis of conventional agricultural engineering experience, as outlined, for example, in Boxes 6.2 and 6.3. Further ideas about the layout of contour bunds will be presented in the next chapter, together with details of a surveying technique that will ensure their accurate alignment with the contour (Box 7.1), and it will be possible to see in more detail how 'modern' and 'traditional' ideas may interact.

7. REPLICATION OF RUNOFF FARMING

COMPLEMENTARY SURVIVAL STRATEGIES

In the chapters on rainwater collection from house roofs, it was argued that effective promotion of the technique may often depend on offering a very comprehensive technical assistance package, including help with organization, training, bulk purchase of materials, loan of equipment, and financial support. The balance struck between these different forms of help would depend on whether the constraints likely to restrict construction of rainwater tanks are lack of skills, shortages of materials, high costs, or some combination of these.

The promotion of runoff farming calls for a somewhat different approach since it is concerned much more with the management of soil and water resources which farmers already possess, and does not usually require large quantities of additional materials. Thus in analysing the constraints which may discourage the spread of runoff farming practice, one is less likely to identify a need for special purchases of materials or equipment (although seed and farm tools may sometimes be needed). Instead, there are more likely to be constraints relating to organization and seasonal labour shortages — or relating to complementary activities such as livestock or grain trading.

It is also important to be aware of constraints which programme organizers can themselves create by ignoring traditional techniques, by closing options prematurely, or by insisting on over-elaborate design procedures. These points involve questions of what Biggs *et al.* (1984) refer to as 'technology responsibility', meaning the responsibility of an agency to make its own selection of the techniques it promotes. The agency must make its selection with an awareness of where its own prejudices lie, and with a willingness to modify its choices in response to local reactions and local needs. To present a large range of alternative techniques and leave the poor to select those which are most suitable is 'unrealistic and irresponsible'. But to suppose that an external agency is likely to make a good choice on its own, without discussion among local people, is equally mistaken. Biggs *et al.* comment that the best agencies are those which willingly admit to changing their minds in the light of local conditions, and this chapter will document one instance where an agency abandoned its preference for microcatchment techniques in favour of methods relating to traditional runoff control practices in the area where it was working.

'Technology responsibility' might also involve a willingness to step outside the conventional specialisms to consider needs in a community which have nothing directly to do with rainwater, but which may significantly affect prospects for its utilization. For example, in the context of rainwater collection from roofs, it was suggested that some people might need help with house improvements as well as with water tanks — and there is one programme in Kenya which links the provision of rainwater tanks to the installation of improved cooking stoves.

It is even more likely that technical assistance for runoff farming will need to operate in a context of other, complementary developments. This is because runoff farming may be an important survival strategy in a drought-prone environment and may impinge on many aspects of the livelihoods it helps to sustain. The importance of this is very evident from the African case-studies which occupy much of this chapter. In these instances, runoff farming is one of several methods for the insurance of food production against the effects of erratic rainfall. One example is a programme in a part of West Africa where average rainfall is 680mm. It might be thought that with such ample rains, which come within a single season, runoff farming techniques would be superfluous. Indeed, it might be expected that enough soil moisture to support a crop would be provided by the rain falling directly on the cultivated land, without need of extra water from a separate catchment area.

In the area concerned, which is the Yatenga region of Burkina Faso (formerly Upper Volta), it is certainly true that when rainfall approaches the average level, runoff makes little difference to crop yields. During the 1982 growing season, rainfall in part of the area was 400-500mm, and in fields where runoff farming was practised, yields were only marginally higher than elsewhere. However, in 1983, there was a drought with rainfall down to 350mm, and under those conditions, fields receiving runoff yielded 48 per cent more than control plots. In drought years, then, the extra soil moisture from retained runoff might make all the difference between the production of a reasonable crop and a catastrophically poor harvest. It has been noted that in some years, the biggest advantage is gained at the beginning of the season. Early sowing is more successful on land receiving runoff, and sometimes the crop is established a month earlier than on other land. This extends the length of the growing season, and ensures some minimum production even in years when the rains finish early.

These conclusions are paralleled by the results of runoff farming experiments in North America. In regions where average rainfall is relatively high, the main benefits of runoff techniques are not high production in an average year, but improved reliability of yield in drought years (Jones and Hauser 1975). In the very worst seasons, needless to say, crop failures are likely even with runoff farming.

Since runoff techniques have this significance as crop insurance strategies, it is not surprising to find that there are traditional forms of runoff farming in the parts of Yatenga from which the foregoing figures are quoted. One consists of the excavation of small soil depresssions, about 0.2m in diameter spaced about 1m apart. Much runoff which would otherwise be lost is captured this way, and is concentrated in the root zone of plants sown in the depressions.

The technique is comparable to 'pitting', a method of retaining runoff used on dry rangelands in Mexico, in other parts of North America, at one time in Kenya, and also tried on arable land in Zimbabwe. In some Mexican work, the pits were made with a modified disc plough, and were effective for range seeding in areas with 200m average rainfall. In the experiments most directly comparable to the Yatenga technique, 'pits' covered about 20 per cent of the land and filled with runoff from the remainder (Fierro 1981). An ox-drawn implement was devised for making pits of this sort in Zimbabwe (Hlekweni 1975).

The Yatenga approach differs in many details from conventional pitting. For example, manure may be placed in the bottom of each soil depression before the planting season. Pits also effectively trap windborne leaves as mulch. Termites come to feed on this and leave tunnels behind them which facilitate root growth and increase water infiltration (Fig. 7.1). The termites have usually gone before the crop is sown and have not been observed to do it any harm.

Rainfall in the Yatenga is erratic in more than one sense. Riesman (1977) quotes the 1969 rainfall figures for two places only 25km apart. Despite this proximity, and despite fairly ample rainfall in total, monthly amounts were very different (Table 7.1). At Djibo, low rainfall in July had a very bad effect on the immature crop, making this a 'near famine year', while Pobé had a reasonably even distribution of rain throughout the growing season and yields were good. Runoff farming at Djibo would perhaps have

Table 7.1   Rainfall (mm) recorded at two stations in Burkina Faso during the **1969** growing season. The two stations are only **25km apart, but monthly rainfall varies considerably.** (Riesman, 1977, *Freedom in Fulani Social Life*. University of Chicago Press.)

	May	June	July	Aug	Sept	Oct	TOTAL
Djibo		137	33	174	33		500
Pobé	56				76	45	553

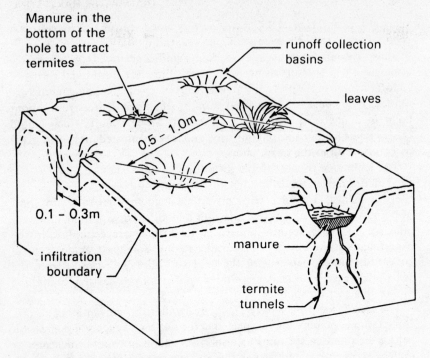

Fig. 7.1   Soil depressions within which seeds of cereal crops are planted – a traditional method of using runoff to support crops in the Yatenga region of Burkina Faso. (Wright 1984)

enabled enough extra water to infiltrate the soil in June to tide the crop over the dry weeks of July.

When average rainfall figures are plotted on a map (Fig. 7.2), it can be seen that isohyet lines are very close together. This indicates that quite small disturbances in the 'normal' geographical distribution of rainfall can make a big difference to the amount of rain received at any one place. The map also shows that average rainfall is consistently higher in the southern regions of Burkina Faso. In 1983, although 'the north had almost no harvest . . . because of drought, in some parts of the south, barns were overflowing with millet after a bumper harvest: farmers were worried about the low price they would receive for their crop on the saturated local market' (Twose 1984).

Across the border in Mali in an area where average rainfall is quoted as 600mm (but where rainfall has been below this nominal 'average' for seventeen years — 1968-85), actual rainfall in most areas during 1984 was typically around 200-250mm. This rain was again patchy and among a hundred and more drought-stricken villages, there were actually *seven* whose fields received ample rain, producing excellent crops (Brittain and Toulmin 1984).

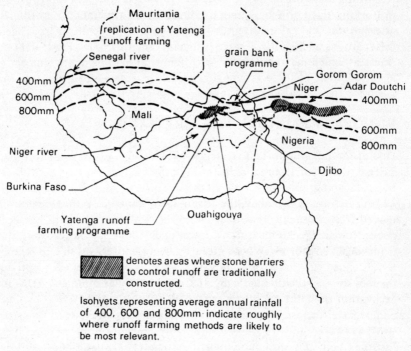

Fig. 7.2   Location of the West African programmes discussed in the text.

Strategies for coping with this extreme patchiness in rainfall, all of which affect the prospects for runoff farming, may involve livestock, migrant labour, choice of crop varieties, grain storage, and food trading. For example, quick-maturing varieties of millet provide some insurance against the rains finishing early and such varieties were increasingly sown during the 1970s. Another strategy is that women customarily travel to villages which have had good crops to help with harvesting and threshing, and to glean on their own account (Brittain and Toulmin 1984). Men travel further afield to seek paid employment, so that they have money to buy food.

Prior to 1920, it was common for cultivators in Burkina Faso to maintain granaries capable of holding three years' requirements of millet, so that after a good harvest, they could survive two successive bad ones (George 1980). The practice declined as a money economy developed and people increasingly needed cash to pay taxes and to buy the necessities they did not produce themselves. Now the tendency is for farmers to sell a large part of their crop soon after harvest and then buy food later in the year. This makes them very vulnerable if food prices rise steeply especially as merchants tend not to release grain until the prospects for a high profit seem good. Locally-run grain banks have made some headway in overcoming this problem.

According to Twose (1984), more than 500 co-operative and village groups in Burkina Faso now buy grain produced by their members immediately after harvest. They store the grain locally, and resell it to members as needs arise, always at the official price (which is generally much lower than the prices at which merchants sell). With financial help from government or agencies, some of these groups now travel to areas with surpluses to buy grain for their village grain banks, so bypassing traders.

RUNOFF FARMING IN PASTORAL AREAS

One of the most important strategies by which people have traditionally safeguarded their livelihoods is through the balance they strike between livestock and grain production. In the situation illustrated by Table 7.1 in which rains are very patchy, the advantage of livestock is that they can be moved from drought areas to graze in districts where rainfall has been good. Nomadic pastoralists track down 'pockets of good pasture' resulting from localized storms. Where groups depend entirely on livestock, they have tended to suffer as cultivated areas have expanded, depriving them of some of their best grazing. In Chapter 3, it was commented that the excavation of hafirs or ponds which fill with rainwater can sometimes compensate for loss of grazing by allowing new rangelands to be used.

Many people, however, have traditionally depended on a combination of livestock activities with cultivation. Riesman (1977) describes how some communities in the north of Burkina Faso are primarily cultivators and how their cattle are effectively treated as extra fields — 'fields on the hoof' — which can be moved to places where rainfall is good, even when drought blights grain crops in conventional, static fields. Although these people think of themselves as herdsmen, their crops provide the greater part of their food in a normal, rainy year, and their livestock are partly a form of insurance. Cultivation is not left to the women, as so often among cattle-raising groups, and active men spend more time with their millet than with their herds.

In the Turkana District of Kenya, the balance between livestock and crops is struck differently. Average rainfall is much lower, and it is therefore logical that crops are less important. Indeed, some years may be so dry that no crop is planted at all. One result is that the people move more, and fields are used intermittently. Thus although the basic principles of runoff farming influence people in their choice of sites for cultivation, building permanent structures to capture runoff has seemed pointless to these farmers, and they have been content with natural concentrations of runoff in dips and hollows. As Hillman (1980) puts it, they regard the rainfall as too erratic to justify construction of bunds and the like.

Yet there is no denying their interest in using runoff. Fallon (1963) has reported on the enthusiasm with which local people participated in a water-spreading project near Lorengippe, planting their own sorghum plots 'haphazardly' after the first season of formal cropping was over. Despite this encouraging start, however, the land was subsequently used by the government Range Management Division for the production of grass seed. Local herders were given some limited access, but after a number of seasons moved away. Indeed, with all programmes in Turkana, the necessarily unpredictable movements of herds have created problems for those attempting to promote permanent runoff cultivation.

More recently, in a report commissioned by FAO, Finkel has stressed that for success with runoff farming in Turkana, techniques must be consistent with the cultural patterns of the pastoralists, and thus should not require permanent settlement near the site. Fields should be designed to require only seasonal attention, without need for maintenance during periods when no crops are in the ground. With this in mind, Finkel recommends that structures should be overdesigned, and that schemes should be as similar as possible to traditional runoff farming practices. As a practical illustration of what might be appropriate, he suggests a series of small cultivation plots enclosed on their downslope sides by bunds laid out on either a trapezoidal or semicircular plan (Fig. 7.3).

The idea is to minimize damage from any breaching of a bund by dividing up the area into small plots, rather than enclosing large areas within a single large embankment. Finkel speculates that herdsmen might prefer to use the plots to grow forage for animals rather than cereals, and suggests that 75 per cent of runoff farming areas might be developed for fodder production.

Clearly, then, technical assistance for runoff farming cannot be narrowly concerned with the design of bunds or microcatchments, but should also be related to the several other methods by which people insure the continuance of their livelihoods. Thus if we were to try and analyse the components necessary in a technical assistance programme (as was done for rainwater tanks in Chapter 4), activities relating to livestock, or in other circumstances, grain storage, might be noted as needing attention. However, there are few programmes in which these varied elements have been put together. In one place there may be an exemplary runoff farming experiment, and in another, encouraging development of grain banks, but rarely are methods of insurance for food supplies dealt with in an integrated way.

EROSION CONTROL

Runoff farming as an insurance measure for areas of erratic rainfall has so far been described in terms which imply stability in the relationship of people to the land, whereas in practice, degradation and erosion of soils is widespread in many of the areas where runoff farming might be used. In

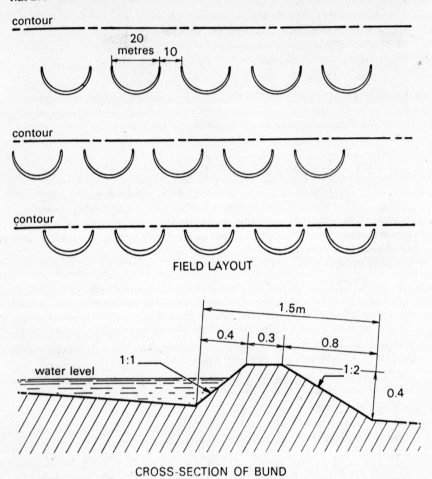

contour

20
metres 10

contour

contour

FIELD LAYOUT

1.5m

0.4 0.3   0.8

water level   1:1

1:2

0.4

CROSS-SECTION OF BUND

Fig. 7.3   Semi-circular cultivated plots with curved bunds or 'hoops' to hold back runoff. This is one of several ideas suggested for the Turkana District of Kenya. Hoops have been used for some time in Baringo District. (Dimensions are in metres.) (Finkel 1984)

Rajasthan, while khadins allow cultivation to flourish in some areas, desert sands elsewhere are encroaching on formerly productive land where trees and grass cover have been over-exploited (Eckholm and Brown 1977). In Ethiopia, problems of a similar kind prompted one villager to tell how, when he was a boy, 'we grew water-melons here and we had fruit trees and lots of sorghum and plenty of butter. Today the fruit trees have gone, we cannot grow any melons, and milk yield is down' (Twose 1984).

In the northern parts of Burkina Faso, especially in the Yatenga region around Ouahigouya (Fig. 7.2), there is a comparable situation. Land is literally disappearing as soils erode to leave large barren patches without vegetation. These covered 11 per cent of the landscape in 1973, and continually spread, encroaching on cultivated areas (Marchal 1977). Local farmers and herdsmen are often forced to ask themselves whether the land can support them any longer, and many are leaving. Although efforts were made to halt this creeping disaster during the 1960s and '70s — some as a result of European aid, and others based on farmers' own efforts — little headway was made. However, in 1979, a new initiative was taken by the development agency Oxfam, after one of its staff had visited the Negev to study the operation of runoff farming systems there. On returning to his post in Burkino Faso, he arranged the construction of 200 microcatchments distributed among seven villages near Ouahigouya. Microcatchments like those used for tree crops in the Negev were chosen because it was felt that loss of tree cover was a major factor in the degradation of the environment. Farmers offered their most badly eroded land for the experiments, and catchment plots measuring 10m by 10m were laid out. Trees were planted in basins 2m square and 0.1-0.2m deep located in the lowest portion of each microcatchment. However, as well as planting trees, some farmers deliberately sowed cereals and others accidently introduced sorghum when they manured the basins. The sorghum was very successful, and at harvest, had 'massive heads, comparable to the best in adjacent fields' (Thomson 1980).

This stimulated a change in the aims of the project. The farmers had planted cereals as well as trees because grain crops were a much more immediate priority for them. With its philosophy of encouraging active participation by people involved in its projects, Oxfam was inclined to respond to this priority. At the same time, there was a change in personnel, with a new project leader arguing that the Negev-style microcatchments were inappropriate to the area (Cullis 1984). Whilst they were effective in establishing trees, they also required much labour for construction, particularly in the dry season. Yet at exactly that time of year, many younger men were absent, earning wages as migrant labourers in more prosperous regions to the south.

As the project developed in this new direction, it made greater use of a technique which farmers in Yatenga and adjacent areas indicated by the map in Figure 7.2 had traditionally practised — the construction of stone barriers to hold back run-off. However, whilst such barriers had previously been built in short lengths to intercept concentrated runoff flows, or to divert streams, they were now developed as extended contour bunds. Unlike conventional bunds, though, the stonework of these barriers allowed water to percolate slowly through to the strip of land below. By this means, water was evenly distributed over the fields and excessive inundation of the land above the barrier was avoided.

Some commentators have argued that the diversion of runoff flows onto the land is inappropriate in this area, with its high average rainfall, because the central problem is soil erosion caused by too much runoff. But it is clear that capturing runoff on the fields has led to greater reliability of yield in times of drought, and this has motivated several hundred farmers to adopt the stone barrier technique. By contrast, programmes which have tackled soil erosion only, with no benefit to crop yields in seasons of low rainfall, have failed to make any impact on the farmers. A programme financed from European funds in the early 1960s which diverted erosive flows into established streams rather than retaining them on the land is a case in point.

What was required was a dual-purpose system, capable of exploiting natural runoff flows to ensure adequate crop production in drought years, but capable also of controlling excess runoff and preventing erosion when rainfall is ample. According to Wright (1984) stone contour barriers forming 'permeable' bunds or terraces achieve this dual purpose on land where large runoff flows concentrate. Where there is less runoff, however, he advocates impermeable earth bunds capable of holding back all the water on a terrace up to a point where there is overflow at the spillways. However, there is little emphasis on the deliberate development of extra catchment areas in this work. The aim is merely to use such runoff as occurs on existing natural catchments.

Wright uses a schematic diagram to indicate various options for the layout of contour barriers and suggests that choices must depend primarily on whether sheet runoff or channel flow has to be dealt with, and in what volume. Systems A and B in Figure 7.4 are for sheet flow, while C and D are designed to pass larger volumes of water in a natural drainage channel. System A has no spillways since this is an array of 'permeable', stone-built barriers. In practice, most farmers start with system A, 'and then watch for damage after a heavy rainfall'. If none occurs, and if water distribution is adequate, no further construction is needed. However, if there is damage in a limited number of places, usually where the crest of the barrier is slightly lower than it should be, then those' places can be reinforced, or small spillways can be built (like those described in Box 6.2).

As well as making terraces with stone barriers, grassed terrace borders are also encouraged. Crop residues — especially sorghum and millet stalks — bundled together are staked down on the contour where the terrace is to be formed, and perennial grasses are then transplanted or sown along the upslope side of this barrier which retains moisture and gives shelter to the grass. Both the crop stalks and the grass if protected from livestock will hold back sediments carried by runoff and promote a gradual build-up of the terrace.

It was hoped from the outset that farmers would be able to extend stone or grass borders along the contours on their own initiative, since it was recognized that any arrangement which required them to call in an outside specialist would not be utilized. The problem, then, was to find a method of surveying contours they could use independently, and organize some form of training in its operation. Two simple methods of surveying were

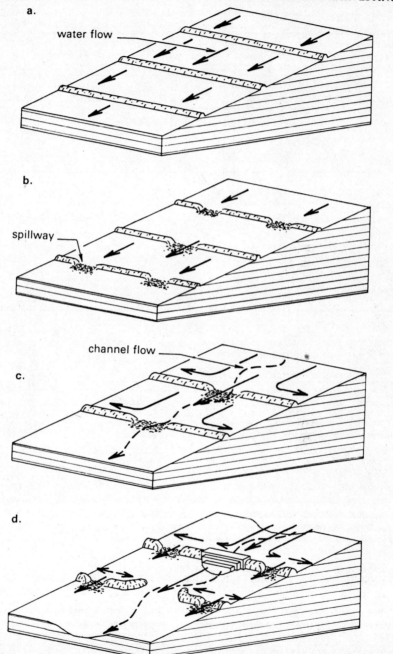

a.

water flow

b.

spillway

channel flow

c.

d.

Fig. 7.4   Options for laying out contour barriers. (after Wright 1984) (a) simple stone barriers for sheet runoff; (b) barriers with spillways; (c) barriers with spillways for channel flow; (d) small dams and spillways for large channels.

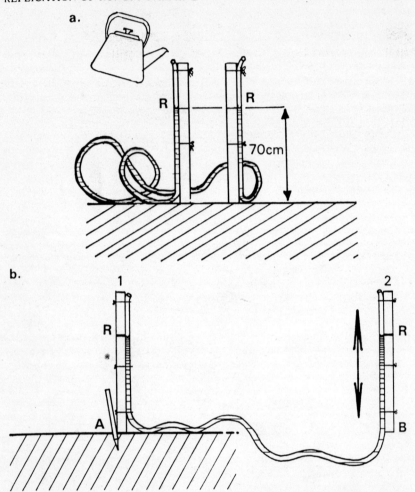

Fig. 7.5   The water tube level for surveying contours. (a) With the poles held vertically side by side, the clear plastic tube is filled with water up to the mark 'R' on each pole. (b) One pole is held vertically at a known point on the contour (marked by a peg) while the other pole is moved up or down slope until the water level arrives at mark 'R'. The foot of the pole is then on the same contour as its fellow. (CIEPAC 1980)

considered, one using an A-frame with plumb-line and the other based on observing water levels in a length of tubing. The water tube method was chosen as the easiest to use on the terrain in this area. The principle is illustrated in Figure 7.5 and further detail is provided in Box 7.1.

FARMER TRAINING

Surveying contours appears to be a critical constraint in many soil conservation and runoff farming programmes, and provision of training in a technique which any farmer can use on his own land may be the single most important task which a technical assistance programme can undertake. A range of simple surveying levels appropriate to this purpose has been reviewed by Collett and Boyd (1977).

In the Yatenga work basic training, which has enabled farmers to learn the use of a level in two-day courses, also involves discussion of the functions of contour barriers. A typical training course is likely to include the following:

- a demonstration of model contour barriers;
- practice surveys with the water tube level;
- visits to fields where contour barriers have previously been built;
- discussion of fieldwork.

The model used for the demonstration consists of a sloping plot of soil, 2m square, on which miniature contour barriers are made. A watering can is then used to simulate rainfall so that the effect of different types of barrier can be observed (Plate 10).

For practice in surveying in nearby fields, farmers are divided into groups of three or four, each of which is given a water tube level to work with. If there is a water-course on the site, contour lines are traced from there, spaced at intervals which would be appropriate if contour bunds or barriers are going to be built. Finally, in the discussion session, farmers not only talk over — and, if necessary, criticize — the contour bunds seen during the field visit, but are also asked to consider how they will organize the work on their own land. Will they construct barriers individually, or will they help each other?

The effectiveness of farmer training may depend as much on what it excludes as on the extent of the local knowledge it uses. Thus a programme which can teach a single, crucial technique to a large number of farmers may be of more value than one which promotes many ideas simultaneously but reaches only a few individuals. In the Yatenga work, one omission was hydrological calculation of the spacing of contour barriers, the length of spillways and the like. Despite the advice quoted in Chapter 3 about the need for years of hydrological observation and careful calculation before any earthworks are constructed, insistence on this proviso would, in this instance, create a considerable constraint, sufficient perhaps to bring the programme to a complete halt. Many farmers in the area are illiterate and cannot be asked to perform numerical calculations. Yet they have their own insights into the local problem, and their own techniques of stone barrier construction, and it has been essential that these resources of knowledge and intelligence be fully used.

Wright comments that farmers have developed terrace systems on their own land in stages, adjusting for mistakes as these are detected. They may

Box 7.1 Determination of contour lines with a water tube level. (Wright, 1984)

Components of the level
—One length of clear plastic tubing, 6–10mm inside diameter and 10–20m long.
—Two poles about 1.5m long.
—Four rubber straps made from inner tube to attach tubing to poles.
—Two rubber straps to mark the water levels in the tube.
—One to two litres water.

Method of use (see also Fig. 7.5)
1. Uncoil the tubing and lay it on the ground, stretching out any bends.
2. From a container of water held at shoulder height, siphon water into one end of the tube, sucking from the other end—or fill the tube by pouring into a funnel at one end.
3. Remove any air bubbles.
4. Tie each end of the tube to one of the poles. Then place both poles together on a flat, smooth surface and hold them vertical side-by-side. Add or remove water as necessary to ensure that the water levels are about 0.4–0.5m below the tube ends.
5. Attach a rubber strap to each tube so that it marks the position of the water level.
6. Place one of the poles so that it marks the end of the contour whose

alignment is to be determined. Take the second pole along the suspected line of the contour, moving it up and down the slope until the water level matches with the position of the rubber marker. The second pole is now standing on the same contour as the first, and a peg should be driven into the ground to mark the spot.
7. The second pole now remains stationary while the first one is carried forward to look for a third point on the contour line.
8. Proceed in the same manner until a suitable length of contour has been marked out.

Hints
1. Work during the coolest time of day, because heat causes the tube to stretch, requiring frequent realignment of the rubber straps which mark the water level. To re-adjust, repeat steps 4 and 5 above.
2. Raising one end of the tube much higher than the other can spill water. If this occurs, repeat steps 4 and 5.
3. When starting on a new site, begin by tracing the highest contour line required. If there are water-courses visible, start each line on the main water-course and work away from it, first on one side and then the other.

begin with a single bund or barrier of the simplest type. The 'empirical experience' gained then enables them to develop more complicated structures within a couple of seasons, 'without the need for calculations and with a minimum of frustration. Runoff from watersheds of up to 10ha have been exploited by "second year" farmers in the Yatenga'.

Textbooks discuss the proper spacing of contour bunds in considerable detail. Much depends on optimizing economic as well as hydrological variables. In the Yatenga, Wright says, 'illiterate farmers make economic choices right along with the rest of us and they should be allowed and trusted to do so'. For optimum water infiltration, the top of each barrier should be level with the foot of the next bund upslope. Thus spacing will tend to be closer on steeper slopes. This is discussed with farmers during training sessions, and they understand it well. However, they may initially space barriers at wider intervals, often as much as 50m apart. Although this is not ideal, it confers some benefits, especially erosion control, and is often a response to shortage of labour when members of the family are working away from home. As one farmer said of his newly constructed terraces: 'If I see during this season that they are too far apart, I'll add some new ones in between them next year'. Because farmers can assess their economic priorities better than anyone else, 'it has been found preferable to allow them to resolve such questions on their own rather than trying to teach complicated formulas that will cause confusion'.

It took a year of trial and error to work out the details of this training programme and to modify procedures for using the water tube level. The next two years were spent teaching the use of the level, and 500 farmers from over 100 villages in the Yatenga region have learned the technique. Twose adds that the experience gained has been used in replicating the work in Mauritania.

The most active groups of farmers in Yatenga have been those experiencing the most severe soil erosion. This is illustrated by a survey of over 100 fields where contour barriers had been built, many of which had clearly been selected for treatment because of the large volumes of erosive runoff to which they were subject. In some fields, it was clear that heavily degraded land was being successfully reclaimed for agriculture.

Reporting this, Wright attributes the success of the project to the urgency of the problems of drought and erosion faced by farmers who could see the productivity of their land falling year by year. He argues that farmers have built contour barriers because the technique offers an immediate increase in yield and reduction of drought risk; he adds that soil conservation measures and tree-planting schemes — which do not show immediate benefits for crops — are taken up far more slowly. This is a cause for concern, because it is doubtful whether soil fertility can be maintained under continuous cropping with the manure available unless tree planting and other measures are pursued. But farmers are occasionally to be seen gathering dead leaves to mulch their fields, and some farmers have planted trees along their contour barriers. Indeed, Twose (1984) mentions a local tradition of planting acacia trees on cropped land because of their ability (as leguminous plants) to restore soil fertility. There has also been some natural regeneration of trees and bushes where contour bunds have stabilized the soil. Thus there is cause for 'guarded optimism' (Wright 1984).

On this analysis, the effectiveness of the Yatenga programme in replicating runoff control and farming techniques is attributed to its direct relevance to an urgently felt need. That in turn was a result of farmer involvement in making choices about which of a number of options should be pursued — microcatchments or contour barriers, trees or cereal crops.

COMPONENTS OF TECHNICAL ASSISTANCE

At this point, it seems worth putting together the details of the various technical assistance programmes discussed. Both in connection with runoff farming, and in relation to rainwater tank construction, there have been three major topics to consider: firstly, how *technological options* are presented; then what *practical help* is given; and finally, what *organization* is necessary (Table 7.2).

With regard to technological options, it is always necessary for the responsible agency to make some initial choices, but it is equally necessary for it to be willing to learn from existing techniques used by local people, and to modify its own methods accordingly. In the Yatenga, some options were introduced by Oxfam (and Peace Corps) personnel with their specialist knowledge of Negev microcatchments and of surveying techniques; other options were rooted in the farmers' own experience of attempting to control runoff using stone barriers and soil depressions. The emergence of an effective technique arose from an innovative dialogue between these two kinds of knowledge and was due to the flexibility of the programme in responding to the farmers' own judgements. A third type of option might have been included, concerning complementary means of insuring against food shortage (Table 7.2).

Ray (1984) indicates a good deal about how such options should be considered when he talks about the need for 'dynamically appropriate' technology to overcome the problems of static poverty. By this he means technology which 'can be altered' in response to local needs, and whose management can develop to accommodate new resources and opportunities. Programmes which Ray picks out as 'dynamic' are those which are capable of changing direction, like the work in Yatenga when it shifted its emphasis from microcatchments to contour barriers. Those which he identifies, by contrast, as static include some in India which offer a single technique, such as irrigation from 'tanks', or a standard set of improvements to khadin agriculture. The latter he sees as unlikely to adapt to social change, and looks on as weak in many of the wider aspects of development.

Reviewing other components of effective technical assistance programmes (Table 7.2), we may note that the work in Yatenga also included a highly relevant *practical assistance package*, centred on the two-day training sessions described above. No significant help to farmers was needed in terms of supplies or finance except that the basic components of the water tube level had to be provided — that is, 10-20m lengths of clear plastic tubing. Wright also mentions that provision of picks, shovels and food for

Table 7.2 Components of technical assistance programmes for runoff farming (compare Table 4.1). Examples cited refer to the Yatenga programmes in Burkina Faso (and occasionally to the Gram Gourav Pratisthan or Pani Panchayat programme in Maharashtra, India).

COMPONENTS	EXAMPLES
TECHNOLOGICAL OPTIONS	
- options selected by professional fieldworkers and agency staff	e.g. microcatchments
- options based on local techniques and skills	e.g. stone barriers, including their construction and spacing
- options for complementary developments	e.g. livestock projects or grain banks
PRACTICAL ASSISTANCE PACKAGES	
- training, including training for women farmers where they exist	e.g. training farmers to survey contours; (in GGP, India, one group of women farmers, the 'widows')
- materials and equipment	e.g. water tube level supplied
- financial help, credit facilities	(in GGP, India, grants from government and foreign sources negotiated by 'parent body')
- follow-up work	e.g. agricultural extension, continued advocacy of tree-planting
ORGANIZATION AND INSTITUTIONAL DEVELOPMENT	
- village-level institutions and organization	e.g. potential for mutual help, co-ops, development of female versus. male roles (in GGP, India, 30–40 family groups of irrigators)
- 'parent organizations'* giving support to village-level groups, making contact with banks, government, etc.	e.g. local voluntary agencies (in GGP, Pani Panchayat meetings linking local groups)
- government institutions and development agencies	e.g. agricultural extension services, government irrigation departments.

* *Biggs et al., 1984*

working parties can help in encouraging co-operative effort, but suggests that the group work can often be organized so that each member contributes to a stock of tools and materials which are shared during the project.

That raises the question of how replication of runoff farming systems is best *organized* among the farmers themselves, and at a higher level, what *institutional structure* is required to support it. In the Yatenga training sessions, farmers were invited to consider four ways of organizing the work:

(i) they could work separately on their own land;

(ii) an individual farmer might invite a group of others to help him, paying them in cash or food;

(iv) several farmers could work collectively on individually owned fields;

(iv) several farmers could agree to share their land, planning its use and carrying out work collectively.

Despite efforts to encourage mutual-help groups of the latter two types, it appears that the trend is for individual farmers to survey contours and construct barriers on their own, especially in times of famine when migration in search of work fragments the group structure.

The most successful villages, however, are those who work collectively, which allows for the informal training of uninitiated farmers as well. In terms of the wider institutional structure, efforts were initially made to interest the appropriate government body, the Organisation Régional de Développement (ORD). However, this agency did not respond, and thus the training programmes and other work have been promoted mainly through an informal project organization co-ordinated by Oxfam. As the success of the techniques becomes apparent one finds the ORD taking a much more active role in training, and it is now expected that they will eventually take over all aspects of the project if funding is available.

A range of more general institutional issues affect the availability of labour for such tasks as building bunds or cultivating runoff-fed land, and include such basic matters as the division of labour between the sexes. Those who plan technical assistance programmes rarely give enough thought to this, and often have no realistic view about how improved farming methods are to be promoted in communities where runoff agriculture is chiefly the province of women. Few agricultural extension services are oriented toward working with women, and very few women are employed as extension officers. Moreover, it might well be found that the amount of time which women must spend on domestic work seriously limits their opportunities to attend training sessions or to construct earthworks. The informality and lack of engineering structures on women's sorghum fields in Kenya (see Chapter 6) may partly be a reflection of time shortage. Thus, a very different approach to the organization of the work may need to be developed, perhaps after exploration of local attitudes to male and female roles with a view to securing male co-operation in time-consuming construction work.

Availability of labour for construction is in practice an important factor influencing the choice of runoff farming technique for a particular site. A system with an external catchment constructed in the sophisticated manner typical of those in the Negev may require 600-800 man-days per hectare to complete, with a continuing requirement for maintenance afterwards. Evenari *et al.* (1982) even record a figure of 2,000 man-days per hectare for the reconstruction of a runoff farm in the Negev. By contrast, contour barriers, bunds or terraces having within-field catchments may call for only 40-100 man-days of construction work per hectare, depending on soil conditions.

Where people leave home at certain times of the year in search of paid work or to care for livestock, ambitious works cannot always be attempted because of shortage of labour. By contrast Cullis tells of famine relief schemes in Kenya since 1981 where earthworks for runoff farming have been constructed as a 'food-for-work' exercise, and more labour was available than could be purposefully employed. Inadequate planning, design and supervision has resulted in many of the earthworks being washed away. Structures have been generally poorly maintained and the impounded land under-utilized because food handouts rather than food production has been the motivating factor.

Another aspect of the organization of rainwater harvesting is raised by Ray (1984) when he comments that in India especially, 'the rural poor are reluctant co-operators'. Where survival is at stake, collective action is much more acceptable than otherwise. After analysing a number of Indian projects, he suggests that important factors in the development of co-operation are strong local leadership, official encouragement, and access to outside finance. This emphasizes the point made earlier that local mutual-help groups are unlikely to get very far without some sort of higher-level institutional support to provide advice and encouragement and to assist negotiations with banks and grant-giving bodies. The latter point is important because one reason for encouraging co-operative action is so that groups of poor people can obtain the same advantages as rich farmers in terms of marketing, access to credit and economies of scale. In Burkina Faso, there seemed to be no particular advantage in co-operative work on contour bund construction. Thus although farmers were encouraged by the programme organizers to work in groups, the trend was for them to work individually. While the majority of this work may still be done individually, the trend is now towards collective action taken on individual parcels of land.

By contrast, the quite separate programme for insurance of food supplies by establishing grain banks does involve poor farmers co-operating in group action. This is necessary so that the farmers can achieve sufficient economic strength to compete with merchants who speculate on grain prices, taking advantage to scarcity to make large profits. As previously mentioned, there are some 500 village groups in Burkina Faso buying and storing grain to meet their members' future needs. In the local runoff farming projects, the economic weakness of the farmer is not an immediate problem and so there is less incentive to collective action.

LOCAL ORGANIZATION AND GOVERNMENT ROLES

Whatever measures are proposed — contour barriers or grain banks — some sort of institutional support for farmers' efforts is likely to be needed. In relation to contour barriers, its primary function is to provide training, and with regard to grain banks, to help with finance. In both instances, any widespread extension of the work may well depend on persuading governments to play a role in providing this necessary support. In India, Ray has noted two states which illustrate government encouragement for water harvesting, Rajasthan and Maharashtra, which have programmes for khadins and 'tanks' respectively.

In one part of Rajasthan, Kolarkar and his colleagues estimate that there were 500 khadins in 1980, whereas Ray thought that there were 700 or more three years later. Thus there is evidence of very effective replication of this form of runoff farming, for which the state Department of Irrigation has been responsible. There is also support for the work from the nearby Central Arid Zone Research Institute, which is carrying out extension work on some khadins to demonstrate improved varieties of wheat and green gram, grown with chemical fertilizer.

In this area, though, one sees the disadvantage of runoff farming on such a large scale. The many small farmers who have plots within a single khadin do not appear to be well organized. They leave management of the system to the Department of Irrigation, which decides when water should be drained off at the sluices prior to planting, and which also handles maintenance. The Department's costs are paid for by a tax on the cropped land. The farmers make representations when they see the need for maintenance or other action, but otherwise do not participate in the running of the scheme. At the same time, there is a strict demarcation between the state Department of Irrigation and the Department of Agriculture, the latter employing the extension officers who give advice to farmers about crops and fertilizers. Ray suspects that lack of co-ordination here impedes extension links with farmers.

Despite achievements in constructing new khadins and in providing new spillways and sluices for old ones, there are doubts as to whether khadin development is proceeding fast enough or efficiently enough to meet the needs of a growing population. Some local experts believe that new canals bringing irrigation water from outside the region will ultimately become more important. Moreover, khadins only provide a limited number of plots for farmers, and leave many of the poorest cultivators uncatered for. Many of these limitations of the system arise from its somewhat cumbersome and bureaucratic organization. From a purely technical point of view, it is a highly effective form cf runoff farming.

In Maharashtra, scene of the other major example of an official programme for replication of a water harvesting technique, the main institution concerned was once again the local state government's Department of Irrigation, and later the administrators of India's Employment Guarantee Scheme. Both have been active in constructing percolation tanks, a form of floodwater harvesting in which water held behind a dam percolates into the ground, raising the water table at wells further down the valley. (The principle was illustrated earlier by Figure 2.4.) In Maharashtra, new percolation tanks have been constructed in the last two decades wherever officials of the Department of Irrigation, 'felt that physical conditions were encouraging' (Ray 1984). However, the construction of new 'tanks' is one thing; their effective exploitation is another. It is striking that the case studies of effective use which have received publicity tend to be examples where voluntary agencies rather than government departments have taken initiatives. One instance concerns groups of poor farmers who share irrigation pumps, and who were mentioned earlier (Chapter 2). Their irrigation water is pumped from wells in which the water table is sustained by a perculation tank some little way upstream. The earlier discussion also commented on the two levels of organization which characterize this project — the groups of 30–40 families that manage their own small irrigation systems — and the parent organization that provides technical assistance and negotiates financial support from more remote bodies to which the poorest farmers would not normally gain access. Initially, government grants were obtained, but when these stopped in 1981, finance came instead from foreign aid and from some Indian industrialists (Biggs *et al.* 1984).

Another case study from Maharashtra again involves the abstraction of irrigation water from wells below a percolation 'tank'. This 'tank' in fact consists of a dam 400m long impounding 300,000m³ of water from a large catchment. Improvements introduced by the project include reafforestation on the catchment, to reduce erosion, and a number of measures to compensate for the poor performance of some wells down-slope from the dam. In places, check dams on streams improved percolation of water into the wells, but a large pump was also needed to raise water directly from the dam for irrigation of some of the land.

Two voluntary organizations jointly run this project which is located near Jalna (Fig. 2.3). One is a local body, whilst the other is Action for Food Production (AFPRO), which is active in many parts of India. Ray (1984) comments that because these are indigenous institutions, they cannot 'walk away from failure', and therefore proceed more cautiously than many foreign aid agencies which seek 'rapid dissemination' of favoured techniques. Both bodies were initially worried by the lack of organization within the local community. People who owned land, about 2–4ha per household, belonged to a co-operative, but there seemed no way of bringing poorer families in. AFPRO and its partner decided to go ahead when they had established that people were at least willing to co-operate in planting trees on the catchment and fencing the area to keep livestock out. In another village, where there was no such co-operation, a similar project was not commenced.

There are obvious lessons in these case-studies about the organization which is necessary, firstly if a project is to succeed at all, and secondly if it is to help the poorest groups of people. The latter, it often seems, only benefit if they are well organized to help themselves. In the last project discussed, landless families in the end did find a way of working together for their own profit. They observed the considerable growth of grass within the newly fenced forestry area on the catchment, and negotiated the right to cut the grass and sell it as fodder to buffalo owners in a nearby town. In the other programme mentioned, however, the groups of irrigators seem to have achieved more — perhaps because their membership of about 30-40 families in each group is near the optimum size for self-management, and brings together sufficient resources for an effective operation.

In the very different circumstances of Africa's arid and semi-arid regions, pastoralists and farmers also need better organization for land and water management as well as to balance the activities of stronger commercial and government agencies. The case is put for grain bank collectives by Twose, and for pastoral co-operatives by Swift (1977), but has not yet been formulated with any clarity in rainwater harvesting programmes. In Burkina Faso, farmers apparently did not feel the need for organization initially.

Sandford (1983) offers an analysis of options for the organization of pastoralists which can be loosely applied to any rural group likely to be involved in managing water resources. Firstly, there are options concerning the functions of different units of organization: government departments, community groups, individuals and commercial firms. All too often, the problem is the weakness of groups at the community level compared with government and commerce. Then there are options as to whether organizations should be multipurpose or specialist. For example, should co-operative efforts in runoff farming be pursued separately from co-operative efforts in other spheres, or should a single village group be responsible both for the local grain bank and the organization of contour bund construction?

There are also questions to ask about how local groups should relate to one another and to sources of professional expertise. One might hope for a self-governing federation of small local groups capable of functioning as their 'parent organization' — that is, negotiating with banks or with government, and employing any professional staff needed (Biggs *et al.* 1984). The Indian groups of irrigators who send representatives to regular Pani Panchayat meetings enjoy a degree of representation, but the programme is in fact run by a local voluntary agency. In other instances, government departments, perhaps through their extension services, may attempt to provide technical and financial advice directly to local groups.

In the context of runoff farming, one difficulty may be a lack of competent professionals for either parent bodies or extension services to employ. There is certainly professional training available, in India, Israel and the United States, and it is supported by textbook material of wider interest.* However, not all this training is fully relevant to tropical areas, nor is it all calculated to make professionals aware of the significance of local traditions in runoff farming, and how these may affect the contribution farmers can make to the development and application of improved techniques. As a result one encounters complaints from some areas where runoff farming is being encouraged that each new 'expert' who arrives promotes his own favourite technique, be it microcatchments, desert strips, floodwater diversions or Negev-style runoff farms, and nobody seeks to encourage a consistent pattern of development, building on existing local traditions of runoff farming. Yet that consistency may often be the key to effective technical assistance.

* Prasad 1979; Shanan and Tadmor 1979; Matlock and Dutt 1984 are relevant teaching texts from the three countries respectively.

8. RAINWATER ECONOMICS AND FUTURE PROSPECTS

THE OUTLOOK FOR RUNOFF FARMING

The arid area of Rajasthan is said to be the most densely populated desert in the world, and significantly, it is the location of several forms of rainwater harvesting. Houses are constructed with basement cisterns ('water-retaining cellars') into which runoff from roofs is directed. Patches of soil with underlying clay are variously dug out or bunded up to form excavated rainwater catchment ponds (called *nadis*). Finally, of course, there are the khadin runoff farming systems described in Chapter 6. In other regions of the world also, one may find runoff farming and rainwater collection from roofs in simultaneous use, notably in some arid and semi-arid parts of the Middle East and Africa. Moreover, a selective technical account of rainwater and of runoff utilization could be written to emphasize how closely allied these agricultural and domestic versions of the technique may be.

However, if we look at the social and economic conditions under which rainwater collection is expected to develop in the modern world, we observe the greatest possible contrasts. Tanks for collecting water from house roofs are constructed of modern materials — galvanized steel or ferrocement — and can be represented as very desirable home improvements. Moreover, the tanks can be bought from contractors or built on a do-it-yourself basis, and the marketing of the tanks or materials for building them can be a profitable activity for small private businesses. Indeed, the suggestion has been made here that development agencies should encourage commercial marketing of tanks as the most effective way of extending or replicating their use whilst continuing to assist poorer families who can benefit from them. In some countries, then — including Kenya, Thailand and probably Indonesia — rainwater tanks have many of the attributes of a modern consumer good, and there are excellent prospects for their promotion.

With runoff farming, the outlook is very different. Whilst it is possible to describe many traditional and historical examples of the technique, only a handful of successful modern programmes can be quoted. Much detailed technical information has emerged from experimental projects in Israel and the United States, but little has been reported about experience of modern runoff farming in regular use. Where traditional runoff techniques in India, the Middle East and North Africa are documented, many reports are pessimistic, describing systems in decline or having been totally abandoned. Rajasthan in India and Tunisia in North Africa were quoted earlier as having official policies of encouraging runoff farming. But in Rajasthan we also noted comments to the effect that irrigation would ultimately produce greater increases in food production, and in Tunisia, planned improvements to terraced wadi systems are made in the context of a deterioration of other floodwater and runoff collection methods. El Amami (1977) speaks of 'inconsistency between inherited practices and new socio-economic needs' in Tunisia. Specific reasons for deterioration in traditional runoff farming he notes are, firstly, over-planting in olive groves so that individual trees receive less runoff, and more seriously, lack of labour to construct and maintain bunds, terrace walls, spillways and so on.

On arid and semi-arid grazing lands, very simple runoff techniques with very low labour requirements are more positively reported. Measures include contour furrowing, pitting, and forming semicircular bunds or 'hoops' (Fig. 7.3) to trap runoff and promote growth of grass, shrub and cactus forage. Tree-planting and re-seeding is also undertaken to hold back runoff, control erosion and establish more nutritious forage species (Sandford 1983). In Australia and the United States, mechanization allows furrowing and pitting to be undertaken with very little manpower. In Kenya, there have been encouraging experiments with 'hoops' (Barrow 1982, Critchley 1984). In Tunisia and other parts of North Africa, treatment has been extended over large areas with planting of forage plants including Acacia trees and the cactus *Atriplex* (Sandford 1983).

Runoff farming for crop production is a very different matter, however, and the amount of labour required for constructing and maintaining bunds and terraces is remarked on everywhere. In several North African and Middle Eastern countries, a movement of labour away from farming to well-paid jobs in tourism and industry has led to a decline in runoff agriculture. Tunisia is one example. Another is North Yemen, where Clouet (1979) ascribes the stagnation of runoff farming to a drift of workers towards high-wage employment in Saudi Arabia. Until 1960, runoff agriculture and floodwater farming enabled Yemen to produce grain surpluses within a feudal system of land tenure. But now, with alternative opportunities not far away, and in the absence of land reform, young and progressive people are leaving the rural areas. As a result, the bunds and terraces of farms are not being maintained, grain production has suffered, and North Yemen has become a net importer of cereals.

Where young Yemenis have retained their interest in farming, and have had remittances from relatives in oil-rich countries to invest, they have preferred to use 'modern' methods, and have replaced floodwater cultivation and runoff farming with boreholes and diesel-powered irrigation pumps. 'Within the last ten years, the number of boreholes has increased tremendously. The per-metre cost of drilling reached the fabulous sum of £600 in the early days and in remote areas, but is now down to £130. Japanese diesel engines can be found everywhere . . .' (Merabet 1984).

In such circumstances, some people appear to think that rainwater collection and runoff farming are too labour-intensive to compete, and are incapable of producing the large increase in food output needed by expanding populations. In many cases, the traditional techniques originated within institutions which few people would wish to perpetuate. Feudal land ownership in Yemen and the zamindar system in India (Chapter 2) restricted individual choices in a way which is now seen as unacceptable. The attraction of the private boreholes which many Yemeni and Indian farmers opt for is that these bring farming more closely under the individual's control, making it not only less subject to difficult weather conditions, but also independent of the decisions of landowners or bureaucratic Irrigation Departments. Advocates of runoff farming should therefore give special attention to techniques which can be used by individuals on their own land (which may have been one factor in the success of the Yatenga programme in Burkina Faso — Chapter 7). Alternatively, where catchments or bunds are best shared by groups of farmers, acceptable forms of organization need very careful thought.

The problem is not just that experience of modern, high-wage economies encourages farmers to take an individualistic view of investments and profits. More fundamentally, some experts believe that low rates of financial return are inevitable in runoff farming, and regard irrigation as the only viable modern method of agricultural production in arid and semi-arid areas.

However, one should beware of such arguments and their implication that runoff farming is simply out-dated. In most places where runoff farming is in decline, there are other symptoms of a deteriorating agricultural ecology, including soil erosion, desertification, failures in food production, and indeed, poor results from expensive modern irrigation systems. A more reasoned point of view might therefore be that agricultural policies are seriously inadequate in these parts of the world, and that the apparently uncompetitive position of runoff farming is merely one aspect of that. More specifically, there is a growing recognition that many governments, especially in Africa, have given insufficient support to basic food production, and instead have given preference to export crops.

Several countries which, like North Yemen, were once exporters of grain now have to import it, and although this is partly due to the growth of population, it also reflects varying degrees of stagnation in local agriculture. Traditional runoff farming in Morocco was so well developed that Kutsch (1982) thought that no further improvements in water management were possible, only improvement in agronomy. Yet he also recorded the negative impact of commercial activities, including tourism, noting particulary how the expansion of towns and their demands for drinking water has disturbed the water balance within some catchment basins and has attracted labour away from farming. It is significant, then, that overall food production showed almost no expansion during the 1970s. In 1980, food production in Morocco was up by 16 per cent on the average of a decade earlier, but in the following year, it fell back to 5 per cent less than the earlier average (FAO 1983).

In Africa south of the Sahara, similar trends are even more clearly evident. Governments have been encouraged to favour cash crops in their agricultural policies by the nature of the technical and financial aid they have received from western countries, and by the need for export earnings to repay loans associated with this aid. Urban elites have done well out of these arrangements, and agricultural research, both international and local, has given technical support, concentrating on irrigation and on crops such as cotton, rice and groundnuts. Meanwhile, food crops such as the sorghums and millets have been neglected by researchers and policymakers alike, and Africa's semi-arid food-producing areas have been 'crucially deprived' of extension services, capital and technology. As Eckholm and Brown (1977) put it, a 'structural transformation' is needed to correct this, but vested interests within the countries concerned, as well as among western aid donors, have so far prevented such a change.

Meanwhile, Twose (1984) notes that although the countries of Africa's Sahel zone have had a consistently poor record in producing food for local consumption over the last twenty years, they have achieved 'steady success' in the cultivation of cash crops such as cotton and groundnuts. Indeed, some have been exporting groundnuts and vegetables whilst simultaneously needing food aid to prevent famine. One problem is that grain yields are dropping because the best land is given over to cash crops, and farming for local food needs has been relegated to marginal areas. In 1920, the average farmer in Niger obtained 500kg of grain per hectare. By 1978, this was down to 350kg, and Niger was only able to maintain some increase in total grain cultivation because a greatly expanded area of land was cultivated — largely at the expense of pastoralists.

Irrigation has often been emphasized in planning for these regions because it has appeared to be the best way of making farmers less dependent on erratic rainfall. However, this policy has had limited success because of a build-up of salt in irrigated soils — a problem which does not usually occur in runoff farming because of the better quality of runoff water from very small catchments. Irrigated agriculture also involves large investments and high recurrent costs and is energy-intensive when water has to be pumped. In order that these costs may be repaid, the authorities responsible for large irrigation schemes must raise a levy from farmers working the irrigated land, who are then forced to grow the crops which will be most profitable in cash terms so that they can pay the levy. Such crops do not usually include the cereals eaten by the local rural population.

It may well be, then, that the policies which emphasize export crops rather than food are a major reason why runoff farming in many countries seems a relatively poor prospect. Export crops bring in the cash resources which can support investments in irrigation. Food crops can be profitable too, but at a lower level of investment. At this level, runoff farming is often appropriate as a means of improving crop reliability, and if further insurance against the effects of erratic rainfall is required, this can in principle be provided by local grain banks. If food crops do not seem profitable, that may be at least partly because governments do not offer the same kind of support in terms of marketing arrangements as they provide for export crops. Farmers in Burkina Faso who had a good harvest of millet in 1983 found prices falling despite shortages elsewhere in the country. They therefore planned to grow cotton in place of millet in the next year because 'they knew that the cotton would be collected swiftly by the Government services and they would get a good price for their harvest' (Twose 1984).

Another factor in the equation is environmental degradation in low rainfall areas where trees have been cut for firewood, and many former pastoral areas have been taken over for cultivation. The resulting losses of natural vegetation expose soils to erosion and to the processes by which productive land turns into desert. The most active agent in this destructive process is uncontrolled runoff, and if the natural vegetation which once retained or slowed runoff and stabilized soils is lost, artificial means of runoff control are essential. A very wide range of techniques is available, including conventional soil conservation at one end of the spectrum (Hudson 1971) and floodwater harvesting at the other (UNEP 1983). The limited range of runoff farming techniques discussed here differ from soil conservation in that they make productive use of runoff rather than merely seeing it as a problem requiring control. These techniques differ from floodwater harvesting (and irrigation) because they use rainwater close to the point where the rain falls, so limiting evaporation and losses.

In India, soil conservation and water harvesting have developed very differently, partly because of an ample labour supply. Whilst individual farmers have invested in private boreholes for irrigation, efforts to find employment for landless labourers have led to construction of large-scale earthworks under 'food-for-work' and employment guarantee schemes. Indeed, it might be argued that the availability of this labour, together with the Indian tradition of large-scale organization and construction, has led to an over-emphasis on tanks, dams, ahars and khadins, and that perhaps conventional runoff farming based on within-field catchments and contour bunding would use land and water resources more efficiently.

To some extent, this is a question of floodwater harvesting versus true runoff farming. In some places, dams and reservoirs (i.e. 'tanks') for floodwater harvesting occupy as big an area of land as the cultivated plots which benefit from the water retained. In such circumstances, it may sometimes be that capturing runoff by contour bunds higher up in the catchment area and nearer to where the rain falls would retain more water for cropping, while enabling the lower ground occupied by dams and 'tanks' to be used instead for cultivation.

QUESTIONS OF ECONOMICS

It is one thing to notice general impressions of the high labour requirements of runoff farming, but quite another to find hard data on the subject. Because many traditional systems are neglected by policy-makers, few figures on labour or other costs have been compiled. As to modern systems, so many are experimental that reports tend to focus on their technical rather than their economic performance.

Farmers, planners and extension personnel assessing any new or modified technology will estimate its gross benefits in terms of yields and the likely price they will obtain for the crop. They will then compare the benefits with the cost of labour, seed and fertilizer inputs required to produce the crop. From this they will estimate the 'net benefit' of the new technology as compared with alternatives and if the net benefit is substantial, they will probably adopt the new approach (Carruthers 1983). Especially where small farmers are concerned, such calculations need to include allowance for risks due to drought, pests and so on. This can be done by repeating the cost/benefit calculations for seasons with the worst likely outcomes.

Costs associated with runoff farming include costs of construction, amortization and maintenance, in addition to the cost of seed, fertilizer, tillage and so forth. Maintenance can be substantial on microcatchments, which need inspection after every storm so that any minor breaks in bunds can be promptly repaired (Shanan and Tadmor 1979). On the other hand, ahars are said to require very little maintenance (UNEP 1983). There may also be costs that are not borne by the farmer but which affect others in society. Many of the latter will arise from conflicts of land use — for example, if runoff farming develops by excluding animals from common pastures which serve as catchments, herdsmen suffer and overgrazing is more likely on such pastures as remain open. Water used for agricultural or commercial purposes by dominant groups may increase their income in ways which are not available for the poor; this can lead to changes which not only worsen the relative but also the absolute position of the poor, such as the severance of arrangements to share food in times of disaster (WHO 1981).

Even confining attention to the direct costs borne by farmers, not all the figures from the case studies quoted have been available to the authors. In Burkina Faso, lack of data is one result of an explicit policy that farmers should be left to make their own economic judgements. When they do, it is evident that they find contour barriers economically worthwhile on those parts of their land where erosion has been robbing them of most production. It is also evident that the labour required is an economic cost that is sometimes difficult to meet, with the result that farmers space the barriers further apart than the technical optimum. It is experiences like this, and figures for the number of man-days required to construct bunds and runoff farms (UNEP 1983, Evenari et al. 1982) which lead to the conclusion that labour requirements are sometimes a major constraint on the development of runoff farming.

In India, more data are available but are often applicable to floodwater harvesting rather than runoff farming, and especially for collection of floodwater in percolation 'tanks'. Particularly good economic results have been recorded in both the Maharashtra programmes discussed in the previous chapter, with production sometimes increased by as much as 300 per cent (Biggs et al. 1984). Such improvements are possible where irrigation aided by a percolation tank has led to double cropping, with millet or sorghum followed in the year by wheat. Farm incomes may be enhanced by factors of two or three. However, it again seems that 'a farming system which includes water harvesting raises the employment requirements per hectare', so the overall increase in farm receipts is to some extent distributed among the extra labour force, and net receipts to farmers may rise by less dramatic amounts. Ray (1984) comments that this benefit is important for poor people and as the Pani Panchayat and similar schemes develop, 'the scope for labour-intensive vegetable production should increase'.

Economic data on the cost of domestic rainwater tanks are more plentiful, though the benefits remain difficult to assess. One study quoted by Pacey et al. (1977) compared different types of drinking-water supply capable of providing a minimal 10 litres per head daily throughout the year. Rainwater tanks were included on the assumption that water from them would be rationed by users to provide an assured daily supply. This somewhat artificial view was taken so that comparison could be made with piped systems which are designed to provide a constant supply. The study was limited to rural conditions and included some very simple arrangements for piping water from springs on hills des to public standpipes at very low cost. The figures that resulted from this study made rainwater tanks look very expensive. Expressed in U.S. dollars at 1971 prices, the range of capital costs was roughly as follows:

Rainwater tanks
  serving 1-5 people: $20-65 per person;
Large rainwater tanks
  serving 20-30 people: $10-$15 per person;
Piped water supplies: $2-$12 per person;
Hand-dug wells: $1 - $5 per person.

This is not a realistic way of comparing costs, however. Rainwater tanks and piped water supplies have such different characteristics that for most purposes, there is no point in saying that one is cheaper than the other. Instead, it makes more sense to ask whether the level of investment required for rainwater tanks is within the same range as other investments being made in the local community. Table 8.1 presents some figures for different kinds of investment in water and sanitation. Where piped water is laid into people's homes, rainwater tanks are unlikely to be built at all, but where water is distributed via public standpipes, tanks still offer advantages in terms of convenience and individual control. Thus the only piped supplies included in this table are those with public outlets. In making comparisons, it must also be remembered that rainwater tanks are usually individual investments by families, whereas a standpipe supply is normally a public investment to which families may only contribute a small amount directly.

The figures in Table 8.1 suggest that the smaller sizes of rainwater tank require about the same level of investment as the construction of a pit latrine. It would be unrealistic to compare benefits, but it might be possible to argue that if families can afford one they can afford the other — or that similar levels of financial support will be needed by those who can pay for neither.

Another point of view noted in Chapter 3 is that because rainwater tanks are so closely connected with a family's house, their capital cost should be in some sort of proportion to the resources invested in the house. The same has also been said about latrines, and Nimpuno (1978) has argued that 10 per cent of the cost of a house is an appropriate limit. However, in many rural areas, the average investment in a house is almost impossible to estimate since so many family homes are extended over a long period of time using the family's own labour for construction. However, the figures for latrines quoted in Table 8.1 appear to be within bounds which Nimpuno would accept, and it is difficult to argue that a greater proportionate investment is justified for rainwater tanks. Thus, while many small tanks fall within an appropriate price range, most 9-10m³ tanks do not. Yet it is clear from what was said in Chapter 3 that many family houses have sufficiently extensive roofs to justify the larger size of tank.

Biggs *et al.* (1984) suggest that the most effective programmes in tackling the problems of poverty are usually those which begin by defining clearly

Table 8.1 Typical levels of investment in water and sanitation in rural communities.
Figures are in U.S. dollars at 1977–8 price levels. (For more detail of rainwater tanks, but at 1981–2 prices, see Table 5.2.) Piped water supply to public standpipes probably receives a higher level of subsidy than most other types of development, but all are partly or largely paid for by beneficiaries.

Nature of investment	Typical investment per family (assuming 6-person family)	
Piped water to public standpipes (IRC 1979)	$60–$180	materials & labour; typical Asia/Africa per capita cost times 6
Pit latrines: Botswana Zimbabwe Nigeria (Oluwande 1978)	$13–$24 $30–$40 $40	materials only
Rainwater tanks 9–10m³ ferrocement tank with cover and gutters, Zimbabwe 7m³ concrete ring tank with cover, Thailand (Keller 1982)	$62–$90 $40	materials only
1.2m³ ferrocement tank with cover (Keller 1982)	$33	materials at 1980 prices

the particular low-income groups they wish to help — landless people, smallholders with less than 0.5ha of land, and so on. Thus instead of discussing average levels of investment in housing, latrines or tanks, the argument should perhaps be based on the needs of people with housing conditions below a defined minimum. Under those circumstances, the advocate of rainwater collection may need to devote a good deal of his or her effort to improving the houses themselves, or at least their roofs. Where rainwater tanks can be introduced, small and cheap factory-made ones— like the unusually economical Jumbo Jar in Thailand — may then be most appropriate. The cost of this at the factory gate was equivalent to only US\$23 at 1984 price levels (Latham 1984b), but whether the same economy and efficiency of production can be achieved in other countries remains to be seen.

QUESTIONS OF LIVELIHOOD

Although it is possible to argue that small rainwater tanks confer economic benefits and are cost-effective, these benefits are always difficult to measure. We can point to the time people save through not having to carry water from a distant source. We can also argue that cleaner water brings better health and enables people to work more productively. These points are significant, but perhaps only during brief seasons when planting or harvest make heavy demands on a family's time and labour. If people use water from a tank at other seasons, its benefits may include better child care or more leisure, but nothing that economists would wish to measure. Thus it may be relevant to recall the point made in Chapter 2 that people's livelihoods do not consist entirely of goods and services which have market value; they depend also on 'home production', defined as activities which improve the quality of life for family members without involving market transactions.

In many cases, the greater convenience of the rainwater supply will show benefits for 'home production' activities such as cooking, housework and child care to a greater extent than benefits measurable in market values. Tanks can also be attractive to people because they are under the family's control and do not involve the conflicts with neighbours sometimes associated with shared facilities. They also have some of the attractions of modern consumer goods and in some communities, acquisition of a tank may seem a definite step forward in modernizing the home. Thus the benefits of rainwater tanks perceived by their owners may be of three general kinds:

- market benefits (time saved for remunerative work);
- home production benefits (cooking, child care, etc);
- non-economic and social benefits (individual control, modernization).

Non-economic factors can influence attitudes to agricultural uses of water as well, but seem to pull in a less positive direction as far as rainwater harvesting is concerned. We have noted how options which offer most in terms of individual control, up-to-date equipment and modernization are sometimes perceived to be boreholes and motor-driven pumps. Undoubtedly, irrigation from boreholes offers market benefits also by enabling farmers to increase their production very greatly, growing two or even three crops a year on the same land instead of being limited to a brief rainy season.

In India, arrangements of this kind may be linked to floodwater harvesting via the recharge of wells from percolation 'tanks' (Figure 2.4). Elsewhere, borehole irrigation may be a straight replacement for floodwater harvesting or runoff farming, and its attraction as a form of modernization can be so great that farmers with spare cash (as in North Yemen) invest in boreholes even when the chances of fully recouping the high drilling charges must be small.

In present circumstances, then, and in the absence of official emphasis on food production or environmental priorities in the policies of many countries, runoff farming is likely only to be attractive in regions where irrigation is not feasible, either because groundwater resources are lacking, or because people cannot afford the high investment involved. In the latter case, where it is people's poverty which makes them look to this technique, their economic assessment of its benefits may be oriented more to basic livelihood than to market advantage. Thus the effect of runoff on the *reliability* of crop yields may be more important to many families than any large production increases.

It is against this background that Ray (1983) sees three features of *both* rainwater tanks and runoff farming as particularly significant. Firstly, he notes that economies of scale offer a financial incentive to build large rainwater 'tanks', dams, khadins and the like, but simultaneously points out the difficulties of efficient management in large projects run either by community organizations or by bureaucrats. He argues that the most successful projects are those which offer the advantages of private ownership without the economic penalties of small scale. He cites the rainwater tank programmes of Indonesia and Thailand as examples, and suggests that domestic rainwater supplies should almost always be based on household rather than communal facilities. As to rainwater collection for agriculture, he might well have cited the runoff farming programme in Burkina Faso discussed in Chapter 7 as an example where farmers can exercise individual control.

The second feature of rainwater collection noted by Ray is its unreliability. Tanks are often empty for part of the year. Crop failures due to drought occur on runoff farms even though yields are *more* reliable than if runoff were not used at all. Thus grain banks or something similar are needed to insure a dependable food supply. An example cited is the trend away from rainwater usage in North Yemen, both for agricultural and domestic purposes, which is attributable to a demand for more reliable systems.

The third distinguishing feature of rainwater harvesting is the poverty of many of the areas where it is practised. A good groundwater supply developed for irrigation and also for domestic purposes offers more options for improved living standards than rainwater harvesting. Thus rainwater techniques tend to be observed mainly on the margins of cultivation, especially the edges of deserts, where they offer modest improvements in the living standards of very poor people. For many advocates of these techniques, that will be a central reason for promoting their development and use. Various technical measures are possible to bring the benefits of rainwater collection within reach of the poorest families. Innovations in low-cost roofing and small, inexpensive tanks have already been mentioned. Similarly, it may be possible to concentrate on low-cost contour bunding which poor farmers can use on their land, rather than more ambitious forms of runoff farming.

However, 'technical fixes' for the problems of poverty are unlikely to be enough. It will often be necessary for poor families to share resources if they are to gain from rainwater collection at all, perhaps sharing a tank, perhaps helping each other meet the labour requirements of construction, or perhaps joining together to bargain for land and water rights. If people feel strong preferences for doing things individually, or if they see one advantage of a household tank that it is under the family's individual control, collective action may not be acceptable. However, few communities are entirely lacking in channels for collective activity. For example, in writing about nomadic pastoralists, Sandford (1983) notes that while they traditionally value the freedom of the individual to manage his herds in his own way, they simultaneously value 'social relations' which limit the damage individuals might do to shared facilities such as livestock watering points; they also have forms of mutual help which improve chances of survival in time of drought. Similarly with other groups, it should be possible to identify areas where individual autonomy is regarded as important, and areas where it is possible for co-operation to secure economies of scale or to bring improvements in water supply within the reach of the very poor.

Thus a United Nations research programme has suggested, with admirable clarity, that 'mutual aid groups' should be considered 'the primary unit of development' for the low-income, 'marginalized' rural sector (UNRISD 1974). Examples cited in this book include 30–40 family groups of irrigators in the Indian Pani Panchayat programme, and groups of pastoralists in Niger with about 20 families in each. The United Nations recommendations are that a group of this sort should be an 'informal, self-selecting set of individuals with confidence in one another, on the basis of kinship, neighbourhood or friendship'. Once established, such groups should be registered and receive official recognition; they should be linked with larger agrarian organizations and peasant movements capable of representing common interests alongside other pressure groups such as those representing big farmers and traders. They should also serve the purpose of advancing grass roots training in technical skills, co-operative organization and self-management. In more practical terms, 'mutual aid groups could act as partnerships for farming . . . as credit societies . . . as

work teams for irrigation maintenance or soil conservation campaigns' —
or for rainwater tank construction and runoff farming.

FOOD AND ENVIRONMENT

For some western commentators, the most significant remark in the last
few pages will be the point that rainwater harvesting tends to be used, 'on
the margins of cultivation, especially the edges of deserts'. There is a school
of thought among environmentalists which sees loss of vegetation and
degradation of soils on desert margins as a far more serious long-term
problem than poverty and famine among the people who live there. Indeed,
Sandford (1983) accuses some of these environmentalists of 'astonishing
inhumanity' in their recommendations for halting and reversing 'desertification', not least because they hold local populations as being chiefly
responsible for the loss of vegetative cover and the spread of soil erosion.
They thus ignore the external pressures which favour cash crops over food
and so compel the extension of cultivation into areas which would be better
reserved for grazing. Having assigned blame this way, the same 'experts'
welcome natural disasters as 'squeezing out the inefficient'.

More positive environmentalist views, expressed by Eckholm and
Brown, stress that many problems of the desert margins would be soluble if
far more emphasis were given to food crops in the areas concerned. If yields
from such crops were to improve, pressures for the expansion of the
cultivated areas could be contained. A policy based on this principle would
undoubtedly involve runoff farming, both as a means of improving crop
production and yield reliability, and to control erosive runoff flows.

Even within this context, though, there could still be conflicts between
environmental concerns and local people's worries about the security of
their livelihoods. This is illustrated by the case-study from Burkina Faso in
the previous chapter. Western advisers wished to control soil erosion by
planting trees, whilst farmers wanted to reclaim eroded land for growing
grain. The solution ultimately arrived at, based on the building of contour
bunds, favoured the farmers's goals. However, it was still an effective
demonstration of how, when the natural vegetation which originally
limited erosion is removed, runoff control by bunds, terraces, check dams
and the like can prove a vital alternative means of controlling erosion.
Thus, on the desert fringes runoff farming can either be regarded as a
crutch to use in re-establishing trees and grass, or as a permanent feature,
allowing trees to be partially replaced by crops without the dangers of
desertification.

An example of runoff farming as a crutch for re-establishing grass cover
was the use of simple 'hoop' microcatchments in Kenya, discussed in
Chapter 6 (see also Figure 7.3). Once perennial grasses are flourishing
within the hoops and begin to spread beyond them, the grass itself binds the

soil together and retains runoff, and further maintenance of the hoops becomes unnecessary.

However, it is not only in marginal areas of Africa that conflicts of purpose between environmentalists and others influence prospects for rainwater collection. In Chapter 2, several reasons why urban policy-makers might favour rainwater collection in remote catchment areas were noted, including 'conservation' and a wish to reduce flood risks in crowded urban areas. In parts of India with relatively wet climates, trees planted on catchments can slow runoff and retain water during rain. Then, 'water harvesting is done by the trees' (Ray 1984), and the aims of policy-makers and environmentalists are met. However, the small farmers who work the land cannot afford the five years or more that it may take to start realizing a useful income from trees.

Where such conflicts between long-term environmental aims and short-term needs of farmers arise, Ray's views on India coincide with Wright's implied conclusions about Burkina Faso. Both agree that the proper role for development agencies is to accept the 'short-term first' strategy based on food production priorities. Experience seems to show that bunds and 'tanks' that provide immediate benefits in terms of cereal crop yield and reliability can be effective in reducing the most urgent erosion problems, and can lead on to tree planting below bunds or on catchment areas later.

The case-studies of rainwater collection presented in this book have illustrated three major aspects of the subject from three geographical vantage points: South-east Asia, India and Africa. One contrast here was between areas where shortage of water is a *resource constraint* for both agriculture and domestic needs, and areas where poor domestic supplies may exert *time constraints* on people's livelihoods. In Thailand and Indonesia, there were the examples of a very positive development of rainwater tanks in areas where rainfall is ample for agriculture, but where domestic water supplies are difficult to provide. In these areas, the main benefits of rainwater collection are neither environmental nor economic (in the 'market' sense), but are more concerned with people's livelihoods on the level of housing conditions and home production. One or two areas in Africa, notably in Kenya and Zimbabwe, illustrate the same points, though with much smaller programmes, and have provided some of the data presented in Table 8.1.

In India, agricultural usage predominates in all forms of water harvesting, but the context is one in which organization and institutional structure have favoured large-scale schemes, many dealing with floodwater rather than runoff — and hence strictly outside the scope of this book. That is true, for example, of percolation tanks in Maharashtra, although they have been quoted for the light they shed on the organization of cultivators and the potential of successful rural development to attract urban migrants back to the land (Chapter 2). Some khadins in Rajasthan (though not all) are true runoff farming devices with hillside catchments and valley cultivation in comparable conditions of landform and aridity to those of the Negev, but with strikingly different techniques to exploit summer rather than winter rains.

The third and most disturbingly problematic area for rainwater and runoff application has concerned 'drought-prone' areas in Africa. Arguably, runoff farming and related soil conversion measures are more desperately needed here than anywhere else, but it is precisely here that 'modernization' has appeared to reduce prospects for runoff agriculture, particularly where irrigation has been developed, where cash crops have been favoured, or where well-paid employment has drawn labour away from farming. Development is also complicated by the need to strike a balance between cultivation and pastoral development. However, growing awareness of the factors linking environmental degradation, food shortages and famine in these regions may result in a more positive view of runoff farming for crops and rainwater collection for pastoral use. Whether that translates into practical measures depends on the extent to which there are policy reforms giving more emphasis to food crops — reforms which would conflict with the vested interests of urban elites and western trading and financial blocs. However, it is to be hoped that the spectre of famine and economic collapse in much of Africa will erode some of this opposition. In its report for 1984, the United Nations Economic Commission for Africa warned of 'unparalleled catastrophe' if policy changes were not made, and if western action did not go beyond the limited food aid currently being given.

It is not, of course, the purpose of this book to campaign for policy changes, but rather to ensure that if they occur, and if they lead to a renaissance in the prospects for runoff farming, fieldworkers and agencies are adequately prepared. Thus, on one hand, they need to be prepared with technical expertise for exploiting what runoff farming and rainwater collection have to offer: greater (but not total) reliability in crop yields, an aid to re-establishing trees and grass cover, drinking water at critical if limited periods, and a more efficient use of water resources by collecting rainwater near to where it falls. On the other hand, many agencies need better understanding of local-level technical assistance — that is, how practical constraints which restrict implementation of new techniques can be identified and tackled. They also need better appreciation of how such assistance should build on traditional technology, and tie in with patterns of organization capable of sustaining rainwater techniques, whilst benefiting low-income groups and small farmers.

REFERENCES AND BIBLIOGRAPHY

Key: * books or papers recommended for *background* information, case-studies, or socio-economic analysis.

** denotes *practical* manuals recommended for details of construction of rainwater tanks, runoff farming methods, and/or related training procedures.

† short booklets or leaflets giving *practical* details of a single technique.

‡ unpublished material. Much of this is stored at ITDG Head Office, Myson House, Railway Terrace, Rugby, CV21 3HT, UK.

NB Volume numbers of journals are italicized whilst part numbers, where relevant, are placed in brackets. Thus 'Volume 3, number 4' abbreviates to *3* (4).

Ahmed, F., 1972 'Design parameters . . . Bangladesh'. Summarized in *Waterlog*, July 1982, pp 4-5. London: Earthscan.

‡Barrow, E. G. C., 1982. 'Use of microcatchments for tree-planting in soil conservation in semi-arid areas'. Soil and Water Conservation Workshop, University of Nairobi, Kenya.

Batchelor, S. J., 1985. 'Introducing appropriate technologies step by step'. *Waterlines, 3* (3), London: Intermediate Technology Publications.

‡Bateman, G., 1972. 'Interim report on a research project on low-cost water technologies'. London: ITDG.

Biggs, S., and Grosvenor-Alsop, R., 1984. *Developing Technologies for the Rural Poor*. London: Intermediate Technology Publications, Occasional Paper 11.

†Botswana Ministry of Agriculture, 1973. *How to Build a Water Catchment Tank*. Gaborone: Agricultural Information Service.

*Bradfield, M., 1971. *The Changing Pattern of Hopi Agriculture*. London: Royal Anthropological Institute.

Brittain, V., and Toulmin, C., 1984. 'The hungry eight in search of aid'. *The Guardian* (*Third World Review*) London, 14 December.

**Bruffaerts, J-C., 1984. *La construction des citernes: recueil et stockage des eaux de pluie*. Paris: GRET (Groupe de Recherche et d'Échanges Technologiques), Dossier No. 4.

Byrne, H., 1983. 'Clean water in Kola', *Waterlines, 1* (3), London: Intermediate Technology Publications.

Calvert K. C., and Binning, R. J., 1977. 'Low cost Water Tanks in the Pacific Islands'. *Appropriate Technology, 4* (3), London: Intermediate Technology Publications.

†Carruthers, I., 1983. (a) 'An economic view of some aspects of rural water investment'; Wye College, University of London; (b) 'Tackling economic issues in appropriate technology publications'. London: ITDG Agriculture Panel.

†CCSK, 1983. *Catching the Run-off Water* (and five other manuals in cartoon form). Communication Centre of Scientific Knowledge for Self Reliance (India) and United Nations University (Toho Seimei Building, Sibuya-ku, Tokyo 150).

‡Chambers, R., 1981. 'Gram Gourav Pratisthan, Naigaon, Pune District; notes on a field visit' Delhi: Ford Foundation.

Chambers, R., 1983. *Rural Development: Putting the Last First.* Harlow (England): Longmans.

Chambers, R., Longhurst, R., and Pacey, A., (eds.). 1981. *Seasonal Dimensions to Rural Poverty.* London: Frances Pinter.

*Chauhan, S. K., 1983. *Who puts the Water in the Taps? Community Participation in Third World Drinking Water, Sanitation and Health.* London and Washington DC: Earthscan.

Chauhan, S. K., and Gopalakrishnan, K., 1983. *A Million Villages, a Million Decades?* London and Washington DC: Earthscan.

‡Childers, L., 1984. 'Water and sanitation project, Yatta Plateau, Kenya'. Nairobi: UNICEF, Technology Support Section.

CIEPAC, 1980. *Niveau à eau: traçage des courbes de niveau.* Paris and Dakar: Centre International pour l'Education Permanente et l'Amenagement Concrete.

‡Classen, G. A., 1980. 'Consultant's report on small-scale Rural Water supplies'. Gaborone (Botswana): Ministry of Agriculture.

Clouet, Y., 1979. Possibilités d'améliorer les techniques agricoles: l'example du Yemen du Nord. *Actes du Colloque du CENECA.*

Collett, J., and Boyd, J., 1977. *Eight Simple Surveying Levels.* London: Intermediate Technology Publications, Agricultural Equipment leaflet No. 42.

‡Copperman, J., 1978. 'The impact of village water supplies in Botswana: a study of four villages'. Gaborone: SIDA Report.

‡Critchley, W. R. S., 1984. 'Runoff harvesting for crop, range and tree production in the BPSAAP area'. Marigat: Baringo Pilot Semi-Arid Area Project, Ministry of Agriculture and Livestock Development, Kenya.

‡Cullis, A. D., 1981. 'Rainwater harvesting in Turkana District: field notes'.

‡Cullis, A. D., 1983. 'Rainwater harvesting: drafts for a fieldworkers' handbook'. Reading, UK: ITDG.

*‡Cullis, A. D., 1984. 'A study of rainwater collection and storage systems in rural Africa'. M.Sc. dissertation, University of Salford, UK (plus supporting documentation).

Cullis, A. D., 1985. Private communication.

Denyer, S., 1978. *African Traditional Architecture*, London: Heinemann.

Doelhomid, S., 1982, 'Rain water cistern systems in Indonesia'. In: *Rain Water Cistern Systems*, see Fujimura, (ed), 1982.

Doody, M. C., 1980. Gibraltar's water supply. *Institution of Water Engineers, Transactions*, pp 151-4.

Drucker, D., 1985. 'Facing the people: the demystification of planning water supplies'. *Waterlines, 3* (3), London: Intermediate Technology Publications.

Dutt, G. R., 1981. 'Establishment of NaCl-treated catchments'. In: *Rainfall Collection for Agriculture in Arid and Semi-Arid Regions*, see Dutt et al. (eds.), 1981.

*Dutt, G. R., Huchinson, C. F., and Anaya Garduno, M., (eds.) 1981. *Rainfall Collection for Agriculture in Arid and Semi-Arid Regions*. Proceedings of a Workshop at the University of Arizona (U.S.A.) and Chapingo Postgraduate College (Mexico). Slough, UK: Commonwealth Agricultural Bureaux.

*Eckholm, E., and Brown, L. R., 1977. *Spreading Deserts: the Hand of Man*. Washington, DC: Worldwide Institute, Paper No. 13.

**Edwards, D., Keller, K., and Yohalem, D., 1984. *A Workshop Design for Rainwater Roof Catchment Systems: a Training Guide*. Washington DC: U.S. Agency for International Development, WASH project, WASH Technical Report No. 27.

El Amami, S., 1977. 'Utilization of runoff waters . . . in Tunisia'. *African Environment, 3* (3-4), pp 107-120. Dakar, Senegal: ENDA.

Evenari, M., 1968-71. 'Runoff farming in the desert' (in five parts with various co-authors). *Agronomy Journal, 60-63*. Wisconsin: American Society of Agronomy.

*Evenari/Mashash, 1975. *Fields and Pastures in Deserts*, edited by 'the management of the experimental farm Wadi Mashash' (M. Evenari, U. Nessler, A. Rogel, and O. Schenk). Darmstadt: Eduard Roether (Enquiries to 6114 Groß-Umstadt, Bodenäcker 10, W. Germany).

*Evenari, M., Shanan, L., and Tadmor, N., 1982. *The Negev: the Challenge of a Desert*. Cambridge (Mass.): Harvard University Press, 2nd edition (1st edition: 1971).

Evenson, R. F., 1981. 'Food policy and the new home economics'. *Food Policy, 7*, pp 180-192. UK.

Fallon, L. E., 1963. *Water Spreading in Turkana* (illustrated booklet). Nairobi: U.S. Agency for International Development, Mission to Kenya.

Fangmeir, D. D., 1975. 'Crop production by water harvesting'. In: *Proceedings of the Water Harvesting Symposium*. see Frasier (ed.) 1975.

FAO, 1983. *The State of Food and Agriculture 1982*. Rome: Food and Agriculture Organization of the United Nations.

‡Farrar, D. M. 1974. 'Aspects of water supply and conservation in some semi-arid regions of Africa'. Ph.D. thesis, University of Manchester Institute of Science and Technology, UK.

‡Farrar, D. M., and Pacey, A. J., 1974. 'Africa Fieldwork and Technology, No. 6., 'Catchment tanks in southern Africa'.

Feachem, R., Burns, E., Cairncross, S., Cronin, A., and Cross, P., Curtis, D., Ichan, M. K., Lamb, D., and Southall, H., 1978. *Water, Health and Development: an Interdisciplinary Study*. London: Tri Med Books.

Fierro, L. C., 1981. 'Water-catchment practices for range seeding in northern Mexico'. In: *Rainfall Collection for Agriculture in Arid and Semi-Arid Regions*. See Dutt *et al.* (eds.) 1981.

‡Finkel, M., 1984. 'Report on water harvesting in Turkana, Kenya'. Rome: FAO, document GCP/KEN/048/MOD

*Frasier, G. W., (ed.), 1975. *Proceedings of the Water Harvesting Symposium, Phoenix, Arizona, 1974*. Berkeley (Calif.): USDA Agricultural Research Service (ref: ARS–W–22).

‡Fricke, T. B., 1982. 'Bamboo-reinforced concrete rainwater collection tanks . . . in Thailand'. Washington, DC: A.T. International Working Paper.

Frith, J. L., 1975. 'Design and construction of roaded catchments'. In: *Proceedings of the Water Harvesting Symposium*. See Frasier, (ed.), 1975.

Fujimura, F. N., (ed.), 1982. *Rain Water Cistern Systems* (conference proceedings). Honolulu: Water Resources Research Centre.

George, S., 1980. *Feeding the Few: Corporate Control of Food*. Washington, DC, and Amsterdam, Institute of Policy Studies.

Gibberd, V., 1969. 'Summary of research and development at Radisele'. Appendix 2 in: *The Introduction of Rainwater Catchment Tanks and Micro-irrigation to Botswana*, London: ITDG.

Gibberd, V., 1981. Contribution to *Serowe: Village of the Rain Wind*, by Bessie Head. London: Heinemann.

Gibberd, V., 1982. Interview. *People's Workbook*. Johannesburg: Environment and Development Agency.

‡Gonzalez, F. J. 1972. 'The water supply in Gibraltar'. Paper presented at the Barcelona conference. Gibraltar: Public Works Department.

Gordillo, T., Gonzalez, E., and Gaona, S., 1982. 'History of Yucatan cisterns'. In *Rain Water Cistern Systems*. See Fujimura (ed.) 1982.

‡Gould, J. E., 1983. (a) Preliminary report on rainwater catchment in Botswana, and four subsequent reports; (b) Rainwater catchment systems in Matabeleland, Zimbabwe; (c) Report on rainwater catchment in Kenya; (d) M.Sc. thesis forthcoming, University of Alberta, Canada.

*Gould, J. E., 1984. 'Rainwater catchment systems in Botswana: past,

present and future'. *Waterlines, 2* (4). London: Intermediate Technology Publications.

Greeley, M., 1978. 'Appropriate rural technology: recent Indian experience with farm-level storage research'. *Food Policy, 3*, pp 39-49, Washington.

‡Grover, B., 1971. 'Harvesting precipitation for community water supplies'. M.Sc. thesis, University of Manitoba. (Verbatim extracts appear in UNEP, 1983, pp 93-113).

‡Guggenheim, H., 1974. 'Fighting the drought'. Report to Wunderman Foundation, Madison Avenue, New York.

Guggenheim, H. and Fanale, R., 1976. 'Shared technology: a project for water storage and irrigation in Dogon villages'. *African Environment, 2*, supplement: Occasional Paper No. 76-1.

Hall, D., 1974. 'Collect rainwater for your house and garden'. *Young Farmers' Club News* (Zimbabwe/Rhodesia), August 1974, p 4.

‡Hall, D. 1975. Private communication.

Hall, N., 1981. 'Has thatch a future?' *Appropriate Technology, 8* (3), London: Intermediate Technology Publications.

Hall, N., 1982. 'Water collection from thatch'. *Waterlines, 1* (1), London: Intermediate Technology Publications.

‡Hartley, B., 1981. 'Lokitaung water harvesting project, Salvation Army'. Oxford: Oxfam, file KEN 109.

Hillman, F., 1980. Water harvesting in Turkana District, Kenya. London: Overseas Development Institute, Pastoral Network Paper 10d (cyclostyled).

Hinton, W., 1984. 'The instability behind the new boom in agriculture'. *The Guardian (Third World Review)*, 27 September, p 11. London.

‡Hlekweni, 1975. (a) Director's Reports, Friends Rural Training Centre, Hlekweni, near Bulawayo: (b) Reports to Oxfam, Oxford from the Friends Rural Training Centre, files RHO 8, RHO 10; (c) Ben Henson, private communication.

Hoey, P. J., and West, S. F., 1982. 'Rainwater supply systems for South Australia'. In *Rain Water Cistern Systems*. See Fujimura, (ed.) 1982.

Hofkes, E. H., 1981. *Small Community Water Supplies*. The Hague: International Reference Centre for Community Water Supply, Technical Paper Series, 18.

‡Hofkes, E. H., 1981. 'Rainwater harvesting for drinking water supply and sanitation'. Draft, revised for publication, IRC, The Hague (1981).

‡Howlett, D., 1983. Soils investigation in Turkana District, N.W. Kenya. Ph.D. thesis, University of Reading, UK.

**Hudson, N., 1971. *Soil Conservation*. London: Batsford.

ICHS, 1972. 'Agricultural use of floods in Africa'. *Liaison Bulletin of the Interafrican Committee for Hydraulic Studies*, (CIEH, Ouagadougou), No. 10, August, pp 13-17.

†Institute for Rural Water. 1982. *Water for the World* (brief technical

notes), e.g. (a) Evaluating rainfall catchments, technical note No. RWS 1P5; (b) Designing a household cistern, technical note No. RWS 5D1. Washington, DC: U.S. Agency for International Development.

Ionides, M. G., 1939. *Report on the Water Resources of Transjordan and their Development*. London: Publications of the Government of Transjordan.

Ionides, M. G., 1966. 'Rainwater catchment tanks'. *ITDG Bulletin*, No. 1, pp 10-12. London: ITDG (reprinted as an appendix by Moody, 1969).

‡Ionides, M. G., 1976. Private communications, (a) with ITDG Water Panel; (b) quoted by G. McRobie, *Small is Possible*. London: Jonathan Cape, 1981, pp 44-5.

IRC, 1979. *Public Standpost Water Supplies*. The Hague: International Reference Centre for Community Water Supply, Technical Paper Series 13.

*IRC, 1981. *Rainwater Harvesting for Drinking Water Supply*, The Hague: International Reference Centre for Community Water Supply, Training Modules Series.

Irish, J. L., Sukarno, and Murdiyarso, D., 1982. 'Reliability of roof runoff in Indonesia'. In: *Rain Water Cistern Systems*, see Fujimura (ed.), 1982.

**IWACO, 1982. *Construction Manual for a 10m³ Rainwater Reservoir of Ferrocement*. Rotterdam: International Water Supply Consultants.

Jones, O. R., and Hauser, V. L., 1975. 'Runoff utilization for grain production'. In: *Proceedings of the Water Harvesting Symposium*, see Frasier (ed.) 1975.

Kalinin, G. P., and Bykov, V. D., 1969. 'The world's water resources, present and future'. *Impact of Science on Society* (UNESCO), *19* (2), pp 135-150.

**Kaufman, M., 1983. *From Ferro to Bamboo: a case study and technical manual*. Yogyakarta (Indonesia): Yayasan Dian Desa.

‡Kay, J. 1983. 'Comments on hydrology . . . on water quality'. Informal paper for ITDG.

*Keller, K., 1982. *Rainwater Harvesting for Domestic Supply in Developing Countries: a draft literature review*, Washington DC: U.S Agency for International Development, Office of Health, WASH Working Paper No. 20.

Kerkvoorden, R. van, 1982. 'Rainwater collectors for villages in West Java'. In: *Rain Water Cistern Systems*, see Fujimura, (ed.), 1982.

Kolarkar, A. S., Murthy, K. N. K., and Singh, N., 1980. 'Water harvesting and runoff farming in arid Rajasthan'. *Indian Journal of Soil Conservation*, *8* (2), pp 113-119.

Kolarkar, A. S., Murthy, K. N. K., and Singh, N., 1983. 'Khadin — a method of harvesting water for agriculture in the Thar Desert', *Journal of Arid Environments, 6*, pp 59-66, London.

Krantz, B. A., 1981. 'Rainfall collection and utilization in the semi-arid tropics'. In: *Rainfall Collection for Agriculture in Arid and Semi-arid Regions*, see Dutt *et al.*, 1981.

*Kutsch, H., 1982. *Principal Features of a form of Water Concentrating Culture*. Trier Geographical Studies No. 5; Trier (West Germany): Geographisch Gesekkschaft Trier. (one of the most valuable available books, but badly translated into English).

Laing, I. A. F., 1981. 'Rainfall collection in Australia'. In: *Rainfall Collection for Agriculture in Arid and Semi-Arid Regions*, see Dutt *et al.* (eds), 1981.

Latham, B. G., 1984. 'Building a Thai jumbo water jar using a brick form'. *Waterlines, 3* (2), London: Intermediate Technology Publications.

‡Latham, B. G., 1984. 'Rainwater collection programme of Yayasan Dian Desa in Indonesia'. Report to ITDG, London

Layton, S., 1984. *Profile of a Small-scale Rural Industry*, Kieta (North Solomons Province): Village Industry and Training Unit. (Summarized in Layton, S., 'Progress with ferrocement tanks in Papua New Guinea, North Solomons Province', *Waterlines, 3* (2),) London: Intermediate Technology Publications.

Layton, S., 1984. 'Progress with ferrocement tanks in Papua New Guinea (North Solomons Province)', *Waterlines, 3* (2), London: Intermediate Technology Publications.

Lee, G. F., and Jones, R. A., 1982. 'Quality of the Virgin Islands household cistern water supplies'. In: *Rain Water Cistern Systems*, see Fujimura (ed.), 1982.

Lloyd, B., 1982. 'Water quality surveillance'. *Waterlines, 1* (2), London: Intermediate Technology Publications.

Luebs, R. E., and Laag, A. E., 1975. 'Water harvesting for barley'. In: *Proceedings of the Water Harvesting Symposium*, see Frasier (ed.), 1975.

McDowell, J., 1976. *Village Technology in Eastern Africa*. Nairobi: UNICEF Regional Office (60 page booklet).

McRobie, G., 1983. 'We're not talking about revolution'. *Ceres (FAO Review)*, no. 3, pp 33-8. Rome: Food and Agriculture Organization of the United Nations.

‡Maddocks, D., 1973. 'Report on rainwater catchment project, Jamaica'. London: Overseas Development Administration.

‡Maddocks, D., 1975. 'Methods of creating low-cost waterproof membranes for use in construction of rainwater catchment and storage systems'. London: ITDG.

Maikano, G., and Nyberg, L., 1980. 'Rainwater catchment in Botswana'. In: *Rural Water Supply in Developing Countries* (Proceedings of a workshop in Zomba, Malawi). Ottawa, International Development Research Centre, document 167e.

Marchal, J. Y., 1977. 'The evolution of agrarian systems: the example of Yatenga'. *African Environment, 3*.

**Matlock, W. G., and Dutt, G. R., 1984. *A Primer on Water Harvesting*

and Runoff Farming. College of Agriculture, University of Arizona, Irrigation and Water Management Institute.

Merabet, Z., 1984. 'How the Yemen is trying to meet the aims of the Water Decade'. *Waterlines, 2* (4), London: Intermediate Technology Publications.

‡Molvaer, R. K., 1982. 'Processes of change involving appropriate technology'. Nairobi: UNICEF Regional Office.

Moody, P., 1969. *The Introduction of Rainwater Catchment Tanks and Micro-Irrigation to Botswana*. London: ITDG.

‡Moody, P., 1971. 'Report on the state of the Botswana catchment tank project after three years of operation'. London: ITDG.

‡Moody, P., 1972. 'Annual report of the water catchment tank programme'. Mbabane (Swaziland): Ministry of Local Administration, Government of Swaziland.

Morgan, W. T. W., 1974. 'Sorghum gardens in South Turkana'. *Geographical Journal, 140*, pp 80-93.

Morin, G. C. A., and Matlock, W. G., 1975. 'Desert strip farming — computer simulation'. In: *Proceedings of the Water Harvesting Symposium,* see: Frasier, (ed.), 1975.

Myers, L. E., 1975. 'Water harvesting 2000 BC to 1974 AD'. In: *Proceedings of the Water Harvesting Symposium*, see Frasier, (ed), 1975.

Nabhan, G. P., 1979. 'Ecology of floodwater farming in arid south-western North America'. *Agro-Ecosystems*, 5, pp 245-55.

Nabhan, G. P., 1984. Soil fertility renewal and water harvesting in Sonoran desert agriculture. *Arid Lands Newsletter*, No. 20, pp 20-28.

*NAS, 1973. *Ferrocement Applications in Developing Countries*, Washington, DC: National Academy of Sciences.

*NAS, 1974. (a) *More Water for Arid Lands*; (b) *Roofing in Developing Countries*. Washington DC: National Academy of Sciences.

Nation, 1984. 'The project that holds water'. *The Nation Sunday Special*, Bangkok, October 21st.

Nessler, U., 1980. 'Ancient techniques aid modern arid zone agriculture'. *Kidma: Israel Journal of Development, 5* (4), pp 3-7.

Nimpuno, K., 1978. 'Criteria for evaluating excreta disposal techniques'. In: *Sanitation in Developing Countries*, ed. A Pacey, Chichester (England): John Wiley & Sons.

Ninez, V. K., 1984. Household gardens: theoretical considerations on an old survival strategy. Lima: International Potato Centre.

**Nissen-Petersen, E., 1982. *Rain catchment and water supply in rural Africa*. London: Hodder and Stoughton.

Nissen-Petersen, E., 1985. 'Water from rocks', *Waterlines, 3* (3): London: Intermediate Technology Publications.

‡Nopmongcol, P., Vadhanavlkkit, C., Thiensiripipat, N., Viwathanathepa, S., Bunyaratpan, V., and Sethaputra, C., 1981. 'Roof catchment

(Thailand), Progress and Financial Report to IDRC for July-December 1981'. Khon Kaen University, Thailand.

Novieku, E., 1980. *Rainfall Harvesting Techniques in Ghana*, (short booklet). Accra: Water Resources Research Unit, Council for Scientific and Industrial Research.

Oluwande, P. A., 1978. 'The potential of the aqua-privy'. In: *Sanitation in Developing Countries*, ed. A. Pacey, Chichester (England): John Wiley and Sons.

‡Omwenga, J. M., 1984. 'Rainwater harvesting for domestic water supply in Kisii, Kenya'. Thesis: Tampere University of Technology.

O'Reilley, C., 1984. Yayasan Dian Desa Rainwater Harvesting case study. Report for ITDG, London.

*Pacey, A., 1980. *Rural Sanitation: Planning and Appraisal*. London: Intermediate Technology Publications.

Pacey, A., 1983. *The Culture of Technology*. Oxford: Basil Blackwell (Chapter 8 is relevant).

Pacey, A., and ITDG Water Panel, 1977. *Water for the Thousand Millions*. Oxford: Pergamon Press.

Parker, R. N., 1973. 'Catchment systems for rural water supplies'. In: *Agriculture in South East Ghana*, Vol. 2, by G. E. Dalton and R. N. Parker. Reading (UK): University Department of Agricultural Economics, Study No. 13.

Parry, J. M., 1981. 'Development and testing of roof cladding materials for fibre reinforced cement', *Appropriate Technology, 8* (2), London: Intermediate Technology Publications.

Parulkar, V., 1982. 'Pani Panchayat can save Bombay'. *Imprint*, April issue, pp 7-16.

Payne, P., 1985, in *Agricultural Development and Nutrition*, ed. A. Pacey and P. Payne, London: Hutchinson.

Perrens, S. J., 1982. (a) 'Design strategy for domestic rainwater systems in Australia'; (b) 'Effect of rationing on reliability of domestic rainwater systems'. In: *Rainwater Cistern Systems*, see Fujimura (ed.) 1982.

‡Perron, Y., 1978. 'Approvisionnement en eau: eaux de ruisellement; système des Meskats du Sahel de Sausae'. Paris: GRET Fiche T.288.

‡Podchivalov, V., 1983. 'Problems affecting growth of various crops under spate irrigation in PDR Yemen'. FAO/World Bank Report, PDY/81/001.

Power, G., 1983. 'Bamboo reinforces Thai roof rainwater tank'. *World Water*, July issue, pp 61-3.

‡Prasad, R., 1979. 'Rural technologies for utilizing surface waters', lecture No. 8.2. Bangalore: Department of Civil Engineering, Indian Institute of Science (verbatim extracts appear in UNEP 1983, pp 149-157, 160-164).

Pratt, D. J., and Gwynne, M. D., 1977. *Rangeland Management and Ecology in East Africa*. London: Hodder and Stoughton.

Rao, A. V. R., 1975. 'Roofing with low-cost corrugated asphalt sheets'.

Appropriate Technology, *1* (4) London: Intermediate Technology Publications.

*‡Ray, D., 1983. 'Rainwater Harvesting Project: Socio-economic case studies, Volume 1'. Report for ITDG, London.

*‡Ray, D., 1984. 'Rainwater Harvesting Project: Socio-economic case studies', Volume 2, INDIA. Report for ITDG, London.

Richards, K., 1972. 'Rainwater harvesting for domestic purposes'. *Rhodesia Agriculture Journal* Technical Bulletin No. 15, Salisbury (Zimbabwe/Rhodesia).

Riesman, P., 1977. *Freedom in Fulani Social Life*. Chicago and London: Chicago University Press.

Robertson, A. C., 1953. *The Hafir: what-why-where-how?* Ministry of Agriculture, Government of Sudan, Bulletin No. 1.

Romeo, C., 1982. 'A water quality argument for rainwater catchment development in Belau'. In *Rain Water Cistern Systems*, see Fujimura (ed.) 1982.

*Sandford, S., 1983. *Management of Pastoral Development in the Third World*. London: ODI, and Chichester (England): John Wiley & Sons.

Saunders, R. J., and Warford, J. J., 1976. *Village Water Supply: Economics and Policy*. Baltimore and London: Johns Hopkins University Press.

**Shanan, L., and Tadmor, N. H., 1979. *Micro-Catchment Systems for Arid Zone Development*, 2nd revised edition. Jerusalem: Hebrew University, and Rehovat: Ministry of Agriculture.

Sharma, K. D., and Joshi, D. C., 1981. 'Nadis, the vital water resource of the Indian arid zone'. *Journal of Arid Environments, 4*, pp 247-251, London.

‡Sinclair, A., 1983. (a) 'Domestic rainwater harvesting, North Kitui, Kenya'. Report for ITDG: (b) 'Present and potential water supply and use in Kyuso Division, North Kitui, Kenya'. Final Report to Action Aid and ITDG.

‡Soedjarwo, A., 1981. (a) 'Traditional technology — obstacle or resource? Bamboo-cement rainwater collectors and cooking stoves'. Paper presented at the Project on Sharing Traditional Technology (STT), United Nations University, Tokyo; (b) 'Bamboo-cement rainwater containers in Ngestireso'. Yayasan Dian Desa Report for 1980, Yogyakarta.

‡Sparkes, K. F., 1974. Interim report by the Water Engineering Adviser, Turks and Caicos Islands.

‡Stern, P. H., 1975. 'Cisterns for the Ogaden area'. Report to the National Water Resources Commission, Ethiopia.

Stern, P. H., 1978. 'Rural water development in arid regions'. *Progress in Water Technology, 11*, (1 and 2).

‡Stern, P. H., 1978. 'Report on Mahweit Town Water Supply and other water projects in Mahweit County'. Report for Save the Children Fund.

*Stern, P. H., 1979. *Small-scale Irrigation*. London: Intermediate Technology Publications.

Stern, P. H., 1982. 'Rainwater harvesting'. *Waterlines, 1* (1), London: Intermediate Technology Publications.

‡Stewart, N., 1960. 'Land and water resources in Tripolitania'. Report for U.S. Agency for International Development.

Swift, J., 1977. 'Pastoral development in Somalia'. In: *Environmental Degradation in and around Arid Lands*, ed. M. H. Glantz. Boulder (Colorado): Westview Press.

‡Swift, J., 1984. Private communication.

‡SWW, 1984. Private communication, South West Water Authority, Exeter, confirming advice to consumers, 'to install rainwater butts'.

Thomas, A., and Lockett, M., 1978. *Choosing Appropriate Technology*, Milton Keynes, UK Open University Press, Course Unit T361 15–16.

‡Thomas, R. G., 1982.(a) Back-to-office report to PDR Yemen; (b) Ancient spate irrigation in Wadi Beihan, PDR Yemen. Rome: Food and Agriculture Organization of the United Nations (FAO).

‡Thomson, J., 1980. Oxfam microcatchment project, preliminary evaluation. Oxford: Oxfam.

‡Tutweiler, R., 1980. 'Social aspects of water distribution and consumption in a subdistrict of Mahweit Province, Yemen'. American Save the Children Fund.

Twose, N., 1984. *Why the Poor Suffer Most: Drought and the Sahel*. Oxford: Oxfam Behind-the-Weather Booklet.

UNESCO, 1981. *Inventaire des techniques appropriées pour l'utilisation et la conservation rationnelles des resources en eau . . . systems de collect des eaux de pluie*. Dakar (Senegal): Regional Office of Science and Technology for Africa.

*UNEP, 1983. *Rain and Stormwater Harvesting in Rural Areas*. ed. United Nations Environmental Programme. Dublin: Tycooly International.

UNICEF, 1979. Sudan Government/UNICEF Co-operative Drinking Water Project: Rectification (clearing of hafirs).

UNICEF, 1982. 'From Kenya — how to make plastered basket tanks for storing water'. *Appropriate Technology, 8* (4), pp 7–8.

†UNICEF, 1984. Compound catchment ferrocement water tank. Nairobi: UNICEF Technology Support Section.

†UNICEF, n.d. *The Bamboo-Reinforced Water Tank*. Nairobi: UNICEF Technical Support Section.

†UNICEF, n.d. *Cement Jars for Storage of Grain or Water*. Nairobi: Village Technology Unit.

†UNICEF, n.d. booklet on 'Bamboo-reinforced Concrete Tank Construction' (in Thai). Source for Figures 4.1 and 5.9).

UNRISD, 1974. *The Social and Economic Implications of Large-Scale Introduction of new Varieties of Foodgrain*. Geneva: United Nations Research Institute for Social Development.

VITA, 1973. *Village Technology Handbook*. Washington, DC: Volunteers in Technical Assistance.

VITA, 1977. *Using Water Resources*. Washington, DC: Volunteers in Technical Assistance, VITA Press.

‡Vogler, J., 1982. 'Field visit to inspect rainwater installations in and around Mandeville, Jamaica'. Report for ITDG, London.

Waller, D. H., 1982. 'Rain water as a water supply source in Bermuda'. In: *Rain Water Cistern Systems*, see Fujimura (ed.), 1982.

‡Water Panel, 1974. Draft leaflet on water catchment from roofs. London: ITDG Water Panel Sub-committee.

‡Watkins, J., 1974. 'Report on rural water supply project, Fundacao Ruralista, Piaui, North-east Brazil'. London: ODA.

Watt, S. B., 1975. 'Water jars from cement mortar'. *Appropriate Technology*, 2 (2), London: Intermediate Technology Publications.

**Watt, S. B., 1978. *Ferrocement Water Tanks and their Construction*. London: Intermediate Technology Publications.

‡Wheeler, D., and Lloyd, B. J., 1983. 'Some microbiological and physico-chemical aspects of rainwater harvesting: a report commissioned by ITDG'. Guildford, University of Surrey.

*Whitcombe, R., 1983. 'A. T. institutions: the missing piece'. *Appropriate Technology*, 9 (4), pp 1-4.

*White, G. F., Bradley, D. J., and White, A. U., 1972. *Drawers of Water: Domestic Water Use in East Africa*. Chicago: Chicago University Press.

**Whiteside, M., 1982. *How to build a Water Catchment Tank* (booklet). Gaborone (Botswana): Government Printer, for Mahalapye Development Trust.

WHO, 1981. Community Participation in Water and Sanitation. Geneva: World Health Organization.

WHO, 1983. Minimum evaluation procedure for water supply and sanitation projects. Geneva: World Health Organization, documents ETS/83.1 and CDD/ORR/83.1.

Wickens, G. E., and White, L. P., 1978. Land-use in the southern margins of the Sahara. In: *Management of Semi-Arid Ecosystems*, ed. B. H. Walker, Amsterdam: Elsevier Scientific Publications.

Winarto, 1981. 'Rainwater collection tanks constructed on a self-help basis'. *Journal of Ferrocement, 11* (3), pp 247-254, Bangkok: RERIC.

World Bank, 1984. *Towards sustained development in Sub-Saharan Africa*. Washington DC: The World Bank.

Wright, P., 1984. Private communication quoting an unpublished paper by P. Wright and E. G. Bonkoungou.

Wright, P., 1984. Report on runoff farming and soil conservation in Yatenga, Upper Volta (Burkina Faso). Report to Oxfam, Oxford.

INDEX *(with GLOSSARY)*

Unusual words, and terms used with special or restricted meanings, are explained in the following two ways:

1. By an explanatory phrase or synonym placed in brackets within the index entry.
2. By page references to fuller definitions where these are given in the text of the book.

Page numbers set in *italics* refer to illustrations and their captions or to information 'boxes'.

Afghanistan, 6
Africa, environmental crisis, 127, 157, 183-4, 195; pastoralists, 25-9, 40, 163-4; run-off farming, *128*, 130, 133, 150-5, 160-2; Sahel region, 28, 128, *147*, 154, 184; *see also* names of individual countries
agencies, *see* development agencies
agricultural policies, 127, 183-5, 191, 193-5
agriculture, *see* crops, farmers, irrigation, livestock, runoff farming
ahars (large contour bunds with inundated land, India), *39*, 41, 131, 139, 186; definition, construction, 135-6, *137*
aluminium foil catchments, 19
animal husbandry, 27-8, 35; *see also* livestock
arid regions, 3, 130, 131, 181; pastoralism in, 31, 57, *58*, 179; *see also* deserts, semi-arid areas
Arizona, 133, 145, 151-2
asphalt, 19, 50
Australia, 6, 17, 23, 135, 150, 182; domestic rainwater use, 59, 60, 75-6; population using rainwater, 3, 20

bacteria, survival in tanks, 63-4, 65
bamboo-cement tanks, 62, 69, 74; construction method, 85, *86*, 116, *120*; cost of, 110, 111; durability, 88, 115, 119-121, 123; inlet filters on, *102*, 105
bamboo gutters, 18, 105, *106*
bamboo matting framework, 119, *120*
bamboo rafters, *18*, *104*
bamboo-reinforced concrete tanks, 49, 62, 74, 75, *107*; construction and materials, 116-118, 121, *122*, 123; costs, 77, 111; design tolerance, 115, 121
Bangladesh, 66
basket-framed tanks, 45, 46, *48*; *see also* Ghala tanks
Belau (Pacific Island), 63
Bermuda, 5, 22, 59, 63, 65, 100, *101*
bitumen, 19
boreholes, 29, 63, 183, 185, 190-1
Botswana, 25, 37, 43, 46, 145, 189; arable lands programme (ALDEP), *94*, 95-7; excavated tanks, 65, 90, *91*, *96*, 126; household tanks, 12, 17-18, 59, 60, 114; school tanks, 91-3, *94*; threshing floors, 19, 20, 55
brickwork tanks, 62, 110, 112, *113*, 114; in Zimbabwe, 74, 82, 84
builders, 72, 73, 80, 83, 94; training for, 97, 99
bunds (earth banks or low dams), *136*, *137*, 139, 142, *156*; construction method, *143*;

stone-built 'bunds', *148*, 166-7, *168*;
  see also, ahars, contour bunds, hoops,
  khadins, microcatchments
Burkina Faso, 154, 159-166, 185, 191, 193;
  Yatenga contour barriers, 170-3, *174*,
  176, 179, 183, 187
business development, 73, 79, 82, 83, 114,
  181
butyl rubber, 19-20, 55, 90, 110, 125

Canada, 23
Caribbean region, 14, 23, 63
catchments (watersheds), 8-9, 15, 17-21,
  55, 125; see also ground catchments,
  microcatchments, roaded catchments,
  rock catchments, roofs
cement, 74, 77, 80, 123; materials derived
  from, 50, 108-110, 114-123; quantities
  for tank construction, 116, 117; see also
  bamboo-cement, ferrocement, sisal
  cement
cement block construction, 112, 113
cement mortar jars, 78, 108; fibre-
  reinforced, 119; unreinforced, 84, *109*,
  115, 117; wire-reinforced Jumbo jars,
  108, 110-111, 116; see also Ghala tanks,
  ferrocement tanks
cement/sand mixes for mortar, 46, *48*, *81*,
  109, 118
cereal crops, 132, 177; grown by runoff
  farming, 136, 138, 139, 140, 166-7;
  reliability of yield, 159-60, 184, 185,
  191, 194; see also millet, sorghum
chemical soil treatments, 3, 19, 55
China, 41, *124*, 133, 135
chlorine, *88*
cisterns (underground tanks), 1, *3*, 15, 63,
  123, *124*; for livestock water, 25, *27*, 28,
  57, 58; under houses, 12, 181; for
  cisterns above ground, see tanks
climate, 3-5, 23, 60, *128*, 128-131
commercial aspects of projects, 73, 79, 80,
  82-4, 87, 97
communal tanks, 5, 45, 51, 125, 190, 191
community workers, 74, 77, 79, 84, 93, 115
concrete, 118, 121; bamboo-reinforced, 49,
  121-3; catchment surfaces, 20, 55, 79,
  80, 96; curing of, *81*, 90, *109*, 115, 121
concrete blocks, 112, 113
concrete ring tanks, 84, 115, 116, 189
consumption (of water), 54, 56-8, 59, 60
contour barriers (permeable stone
  'bunds'), *148*, 166-7, *168*, 170-3, 176, 177;
  benefits of, 186, 187, 193
contour bunds (or ridges), 144-6, *146*, *147*,
  186
contour farming, 144-8

contour lines, surveys of, 167, *169*, *170*,
  171
contour ridges, 144, 145, *146*, *147*, 155,
  182
contour strips, 15, 19, 129, 133, 145, *146*,
  147, 148; definition of, 9, *10*;
  construction method, *147*; see also
  contour bunds, terraces
cooking, 32, 35, 190; stoves, 74, 159
co-operatives, 40, 84, 176, 178
corrugated iron, formwork made from, *81*,
  122; on ground catchments, 14, *16*;
  roofing, *47*, 50, *76*, 77, 100, *107*
corrugated iron tanks, 62, 78, 79, 110, 111;
  see also galvanized iron tanks
costs, see economic analysis, and tanks,
  cost of
cow-dung plaster, 20, 46, 55
craftsmen, 44, 45, 82-3, 110; training of,
  74, 78-9, 83; see also builders, masons
crops, 32, 34, 35, 163-4; cash crops, 184,
  185, 193, 195; early planting with water,
  36, 127; moisture requirements of, 44,
  52, 132, 136, 155; planting density of,
  142, 144, 150, *151*, 155; runoff farming
  and, 129, 138, 159-60, 191; see also
  cereal crops, millet, sorghum, vegetables
crop storage, 44; see also grain banks,
  granary storage bins
curing of concrete and mortar, *81*, 90, *109*,
  115, 116, 121
cuvettes (shallow cultivated basins, West
  Africa), 151

dams, 1, 5, 8, 16, 25, 37; as 'tanks' in
  India, 17, *39*, *40*, 166, 191, 194; see also
  bunds, hafirs, percolation tanks
depression storage, 7
desalination, 16, 23
desertification, 28, 165, 183, 193
deserts, 3, 24, 144, 181, 192, 193; see also
  Negev Desert
desert strips, 145, 147; see also contour
  strips
design criteria, for rainwater tanks, 34, 99,
  114, 116; for runoff farming, 155-7
design tolerance (for poor workmanship),
  115, 116, 121
development agencies, 71, 163, 178, 181,
  194, 195; locally based, 69, 74, 85, 90,
  93, 174, 178; non-commercial bias, 82,
  181; responsibilities in technology
  choice, 88, 158-9, 173, 174; technical
  assistance by, 73, 78, 84, 89, 97, 98; see
  also 'parent' organizations
dew, 6
dissemination of techniques, 23-5, 72-3,

173; *see also* replication of techniques
diversion structures (in floodwater
systems), 8, *11*, 133, 135, 152
downpipes, 82, 100, 103, 105, *106*; adapted
for foul flush diversion, *64*, *102*, 105, *107*
drinking water supply, 15, 61, 65; *see also*
water quality, water supply

economic analysis, 30, 31-2, 37-8; of runoff
farming, 181-3, 186-7
employment opportunities, 31, 36, 38, 110,
114, 116, 185; *see also* labour,
livelihoods
England, rainwater collection in, 6, 23
environmental degradation, 28, 46, 165-6,
183, 185, 195
erosion control, 37, 152, 164-7, 178, 193;
see also soil conservation, soil erosion
Ethiopia, 25, 165
evaluation, 88, 97
evaporation, 1, 7, 55, 185; losses from
tanks, 39, 58, 119; rates of, 52, *53*, 130,
136
excavated tanks, 12, 15, 16, 65, 70, 123-6;
butyl rubber linings, 90; ferrocement
linings, *80*, 95, *96*, 97, *112*; mud/polythene
linings, 90, *91*; unlined, 95; *see also*
cisterns, hafirs
extension officers, 66, 95;
extension work, 40, 73-6, *174*, 180, 182;
see also, replication, technical assistance
external catchments (for runoff farming),
129, 133, *142*, 150, 155; definition, 9, *11*,
15, 132

factory-made tanks, 78-9, 82, 108, 110,
189-90
farmers, 41-2, 158, 177, 178, 185, 186;
learning from, 154-5, *156*, 157, 180, 193;
tanks built for, 95-7; training of,
166-73, *174*; women as, 153, 154, 155,
174; *see also* water management groups
ferrocement linings, 119; for excavated
tanks, 95, *96*, 97, 112; for grain bins, 46
ferrocement tanks, 62, 79, 110, 119-20,
181; construction method, *81*, 117, *118*;
costs, 77, 85, 100, 116, 189; Indonesian
type, 111, *112*; jar type, 75, 108;
maintenance, *88*; Zimbabwe type, 79,
80, 80-2, 83
fibreglass tanks, 110, 111
field capacity (of soil), 132, 133
filters at tank inlets, 63, *64*, 68, 87, *88*,
102, 105
first flush, *see* foul flush
flood control, 37, 194

flood-plain farming, 133, 135
floodwater harvesting (exploitation of
flood flows in gullies, streams and
wadis), 10, *11*, *13*, 15, 182, 185-6;
definition, 8, 132, 185; diversion
systems, *11*, 133, 135, 140, 152;
inundation method, 131-2, 140; 'tanks'
(dams) for, 17, *39*, *40*, 41, 166, 178, 191,
194
food production policies, 164, 183-5, 191,
193-5
formwork (temporary support for tank
under construction), 74, 79, 108, *109*,
115, 117, *120*; metal types, 77, *81*, 121,
122; for tank roof, *118*; structural
aspects, 119-20
foul flush deflectors, 63, *64* , 88, *102*, 105,
107

galvanized iron tanks, 110, 115, 119, 181;
see also corrugated iron tanks
gardens, at schools 91-2, 97; household,
33, 34, 69; irrigation of, 12, 15, 16, 36
ghala baskets (granary baskets, Kenya),
46, *48*
Ghala tanks, 46, 50, 74, 84, 92, 114;
construction method, *48*, 83, 117; costs
and materials, 110, 111, 116, 117, 119;
shape and strength, 108, 115, 119-20,
121
Ghana, 57, 60, 72, 101
Gibraltar, 5, 14, *16*, 20, 22
government, role of, 163, *174*, 175, 177-80,
182; agricultural policies, 183-5, 191,
193-5; development of tanks, *94*, 95, 96
grain banks, *174*, 176, 177, 179; Burkina
Faso, 162-3, 164, 185, 191
grain storage bins, 46, 108, 110, 162
grass, regeneration of, *147*, 150, 167, 193,
195
ground catchments, 7, *14*, *16*, 55, 194;
cisterns and, 1, *3*, 27; classification, 9,
10, *11*, 17-21, 133; for excavated tanks,
91-2, 95-6, 114, 125-6; *see also* external
catchments, microcatchments, within-
field catchments
groundwater, 1, 16, 22, 191; *see also* wells
groundwater recharge, 37, *40*, 178; *see also*
percolation tanks
gully flow, 6, 10, 15, 17, 133, 151
Guinea Bissau, 89
gutters, 18, *47*, 50, 74, 99-107; alternatives
to, *47*, 100, *101*; constraints on use of
rainwater, 72, 82; construction detail,
104, *106*; costs, 100, 103; technical
assistance with, 74, 75, 80, 82, 100;
maintenance of, 65, 87, *88*

hafirs (excavated rainwater reservoirs, Sudan), 15, *26*, 123; definition, 25; in Botswana, 25, *94*, 95; livestock watering at, 57-8, 163
Hawaii, 20
health, 32, 34, 87, 97, 190; water quality and, 63-66
health education, 49, 66, 70
home economics, 32, 33
home production, 32, 35, 36, 190
hoops (small curved bunds), 164, *165*, 182, 193
housing, 36, 41, 43, 49-51, 75, *76*, 194; surveys of, 46, 49, 51; improvements, 72, 99, 181, 188-9
householders, 82, 83; maintenance by, 87, *88*; tank construction by, 79-80, 82
household tanks, *see* tanks.
hydrology, 44, 51-8, 59, 66, 114, 116, 171.
hygiene, 32, 33

India, 17, 21, 22, 31, 37, *39*, 180; environmental problems, 28, 29, 194; Gram Gourav (or Pani Panchayat) project, 38-42, 84, 174, 178, 192; percolation tanks, 39-40, 178, 187, 191; runoff farming traditions, *39*, 127, 130, 135-141; runoff and irrigation policies, 173, 177, 185-7, 190-1; rural poverty, 41, 176, 183, 173; *see also* Maharashtra, Rajasthan
Indonesia, 43, 51, 97, 105, 194; rainwater tanks, 59-62, 74, 116, 119-123; replication and training, 24, 45, 69-70; seasonal water use, 5, 62, 87; West Java project, 23, 37, 61, 110-112, *113*; Yogyakarta district project, 60, 69-70, 84-7, *102*, 191
infiltration into soil, 7, 19, 132, 135, 141
inlet filters, *102*, 105
innovation, 83-5, 89, 93, 97
innovative dialogue, 43, 89-90, 96, 155
instruction leaflets, 74, *76*, 95, 97
Intermediate Technology Development Group, 3, 92, *94*, 96-7
inundation (flooding fields before planting), 131; runoff used for, 135-8, *139*, 140-1;
Iraq, 4
iron sheeting, *see* corrugated iron
irrigation, 39, 40, 178, 184-5; ahars or khadins used for, 136, *137*, 140; boreholes used for, 183, 185, 190-1; dams or 'tanks' for, 17, *39*, *40*, 84, 173, 178, 187; floodwater diversion for, 8, *11*, 13, 15, 133, 135; garden-scale, 15, 16, 36, 61, 89, 91; runoff farming displaced

by, 182, 183, 195; *see also*, micro-irrigation, spate irrigation, water spreading
islands, 5, 22, 31, 34, 35; *see also* Belau, Bermuda, North Solomons
Israel, 2, 146, 180, 181-2; *see also* Negev Desert

Jamaica, 5, 20, 110, 114
jars for water collection, 46, 64, 75, 77; cement-mortar, 108, *109*; ferrocement, 75, 108; pottery, 46, 70-1, 90
Java, 23, 37, 61, 110-13; *see also* Indonesia.
Jordan, 4
Jumbo jars, 108, 111, 189-90

Kenya, 92, 100, 159, 160, 176; Baringo runoff farming, 142, 145, 150, 155, *156*, *165*, 193; excavated tanks, 70, 95, 126; Ghala tanks, 46, *48*, 74, 111, 119; household tanks, *47*, 51, 61, 62, 110, 194; Karai project, 74, 78-9, 83-4, 90; tank types, 84, 89, 108, 113-114, 116; traditional runoff farming, 152, *153*, 154-5; Turkana region, 52, 54, 145, 147, 163-4, 175; Wasini Island, 114, 123, 125-6; water-spreading, *134*, 135
khadins (bunds for seasonal inundation of crop land, India), *39*, 129, *131*, 139-40, 144, 165; definition, 135-6, 194-5; organization, 173, 177, 181, 186, 191
kuskabas (bunds with inundated land, Pakistan), 131.

labour, maintenance requirement, 164, 175, 182; migrant, 37, 162, 166, 176; runoff farming requirement, *147*, 175-6, 182-7; seasonal, 37, 41, 158, 162, 166, 176
Latin America, 22, 23, 66
latrines, 70, 85, 189
laundry, 12, 16
Lesotho, 37, 72
Libya, 28
limestone areas, rainwater collection in, *3*, 5, 114
livelihoods, 30, 31-6, 38, 65, 110, 191; definition of, 32-3; survival strategies for, 158, 162-3, 164
livestock, 12, 16, 17, 20, 23, *174*; as drought insurance, 162, 163; water consumed by, 57-8; watering points, 15, 25, 95, 135-6, 192

Maharashtra, 177-8, 187, 194.

maintenance, 19, 21, 31, 51, 71, 90;
 gutters 63, 65, 87-8, 100; hafirs, 25, 27;
 labour needed for, 164, 175, 182, 186;
 runoff farming, 41, 42, 65, 141, 182,
 186; schedule of, 87, *88*
malaria, 65; *see also* mosquitoes
Mali, 46, 119, 161, *162*
management, *see* organization, water
 management groups
materials for tank construction, 116, 117;
 local and low-cost, 77, 99, 108, 119, 123;
 supplied as technical assistance, 74, 158,
 173, 174
metal tanks, 84, 110, 111; *see also* corrugated
 iron tanks, galvanized iron tanks
Mexico, 1, *3*, 23, 135, 160
microcatchments (plots with crop watered
 directly by runoff), 9, 12, *13*, 19, 129,
 145, 159, 166; definition of, *10*, 149-50;
 design of, 52, *53*, *149*, 149-50
micro-irrigation, *13*, 90, 91, 127
micro-watersheds, 145, *146*
millet, 142, *147*, 160, 162, 163, 184, 185; in
 India, 140, 187; quick-maturing
 varieties, 129, 131, 155
moist climates, 5, 31, 34, 35, 59
monitoring projects, 73, 87-8, 89, 92, 97
Morocco, 130, 133, 144, *148*, 149, 150,
 151, 184
mortar, *see* cement, cement mortar jars,
 curing
mosquitoes, 105, 118; gauze to protect
 tanks against, 65, *81*, 87, *88*
mutual-help groups, 77, 175, 176, 179, 192;
 organizational framework 84-5, 93, 174;
 see also water management groups

nadis (artificial ponds, India), 125, 181
Negev Desert (Israel), 2-3, 24-5, 133, 135;
 cisterns, 12, *27*, 123; climate, 6, 24-5,
 129-131, 139, 195; microcatchments,
 149, 150, 173; runoff farming methods,
 53, 136, 141, 145, 175-6
Nepal, 119
New Hebrides, 126
Niger, 154, *162*, 184, 192
Nigeria, 2, *162*, 189
North America, 130, 133, 136, 138, 147,
 150, 159-60; *see also* Arizona, Canada,
 Mexico, United States
North Solomons (Papua New Guinea), 79,
 83, 114
North Yemen, 41, 131, 182, 183, 191

oil drums (for rainwater collection), 17,
 47, 108

organization, 40-2, 43, 73, 84-5, 140-1,
 158; individual *versus* collective, 174-6,
 178-9, 183, 188, 191; local-level, 71, 177,
 179-80; technical assistance and, 75,
 115-116, 173, 174; *see also* mutual-help
 groups, parent organizations, technical
 assistance, water management groups
overland flow, *see* sheet runoff
Oxfam, 166, 173, 175

Pakistan, *39*, 131, 135
Papua New Guinea, 79, 83, 110, 119
parent organizations (linking local
 groups), 40-1, 84-5, 92, 174, 178-80
participation, 30, 40, 89, 93, 98, 166, 177
pastoral areas, 25-9, 31, 57-8, 127;
 expansion of cultivation in, 184, 185,
 195
pastoralists, 28, 71, 154;
 organization of, 29, 51, 179
payment by instalments, 74, 77, 78
percolation tanks (small dams for
 groundwater recharge, India), *39*, 39-40,
 178, 187, 191, 194
pitting, *see* soil depressions
plastic catchment surfaces, 19, 20, 55
planting density, 142, 144, 150, *151*, 155
polythene, 20, 90, *91*
potters, 45
pottery rainwater jars, 46, 70, 90, 108
poverty, 31, 177, 186-7, 191, 195; action
 for reduction of, 62, 181, 188-9; housing
 aspects, 49-50, 99; impact of technology
 on, 29, 31, 36, 38, 173; organization by
 the poor, 41, 77, 176, 178-9, 192-4
priorities, 43, 49, 50, *68*, 95, 194;
 see also values, conflicts of
promotion of techniques, *see* replication,
 technical asistance, training
pumps, 39, 178;
 in excavated tanks, 65, 80, 92, 114

quality of life, 34
questionnaires, 67

rainfall, 7, 159-162, 163; data on, 45, 52,
 55, 60; intensity of, 51, *53*, 64, 100, *143*,
 155; relation to runoff, 7, 21;
 requirements for runoff farming, 129,
 130, 138-9, 145, *162*; seasons of, 52, *56*,
 58, 127-9
rainwater collection, *see* rainwater
 harvesting
rainwater harvesting (surface water
 collected near where rain falls),

classification, 12-17, 133; conditions
where applicable, 1-5, 22-3, 31, 35;
definition, 5-9; *see also* catchments,
hydrology, tanks, reliability of supply,
roofs, runoff farming, water quality
rainwater tanks, *see* tanks
Rajasthan, 181, 182; khadins in, 136,
138-41, 165, 177, 194-5
rationing of water, 57, 59, 60, 187
reliability of supply, 22, 59, 60, 98
replication (or dissemination) of
techniques, 24, 72-3, 158, 173;
Botswana case-study, 91, 93-8, 99;
commercial impetus in, 73, 79, 82, 83,
181; government roles in, 175, 177-8;
Indonesian case-study, 69-70, 85;
informal processes, 24, 62, 84, 97; runoff
farming aspects, 141, 165-173; for
methodologies, *see* technical assistance
research, 24, 25, 44, 45, 62, 97;
inadequacies of, 127, 129
resource constraints on development, 33,
34, 35, 45, 62, 194
revolving loans, 78, 99
river margin farming, 133, 135, 152
rivers, 5, 12, *13*, 15, 37, 135; flow volume
in relation to rainfall, 1, 7, 22
roaded catchments, 20
rock catchments, 14, 55, 71, 79
roofs, 5, 9, *14*, 43, 54-7, 74; areas of, 54,
55, 59, 60, 75, 188; corrugated iron, *47*,
55, *76*, 77, 100, *107*; flat, 20, 21;
maintenance of, 65, *88*, 99; thatched, *2*,
17-18, *18*, 50, *101*; unsuitable as
catchments, 17, 49-50, 65, 67
runoff (surface water flow during storms),
erosive effects, 9, 12, 144, 185, 193;
measurement of, *53*; relation to rainfall,
7, 9-10, 21, 51; *see also*, ground
catchments, sheet runoff
runoff coefficient (fraction of rainfall
running off a catchment), 54, 55
runoff farming (irrigation by runoff), 1-2,
4, 15, 44, 52, 180; benefits, 159-60, 167,
185, 186-7, 195; bunds for, *142*, *143*,
156; catchment/cultivation area ratios,
51, *53*, 54, 144-5; classification of, 12-15,
132-3; climatic conditions for, 3, 127-30,
144, 145, 162; conventional (Negev)
method, 138, 141-4; inundation method,
39, 131-3, 135-141, 144, 151; prospects
for, 181-5; replication of, 23-4, 141, 158,
165-73; 'simple' methods, 150-7, *156*,
160, 163-4
rural development, 37, 38, 70, 108, 110

Sahel, 28, 128, *147*, 154, 184

sailabas (bunds with inundated land), 131
sand, for mixing mortar, 123;
proportion to cement, 46, *48*, *81*, 109,
118
Saudi Arabia, 182
savings clubs, 77
schools, catchments at, 19, 21, 92; gardens,
91-2; tanks, 91, *94*, 96
seasonal use of water, 5, 23, 31, 34, 35, 56,
87; small tanks relevant for, 57, 61-2, 95
self-help, 78, 110
semi-arid areas, 7, 8, *147*, 154, 181, 182;
pastoralists in, 25-9, 71, 179; relevance
of rainwater harvesting, 4, 5, 31, 34-5,
38
Senegal, *2*, 110, 119
settlement patterns, 1, 5, 38
sheep, *27*, 28
sheet runoff (smooth overland flow of
runoff), 12, *13*, 25, 131, 140, 167; on
small catchments, 8-9, 15, 133
silting basins, 25, *80*, 124
sisal cement, 99, 119
skills, 75, 78, 79, 100, 158; inventories of,
45, 46, 73; *see also* training
snow, 1, 6
social assessments, 44-6, 66, 68, 71, 72, 97
social marketing, 76-7
soil, 7, 19, 129, 151; deposited behind
bunds, *134*, 135, 140; stabilization of, 3,
19, 55, 125; suitability for runoff
farming, 129, 138-9, 141, 151-2; water
storage in, 12, 14, 15, 132, 133
soil conservation, 146, 172, 193; contour
surveys for, 167, 169, *169*, *170*; relation
to runoff farming, 127, 166-7
soil depressions (for runoff collection),
160, *161*
soil erosion, 19, 29, 46, 52, 187; control of,
21, 37, 152, 164-7, 172, 178;
desertification and, 28, 165-6, 183, 193;
effects of runoff, 8-9, 12, 144, 185
soil moisture, 12, 14, 15, *53*, 138, 151
Somalia, 26, 154
sorghum, *147*, 155, 165, 166, 184, 187;
characteristics of, 129, 142, 157;
Turkana variety, 52, *134*, 152-4, 164
South Yemen, 135
spate irrigation, 8, *11*, *13*, 15
spillways, 141-2, *143*, *156*, 167, *168*, 176;
on ahars and khadins, *137*, *139*
subsidies, 36, 74, 76-7, 80, 82, 97
Sudan, 25, 90, *94*, 154, 155; inundation
method, 131-2, 135, 136, 138, 151
summer rainfall, 127, *128*, 129-32, 139,
195
surveying methods for contours, 167, 169,
169, *170*

surveys, *see* social assessments
Swaziland, 60, 65, 66, 92

tanks (large containers for water standing
on or above the ground; for 'tanks' in
India, *see* dams; for tanks below ground
level, *see* cisterns *and* excavated tanks),
capacities of, 34, 43, 54-5, 59-62; costs,
54, 75, 111, 114, 188-90; construction
methods, *48, 81, 86, 109*, 116-123;
design, 54-7, 59-62, 108, 110-115; health
precautions and maintenance, 63-6, *88*;
see also, bamboo-cement tanks,
bamboo-reinforced concrete tanks,
cement mortar jars, corrugated iron
tanks, fibreglass tanks, Ghala tanks,
jars, etc.
taste of water, 17, 34, 64, 66, 69, 70
technical assessments, 44-6, 66, *68*, 71
technical assistance, 72-87, 97-8, 173-4,
177, 195; key components of, 73, 74,
173, 174; materials, tools and finance in,
72-5, 77, 80, 100, 115, 158; organization
and, 75, 115-16, 173, 174; runoff
farming and, 158, 164, 173-6; *see also*,
community workers, parent
organizations, training, village
technicians
technology, options for, 73, 158-9, 173-4
telegas (lined water holes in limestone,
Indonesia), 125
teras (bunds to hold water on cultivated
land, Sudan), 131, 133, 151, 154
terraced wadis, *134*, 135, 182
terraces, 146, *146*, 148, 167, 171, 193;
see also contour bunds, contour strips
Thailand, 24, 45, 46, 70-1, 74-8, 100, 108,
123; Khon Kaen programme, 74-8, 84,
191; materials in tank construction, 110-
11, 116, 117, 123; tank types, 60, 74,
107, 108, 121-3, 189-90; pottery jars, 46,
70-1, 90
thatched roofs, 17-18, 36, 49, 50, 80;
guttering for, *18*, 100, *101*, 105
threshing floors, 19, 46, *94*, 95-6, *96*
time constraints, 32-5, 37, 45, 61-2, 194
training, 44-5, 74, 75, 180, 192; brigades
for, *94*, 96; commercial relevance, 73,
79, 82-3; community workers, 44-5,
66-7, 74, 85; farmers, 169-173, 174, 177;
skills and, 78-9, 83-4, 96-7; villagers, 74,
78-9, 91, 115, 116
trees, 28, 140, 165-6; for fruit, *134*, 135,
149; planting of, 21, 166, 179, 182, 194;
regeneration of, *147*, 172-3, 193, 195
Tunisia, 133, *134*, 135, 145, 150, 182
turbulent runoff flows, 9, 10, 12, 15, 144

UNICEF, 74, *76*, 83-4, 95, *122*
United Nations, 29, 192, 195
United States, 3, 12, 19, 23, 145, 180, 182;
see also Arizona, North America
urban areas, 5, 37, 38, 50
users of rainwater, 43, *56*, 70; innovation
by, 44, 83, 85, 89; dialogue with, 45, 49-
50, 67, 73
use of water, evaluation of, 97-8; *see also*
seasonal use of water

value of water, 33, 36
values, conflicts of, 29, 30, 37; *see also*
priorities
vegetables, 33, 34, 36, 127, 187; grown at
schools, 92, 97
vegetation on catchments, 7, 19, 21, 194
village organization, 24, 40-1, 83, 174
village surveys, 66-7
village technicians, 77, 78-9, 85, 88, 93
villagers, 74, 115; learning from, 85, 89,
94, 96-8; participation, 29, 66-7, 69

wadis (dry desert valleys), 8, 15, 133, 135
water carrying, 5, 33, 35, 37, 61-2
water consumption, 54, 56-8, 59, 60
water harvesting, 6, 8, 17, *40*; *see also*
floodwater harvesting, rainwater
harvesting
water holes, 25, 29, 57
water management groups, 29, 38, 40-1,
178; *see also* mutual-help groups
water quality, 33, 63-6, 89, 98, 126
watersheds, *see* catchments
water spreading (irrigation by floodwater
without ponding), *11*, 15, *134*, 135, 154
water storage, 15, 132-3; *see also* cisterns,
dams, groundwater recharge,
percolation tanks, soil moisture, tanks,
etc.
water supplies, cost of, 187-9
weather, *see* climate, evaporation, rainfall
weather stations, 52
wells, 1, 12, *13*, 36; below dams, *40*, 178;
below khadins, 136, *139*; cisterns similar
to, 124
winter rainfall, *128*, 129-32, 139, 144, 195
within-field catchments, 144-50, 155, 157,
186; definition, 9, 132; *see also* contour
strips, microcatchments
women, 34, 69, 162, 163; as community
workers, 69; as farmers, 41, 152, 154,
155, 174, 175; fixing gutters, 72-3; water
carrying, 37, 72
World Bank, 127
World Health Organization, 97

Yatenga, *see* Burkina Faso
Yemen, 8, 131-2, 133, 183; *see also* North
  Yemen, South Yemen

Zambia, 77
zamindars (land-holders with tax-collecting
  role, India), 41, 183

Zimbabwe, 14, *94*, 96, 100, 124, 160, 194;
  brickwork tanks, 74, 82, 84, 112, *113*
  excavated tanks, *80*, 95; ferrocement
  tanks, 79-80, *81*, 83, 111, 118, 189;
  Hlekweni project, 74, 79-82, 90, 93, 112;
  savings clubs, 77, technical assistance,
  74, 80, 83, 100